THE
ENGLAND
MANAGERS
The Impossible Job

THE ENGLAND MANAGERS
The Impossible Job

BRIAN SCOVELL

TEMPUS

All illustrations are courtesy of Empics.

Front cover: Clockwise from top left: Terry Venables, Sir Bobby Robson, Sir Walter Winterbottom, Sir Alf Ramsey, Sven-Goran Eriksson and Glenn Hoddle.

Back cover, top: Alf Ramsey celebrates with England captain Bobby Moore following his team's victory in the 1966 World Cup. *Bottom*: Sven-Goran Eriksson during a training session ahead of Euro 2004.

First published 2006

Tempus Publishing Limited
The Mill, Brimscombe Port,
Stroud, Gloucestershire, GL5 2QG
www.tempus-publishing.com

British Library Cataloguing in Publication Data.
A catalogue record for this book is available from the British Library.

ISBN 0 7524 3748 8
ISBN 0 7524 3963 4

Typesetting and origination by Tempus Publishing Limited
Printed in Great Britain

CONTENTS

DEDICATION

This work is dedicated to the ten full-time managers of England who were in the firing line in the impossible job. Unless they won, they were castigated and ridiculed.

Sven-Goran Eriksson said: 'I think you should be a saint sometimes in this country, or at least a monk. You shouldn't earn so much money and you should win every game. It is not like other countries. Here they want to go into my private life.'

Sir Walter Winterbottom, Sir Alf Ramsey, Ron Greenwood, Sir Bobby Robson, Graham Taylor and Kevin Keegan were happily married and there was little to be pried into and Glenn Hoddle was unlucky. He survived a divorce but not an anti-PC remark about the disabled. Don Revie's marriage to Elsie was a love match but, like Terry Venables, his financial dealings were deeply probed, which upset a section of the critical media.

I knew all of the England managers and they are, or were, decent men doing their best with some limited players and a few great ones. England gave football to the world but through arrogance they were one of the last countries to take up coaching and to appoint a national manager.

2006 is the sixtieth anniversary of the first appointee, former RAF Wing Commander Walter Winterbottom, and it was recorded by a dry paragraph in the minutes of the FA in March 1946. Winterbottom was the nicest, most enthusiastic man anyone could meet and his passion for coaching inspired many English managers and coaches. Sir Stanley Rous founded the FA Coaching Scheme, which was derided for decades until a more educated public realised that most players needed to be taught (there aren't many geniuses), and Winterbottom turned it into the best in the world.

A successful international manager needs to be a professor-like figure such as Arsène Wenger, who can inspire their players, speak other languages and has the personality to handle extreme temperaments. He needs to love the game and pass that feeling on to his pupils. And he doesn't have to have played at the highest level. This is where the English got it the wrong way round. 'How many caps have you got?' they asked. Those with the most caps, like Bobby Moore, Bobby Charlton and Peter Shilton, were unsuccessful as managers.

Because too many of our managers are insular – Revie, Keegan and Hoddle never took the highest UEFA coaching examinations – English football still lagged behind as the twenty-first century dawned. Other countries picked their managers from the best of the world's nations. It took the FA two lifetimes to appoint the first foreigner. Eriksson was hammered from the start yet his record of fourteen major trophies in three different countries compares well with the nineteen of the nine other managers combined.

The manager attracts all the flak when things go wrong but there are other guilty parties, including the amateurish, overladen, incestuous FA who doubled Eriksson's salary when there was no need for it, and some sections of the media who devalue the game with ill-informed, vicious abuse. The excessively criticial coverage of the England team has led to frenzy among parts of the population, almost as ferocious as in Turkey or Argentina.

Greenwood, Taylor, Hoddle and Keegan were brought down by it. Don Howe could have taken the job but he didn't like the thought of 'all that hassle'. Now we are in a position where hardly anyone wants the post unless he is paid fortunes. Perhaps it is time for some Corinthian values to be restored like fair play and balance. In that environment players can enjoy

DEDICATION

the game and maybe England can win a second World Cup to catch up the Argentinians and Urugayans on two wins each and make up ground on the Germans and Italians (three each) and the Brazilians (five).

We claim that the Premiership is the best league in the world but with sixty per cent of the players hailing from overseas, does that benefit the England team? It is the foreign managers that are regularly winning the major trophies and it is an indictment of English football that not one coach from the British Isles was in charge of a national side in the 2006 World Cup Finals. Standards need to be raised to produce better coaches. A new Winterbottom might do it.

Brian Scovell
Bromley, Kent
March 2006

WALTER WINTERBOTTOM

1946–1962

The Man Who Started it for Others, Not Himself

P 137   W 78   D 32   L 27   56%

English football was almost twenty years behind the other major football-ing countries when they first appointed a full-time manager in 1946. Romania, one of the original thirteen entrants in the inaugural World Cup in Uruguay in 1930, had a man in charge even then – King Carol, who paid for the squad to go to South America. As the inventors of the game, the English didn't believe in having someone in charge. They thought English football ruled the world and it had a team of natural talents like Stan Matthews, Tom Finney, Raich Carter, Wilf Mannion and many more. They knew what they were doing so there was no need to worry.

But a headmaster from a small village in Suffolk, a giant of a man named Stanley Rous, standing 6ft 4ins tall, convinced the members of the Football Association that even geniuses needed a teacher and a leader. There was a lot of resistance to the idea, especially as Rous's nomination, Walter Winterbottom, lacked credibility in the eyes of the leading players and the majority of the FA councillors. Winterbottom had played a few matches for Manchester United as an amateur, playing in midfield before the Second World War, and had guested occasionally for Chelsea in wartime friendlies.

After he was appointed, he organised a training session for the England players, who were picked not by him but by twelve selectors, at Southport before a match against Ireland. Derby County's Raich Carter, christened Horatio after Lord Nelson, lost patience at one of the routines. 'I was doing this when I was ten,' he said. 'What's the f——ing point?' Other players were heard to ask at other times how many caps Winterbottom had.

But Winterbottom soon won their support because this tall, bespectacled academic had many qualities which helped him to become the father of English football, introducing many of the innovations which revolutionised

12

the domestic game, including the FA Coaching Scheme which fostered a generation of great coaches and managers, including Ron Greenwood, Bobby Robson, Don Howe, Bill Nicholson, Malcolm Allison, Jimmy Hill and countless others. He had a poor record in four World Cup tournaments and failed to win a trophy, but his success came from ideas and a passionate cause: persuading talented footballers to exercise their minds and muscles to reach the very highest standards. He talked excitedly about Bobby Charlton's 'fast muscle, like the Brazilians' and Charlton was one of his heroes. Duncan Edwards, who died in the Munich air crash in 1958, was another. Winterbottom was always talking about him because he believed he could have been the finest all-round footballer these islands have produced. Out of these ideas and thoughts came the players who won the World Cup in 1966. Greenwood was one of his chief disciples and Greenwood's leading pupils were Bobby Moore, Geoff Hurst and Martin Peters.

Winterbottom's greatest achievement was to lift England's footballers out of isolation and take them into their first World Cup, the 1950 tournament in Brazil (which turned out to be a disaster). With his courtesy, sheer niceness and enthusiasm he inspired many doubters and filled them with his own enthusiasm. If there is anyone today of his kind it is Arsène Wenger, the professor-type figure who raised fast, flowing football at Arsenal to new heights. But Wenger lacks Winterbottom's vision and burning passion to teach. Unlike Wenger, Winterbottom was too polite, too caring to argue with anyone, especially in public. He was a real gentleman, a devout Christian and, in the words of one of his disciples, Jimmy Armfield, 'no one ever said a bad word about him.'

Not everyone liked Walter. Brian Clough hated him. The reason was that Winterbottom preferred West Bromwich's Derek Kevan to him in his squad for the World Cup in 1958 and Clough's international career was cut short after just two caps. Clough's bitterness lingered on right until his death. In one of his many autobiographies he wrote:

It was criminal. I was cast aside at the age of twenty-four by a manager who, in my opinion, didn't know his job. He was a pleasant, charming man. A soft man. Not like me – I have been a harsh man on many occasions. I am not sure if he had the first idea about management, though. He captivated people with his eloquence but it did nothing to change my mind. I regarded him as a man who did not possess the moral courage to stand up for what he thought should be done. He had used Bobby Charlton, Jimmy Greaves and me in the middle of the attack together. It didn't work, it couldn't work, but it was his job to find a way of producing a combination that made the best use of us. He failed.

Winterbottom was born on 13 January 1913 in Oldham and, then as now, Walter wasn't a common name. It originated from Germany and meant 'warrior leader', which wasn't quite fitting for England's first manager. He was a persuader more than a leader and certainly not a warrior. Walter Hammond, the great all-rounder cricketer, was called Wally and, similarly, Wally Barnes, the Arsenal and Wales full-back, was never called by his full Christian name. But Walter Winterbottom was always Walter and no one coined a nickname for him.

He went to Oldham Grammar School, then to Chester College. There he came under the influence of a man named Eddie Lever, whose footballing career had been cut short through injury. Lever was a student of the theory of football and it was a coincidence that Winterbottom's playing career was also ended by an injury, in his case a spinal one. Winterbottom went on to Carnegie Physical Training College in Leeds and while there he organised one of the first major FA coaching courses, which had been created by Stanley Rous. The FA secretary saw the studious twenty-five-year-old as a man with a future. He was impressed with his willingness to talk about tactics and the new developments in sports science. At the major football clubs there was little said about tactics or fitness. The players did a few laps round the pitch and rarely trained with the ball. One well-known manager once said, 'If you keep the ball away from them in training, they'll be hungry for it when the game starts.' There were no coaches, fitness trainers or sports psychologists, only a trainer, the man who came on to the pitch holding a wet sponge to 'treat' the players. Winterbottom wrote:

There were managers but they didn't manage, they signed cheques. It was player power with the older players deciding the tactics. Goalkeepers rarely came off their line, so Dixie Dean was able to head goals standing only two or three yards out. The game was nearly all long balls, and there was a loosely created midfield. Final passes were laid on from the centre circle. Nobody had worked out even simple things.

During the Second World War Winterbottom became head of physical training at the Air Ministry and reached the rank of Wing Commander. When he was demobbed, he was about to apply for the post of the principal at Carnegie College when Rous came for him. Rous wanted him as England's first manager and, if possible, the national director of coaching as well. The England team was under the supervision of an FA councillor who alternated with other councillors seeking the limelight, and under them were their club's trainers, who had little expertise.

To the FA rulers the word 'coaching' was anathema. One senior England international said, 'Unless this coaching monster is seized firmly by the throat it will strangle the living grace out of our game.' Winterbottom's appointment as England's manager was shrouded by secrecy. Rous was his most powerful backer, the only one, and he convinced the others at 22 Lancaster Gate, the FA headquarters, that he was the only outstanding candidate. FA minutes recorded a two-line mention from a meeting of the Finance and General Purposes Committee, dated 8 July 1946, saying, 'Recommendations with regard to the appointment of Walter Winterbottom to the staff were received and approved for submission to the FA Council.'

The minutes of the next meeting of the FA Council, which consisted of more than eighty members, failed to mention Winterbottom's appointment. The chairman, Amos Brook Hirst, a Huddersfield lawyer who loved rugby, accepted Rous's recommendation without demur. The salary seems to have been an obstacle but Rous circumvented the opposition by suggesting that Winterbottom could take both jobs. Everyone agreed. Afterwards, there was no televised press conference or even radio interview. No media scrum. No awkward questions. Outside the FA offices, a lone photographer asked Sir Frederick Wall, the previous FA secretary, who had held the job for thirty-nine years, if he could pose for a picture with Winterbottom. 'Why should I?' asked Wall, with his starched collar, bowler hat and a walking stick on his arm. Rous had had a similar experience with Sir Frederick when he took over in 1934. Rous had asked him if he had any advice and Wall replied, 'The job's straightforward. You can read up on the files. There is nothing I can tell you.'

The moustachioed Rous, who always wore City-style suits and ties – unlike latter-day FA secretary Adam Crozier, who turned up on his first day's work without a tie – formed a lifelong friendship with Winterbottom, who said of him in 1972:

He is the great man of football, a man who is held in high esteem the world over for his immense contribution to the organisation and development of the game he so dearly loves. Stanley came to football from a career in education [he was Headmaster of Watford Grammar School] with the qualification of being an outstanding referee [he refereed the 1934 FA Cup final and many internationals].

When I first met him at an FA course just before the Second World War, he revealed his keen interest in teaching methods and his inspirational leadership. Not for him the many proposals to alter the basic simplicity of the game by fashioning more complicated laws and regulations. It is remarkable now much he fitted into his life and he fulfilled all his tasks with style, dignity and human understanding.

Winterbottom might well have been writing about himself.

Rous was the son of a grocer, born in the village of Mutford in Suffolk, population 300, in 1895 and until he arrived no one played football in the small community. It is something of a coincidence that England's second manager, Alf Ramsey, wanted to be a grocer when he was a boy. Rous played in goal for his school, Beccles, and asked the school if he could be given a football to start a team in Mutford. The ball was duly handed over. The husband of the school headmistress built the goals and the fourteen-year-old launched the new club. There were no handouts in those days, no Lottery money. It came from one very tall boy who had a dream.

In one game Rous had several teeth knocked out as he dived at a forward's feet and went to the dentist next day carrying his teeth in a handkerchief. He recalled:

> The dentist forced the teeth back into the gum and told me they would eventually go black. But they served me well for another twenty-five years until I was told to have them out as they were too unsightly when invited to appear in TV programmes.

By this time he was secretary of the FA, on a miserly £800 a year from 1934 to 1962, and at the age of sixty-seven he took over as president of FIFA, the world ruling body, for the next thirteen years. He was a colossus in every sense of the word.

The FA was a quaint body then – in many ways they still are – and Rous partly attributed his appointment as secretary in 1934 to his training at Watford Grammar School when he coached football at a nearby deaf and dumb school. Sir Charles Clegg, the elderly FA president, was deaf and everyone had to shout at meetings. At the appointment panel, Rous said to him, 'Is the job pensionable?' framing his words carefully so the president could understand. Clegg, highly impressed, said, 'Your predecessor was well awarded for his services.' Rous said, 'My predecessor? Am I appointed then?' Clegg replied, 'not so fast, young man, that was a slip of the tongue.' At a later meeting, when Rous was in charge as secretary, the Surrey representative had previously raised a contentious matter and Clegg kept interrupting, saying, 'Where is he? He should be speaking on this matter!' 'He's dead,' shouted another member. Clegg, still not hearing, shouted, 'This item must be adjourned until he is present.' Rous pushed a note in front of him: 'We had a minute's silence already for the Surrey man who died last week.' 'Why didn't someone tell me?' asked Clegg.

Wembley's Royal Box must have yielded wonderful stories before it was demolished and Rous, who was renowned for his humour, told one about Winston Churchill, who had a profound dislike of football:

> The match was in aid of Lady Churchill's Aid to Russia Fund. The Prime Minister was just back from a wearing trip to [visit US President] Roosevelt and spoke little during the game. At the end he started going down the narrow staircase and I put my arm out to steady him, warning that it was easy to fall. He shrugged me aside saying, 'Leave me be. I am perfectly capable of falling downstairs myself, thank you.'

Arthur Drewry, a former president of the FA who preceded Rous as FIFA president, was chairman of the England selectors who picked the side for Winterbottom's first match as manager, a game against Northern Ireland in Windsor Park on 28 September 1946. Drewry made his money out of fishing, based in Grimsby. He was an expert in judging North Sea cod and mackerel but was less qualified about assessing the various abilities of Stan Matthews and his mates. Winterbottom, tall and handsome, like Rous, wasn't allowed to be present at the meeting of the twelve-man selection panel. The match was won 7-2 with Wilf Mannion scoring a hat-trick. Some of

England's greatest ever players appeared in the team list. Has England ever put out such a wealth of talent as on that day – Frank Swift, Laurie Scott, George Hardwick, Billy Wright, Neil Franklin, Henry Cockburn, Tom Finney, Raich Carter, Tommy Lawton, Wilf Mannion and Bobby Langton? Matthews had a sore knee and Tom Finney played in the number 7 shirt. It was six months later, in the 1–1 draw against the Scots at Wembley, before Matthews came back – and that was for only one game before Finney returned. It provoked one of the leading controversies of the day: who was better, the magician Matthews or the Preston Plumber?

Although Winterbottom didn't have a say in selection, he must have influenced the committeemen because between 1949 and 1952 Matthews made only three appearances to Finney's thirty-three. Matthews, born in 1915, was the older man by seven years and Winterbottom said in David Miller's authorised book on Matthews, published in 1989:

> I thought at one time Stanley was going to stop playing because of injuries, on top of which we'd begun a policy of trying to bring players through from the Youth and Under-23 teams. Finney tended to have more assists with goals than Matthews, a higher effectiveness, but Matthews gave the entertainment. Stanley tended to have either great games or ordinary ones. He was the matador, goading and provoking the opposition. In the year before the War, he was without parallel, he was the Maradona of his time. His crosses were devastating. It was extraordinary how he could get the ball to float.
>
> Yet wingers were isolated figures within a team and could only dictate the play if they were given the ball. Great players like Puskas, Di Stefano, Sivori and Cruyff achieved things because they played in the middle of the field. Cruyff was everything, captain, coach, leader, scorer.

Finney played in all five forward positions for England, Matthews just one. That was the answer really; that and the age difference. There was no animosity between the two men. They usually travelled to London for matches on the train together and sometimes shared a room. Finney remains the nicest, most loved footballer of his time and his generous nature must have been conditioned by the death of his mother when he was four. His father, a clerk, had to bring up six children, of which Tom was the fourth.

Winterbottom started pre-match training sessions and after-match meetings to discuss what had gone wrong. He also introduced blazers. Some thought he was treating his players like schoolboys but most of them supported him. Billy Wright, later appointed as captain, said, 'He's a man who thinks deeply about the game,' and Alf Ramsey, his right-back, said, 'his tactical knowledge and outlook left a lasting impression.' It was a good time for Winterbottom to start his pioneering work. He believed all great teams needed a core of exceptional players and he had plenty to choose from; a group of players who were the best in the world at the time. In his first four years in charge England won 22 of 29 matches, losing 4 and drawing 3 with a goals tally of 90 for, 31 against. Scotland had a quota of outstanding players as well and the Scots provided the toughest opposition.

The zenith of Winterbottom's career came on 25 May 1947, with England beating a demoralised Portugal 10-0 at Lisbon, with Tommy Lawton and Stan Mortensen scoring four apiece and Stan Matthews and Tom Finney scoring one each. A splendid banquet had been laid on and the Portuguese went straight home from the game and boycotted it. Not far behind was the 4-0 victory over Italy in Turin with Finney scoring twice.

Without any doubt, the lowest point was 29 June 1950 – England 0, USA 1 at Belo Horizonte on a day that, in the words of President Roosevelt on an earlier occasion, 'went down in infamy'. Having decided to enter the World Cup tournament, England duly qualified from the four home countries and on 19 June – Ramsey had ringed the date in this diary – the squad assembled at London Airport for the thirty-one hour flight to Rio de Janeiro via Paris, Lisbon, Dakar and Recife, accompanied by Winterbottom, two trainers, Bill Ridding of Bolton and Jimmy Trotter of Charlton; English referees George Reader, who refereed the final, Arthur Ellis and Reg Leafe; various officials and eight journalists including Charlie Buchan, the former Arsenal star, the first player-writer. The quickfire northern humour of Stan Mortensen and Bolton's Bill Eckersley and the Cockney wit of Eddie Baily, for whom 'The Barrer Boy' became a signature tune, provided plenty of entertainment. (These days there is nothing like this when England fly to matches. The Beckhams and Owens sit there with their music pumped into their ears, hardly exchanging a word.)

Finney mislaid his health certificate and the plane was almost held up, Mortensen fell down a hole on a path close to Copacabana Beach and Jackie Milburn fell and injured his neck, ending up with it in a brace. The opening game, a 2-0 win over Chile, went off painlessly and the group set off by air to the newly built mining town of Belo Horizonte. They were given a rapturous reception and many of the 2,000 English people working there had turned up to applaud. England's exhausted players were delighted but their mood changed on the fifteen-mile drive to the St John d'el Rey Mining Company's Morro Velho camp. 'Never will the England footballers forget this nightmare experience of being driven around 167 hairpin bends on a road which seemed to cling to the side of the mountains, overlooking the valley hundreds of feet below,' wrote a shocked Ramsey.

The chalets were acceptable, the hospitality was superb but when the team arrived at the packed, concrete-built stadium they noticed there was a 12ft-high wall around the entire playing pitch. Goalkeeper Bert Williams said, 'This is the first time I've ever played in a prison.' Winterbottom was upset to see the state of the dressing rooms and ordered the players to be driven to the Minas Athletic Club, a five-minute journey, to change in a better, less smelly facility. He was also unhappy to learn that England had to play in blue shirts while the USA wore England's traditional white shirts. Eddie McIlvenny, born in Glasgow in 1924, had been playing for Wrexham and Manchester United not long before and for some unaccountable reason he was now qualified to play for the USA. Several other bogus 'Americans' also appeared in the line-up. Winterbottom and Arthur Drewery, the only selector, raised no objection. They thought England would have no worries about the outcome.

It turned out to be one of the most one-sided matches ever played in a World Cup. The American goalkeeper 'Bounding' Borghi stopped dozens of shots, including one with his face and, in the words of Ramsey's ghost writer in his book *Talking Football*:

> ...then, tragedy of tragedies, with five minutes from half-time, the right-winger swung over a cross and Joe Gaetjens from Haiti tried to duck and by a million to one freak, the ball came off the back of his head, or more precisely his left ear and went into the net. If there had been an earthquake at Belo we could not have received a greater shock.

The second half was even more one-sided. Mortensen's shot was well over the line before the goalkeeper scooped it back into play, reminiscent of the

Pedro Mendes 'goal' in the Manchester United *v.* Tottenham game at Old Trafford in January 2005. Then Mortensen was manhandled and brought down in the penalty area. No penalty! Immense cheers from a pro-US crowd. Nothing went England's way. 'Cheer up Billy,' Ramsey said to skipper Billy Wright afterwards. 'All we have to do now is beat Spain and we can still win the World Cup.'

Back in Rio, Winterbottom brought his jokers, Eckersley and Baily, into the side. One oddity was that only one member of the FA council was present at the Spain game – the Grimsby fish merchant Arthur Drewry. He picked the teams and Winterbottom trained them and gave them their instructions at matches. In later tournaments there were dozens of FA councillors and staff at England's away matches, costing huge sums. Neutral journalists thought England played some of the best football they had ever seen but Spain won 1-0 and England were back on the Pan-Brazil flight to London.

Ramsey, to his credit, admitted that he was the guilty man when Zarre, the Spanish centre forward, scored the goal. He was incensed about the Spanish tactics:

> Long before the end I think the Spanish were playing basketball not football, for our rivals used their hands far more than their feet. Apart from that, they body checked our players, pulled shirts and we were denied an obvious penalty and a disallowed goal 'scored' by Jackie Milburn. The films of the incident later proved that we were robbed of a perfect goal.

Back at home everyone in the party complained about misfortune instead of examining the inadequacies of the selection and preparation of Winterbottom's squad. Pressure by Rous persuaded the FA council to set up a technical committee to seek the views of directors, managers, players and even pressmen. The members of the committee looked into coaching, training, the development of young talent, systems of play, tactics and refereeing. There were no recommendations of any importance, except the clubs promised to give more help to the international team in future. These promises are still being made but still not kept.

In the aftermath of the World Cup, England's results were reasonable and the team was constantly changed by the meddlesome selectors. This was because they used to go for their own club's players and didn't have any regard for the team's understanding.

England had still never lost at Wembley to a foreign side and this was a proud record they wanted to keep. On 21 October 1953 a Rest of Europe XI, chosen by FIFA, took on England to celebrate the ninetieth anniversary of the founding of the FA. A few minutes from the end, the Rest led 4–3. However, England were awarded a penalty. Ramsey put the ball on the penalty spot and, with his nerves jangling, put a low shot into the corner of the net. The old masters were getting closer to the edge.

Just over a month later another prestige match took place at Wembley. The date was 25 November 1953 and it went down as one of the most decisive days in the history of English football. Hungary were the Olympic soccer champions and they were the favourites to win the next World Cup in Switzerland a few months later. More disturbingly, they hadn't lost a game for three years. Sir Stanley Rous, now knighted for his services to football, suggested that England should be tested by the leading side of the day. Winterbottom admitted he was apprehensive. The Hungarians, supposedly amateurs, had been trained by experts who specialised in sports sciences.

A small number of privileged people went to Wembley to watch the Hungarian players train and they were astonished by their skill and speed of thought. They realised that England were suddenly vulnerable. The selectors gave new caps to Blackpool's Ernie Taylor and George Robb, the amateur who played for Tottenham Hotspur. Wright was still there, so were Matthews, Mortensen, Harry Johnson and the reliable Jimmy Dickinson. There was the usual bravado in the newspapers about England's unbeaten record but the score was 6–3 and England were lucky to get one, let alone three. Byron Butler, the former BBC football correspondent, wrote these words in *The Official History of the FA*:

> The scoreline hurt but the manner of the Hungarian victory wounded deeply. It touched the inner heart of English football because it confirmed, beyond excuse and smokescreen, that the country which had organised the game for the world did not understand its finer points. The 'masters' were using old text books.

Geoffrey Green, *The Times'* football correspondent, wrote, 'England were strangers in a strange world.' Frank Coles of the *Daily Telegraph* argued that 'this was the most brilliant display of football ever seen in this country.' Eyes were suddenly opened.

Winterbottom was enthralled by the wonderful team skills of Ferenc Puskas, Josef Bozsik, Sandor Kocsis, Nandor Hidegkuti and their colleagues. They were all stars. He spoke to his pupils at his FA courses in the summer, the likes of Dave Sexton, Ron Greenwood, Bobby Robson and Don Howe, and told them it was like seeing the light when it had been half lit. People at home were stunned and called for answers.

Seven new players were called up for the next ritual slaughter, the return in Budapest six months later. Ramsey, Mortensen, Johnson and Bill Eckersley were out – they had played their last game. The result was more horrifying: Hungary 7, England 1. Someone said, 'something has to be done.' Someone else asked, 'Do we really need a panel of nine to pick a team of eleven?'

The FA council came up with a compromise: only two of their members would serve as the sole selectors but the FA had the right to change it. Winterbottom's position was strengthened, insisting on more money spent on the coaching scheme. Forty players had been called up in the two previous years, far too many. He wanted a settled team and younger players picked from the Under-23 side groomed by himself and Bill Nicholson.

England's players went into the World Cup in 1954 only a month after the 7-1 rout at Budapest. The two selectors bowed to public opinion, recalling Stan Matthews at the age of thirty-nine, with Winterbottom's full support, but there were two questionable choices: Portsmouth's speedy but inexperienced right-winger Peter Harris and the even less experienced Fulham centre forward Bedford Jezzard. Neither played. Billy Wright was moved from wing half to centre half, despite his lack of height, and he emerged as Winterbottom's aide de camp in the dressing room.

It was the first televised World Cup. Until then the supporters at home had to be content with snippets of football on Pathé News shown in cinemas, several days after the match. The few cameras at the stadium in Berne were able to catch most of the malevolence of the Brazil *v.* Hungary quarter-final in the so-called 'Battle of Berne' which the Hungarians won 4-2. English referee Arthur Ellis sent three players off and *Corriere della*

Sera reported that the watching Puskas, kept out through injury, smashed a bottle into the face of Brazilian defender Pinheiro as he came into the dressing room.

The portly Puskas, the man who should have dominated the tournament, had been kicked by the West German defender Werner Liebrich in an earlier match (Hungary won 8-3 over the side that eventually won in the final) and Liebrich's challenge was termed by the critics as 'the kick that won the cup'. Puskas insisted on playing in the final but was clearly unfit and the Germans won 3-2 amidst flying tackles and bitter recriminations. In 2004 a film called *The Miracle of Berne* was made and it became the most popular film of the year in Germany. It cheered the nation at a time of gloomy economic forecasts.

Winterbottom experienced the worst of his four World Cup campaigns. Luton centre half Sid Owen and Birmingham goalkeeper Gil Merrick were blamed for a 4-4 draw after England had been 3-1 up against unfancied Belgium. The decision to move Wright to the centre proved inspirational and England won an unexciting game at Berne 2-0 against the hosts Switzerland. In the quarter-final, Matthews was at his tantalising best but the cup holders Uruguay emerged with a worthy 4-2 victory before they went down by the same score against the Hungarians in the semi-final, a match hailed as one of the greatest matches of all time.

There were more mutterings about Winterbottom's failures on the world stage but in those days the press, though critical, was never hysterical. Rous had set up a press room at the FA and helping Fleet Street's writers proved a smart move. Winterbottom planned another final assault ready for the tournament in Sweden four years later, promoting younger players from his Under-23 squad, including the strong-willed left-back Roger Byrne, the precocious centre forward Tommy Taylor and the incomparable Duncan Edwards, the midfield player Winterbottom thought would soon become England's greatest all-round footballer.

On 6 February 1958 – another date which will never be forgotten – all three of them died in the Munich air crash. Twenty-one players, officials and journalists died, wrecking Manchester United's, and England's, chances of imminent success. Bobby Charlton, who had just established himself in the England team before making way for Bobby Robson, survived the disaster but it was ten months before he was back in the England side.

WALTER WINTERBOTTOM

Don Howe, an England coach at 129 internationals under three England managers, Ron Greenwood, Bobby Robson and Terry Venables, was included in the squad in Sweden. He played twenty-three internationals between 1958 and 1960 and he gave a wonderful insight into Winterbottom's personality and his methods.

He was a really nice, intelligent man, similar to Arsène Wenger. He would always ask questions to the players, especially the quieter ones, to bring them out. He would say, 'What do you think about this or that?' to get everyone involved. He'd make friends, get them on his side – Bobby Robson and Terry Venables were the other England managers who were great at that. I think Sven does it, too.

Walter – we used to call him Walter – would move around in the coach, sitting down and talking to all the players. He was years ahead of his time, like working on the mental side, and getting players in the right frame of mind. He talked for hours and hours about the Brazilians because they were miles ahead of us in preparation. By the fifties, they had a sports psychologist and a masseur before anyone else thought of them. They held hands, bonded, as they say these days.

Walter never fell out with anyone. There were no awkward customers in those days. He did all the bookings, the travel, the food, almost everything. He used to give his requirements to the chefs at the hotels. Bill Nicholson and Jimmy Adamson, the Burnley captain, were his coaching assistants and Harold Shepherdson was the trainer. That's the lot. These days England go abroad with a huge number.

Walter introduced afternoon tea to footballers He loved to sit down and have meals with the players. After breakfast, they would train, come back for lunch at 1 p.m. and one day he told them afternoon tea was going to be served at four. A player said, 'What? We don't eat all that. It's fattening.' But Walter had them down for tea and scones and cake. He just liked chatting and exchanging ideas. No one was bored.

He never disciplined anyone. No one got into trouble. We stayed in a luxury hotel in Gothenburg and we used to walk across a park to train at a small ground nearby. One day we noticed the Brazilians were walking in the park, arm and arm with the local girls. 'What's going on?' said one of our players. 'They've got a day off,' said Walter. Someone asked, 'Can we have a day off, too?' The Brazilians were more used to it, he explained.

England failed to win any of their four matches and again went out, but with honour. From the outset, questions were asked about the selection. Matthews and Nat Lofthouse, though in good form, were left out and only twenty players came instead of the permitted twenty-two. England were 2-1 down against the USSR when Finney was injured and, with no substitutes allowed, he stayed on and equalised from a penalty. Howe recalled:

> The next game, also at Gothenburg, was against the favourites Brazil. Garrincha was probably in the best form of his life and Didi and Zagallo, the left-winger, were outstanding players. And Pelé turned out to be a star although he was only seventeen. Walter sat next to me and asked, 'What do you think about Zagallo?' I told him I'd heard about him but not much more. 'Well,' he said, 'Bill Nicholson saw him and Zagallo will play deep and I don't want you to go that deep. I want you to tuck in with Billy Wright in the centre and leave Zagallo to somone else.' It worked. We stopped Zagallo and the game ended at 0-0, the first time the Brazilians had failed to score. Walter was really chuffed, putting his arm round the players. He was as proud as any result he'd ever had.

England came from behind to draw 2-2 with Austria and went out 1-0 against the USSR in a play-off. Wales went just as far, losing 1-0 to Brazil in their quarter-final. 'Wales had some very good players, like Jack Kelsey, Ivor Allchurch and Cliff Jones,' said Howe. The chorus of criticism started up again. The FA and Winterbottom were blamed for putting the England players in a swish hotel in the city centre. Next time they would go into the outback of Chile.

The manager enjoyed visiting the capitals of Europe and a trip to Madrid the following year provided an interesting insight into another side of his well-rounded personality. Geoffrey Green, *The Times*' football writer who used to pick up a telephone and ad lib 600 words on the final whistle of a game without writing down a single one, was invited to join two friends in the Anglo-Hispana club for a drink. (In Winterbottom's day it was common to see football writers entertaining the players and, sometimes, the manager – not like today, when the writers are kept well away from the manager and players except for well-policed, boring press conferences lacking any interest. Managers rarely make journalistic friends these days, which is why the press criticism is so damaging and often unfair. As Winterbottom used to say, we learn from each other.)

The night before the Spain game Green saw a rather beautiful Spanish woman in her forties sitting nearby and one of his friends introduced her. 'And what are you doing in my city?' she asked in perfect English. 'I am in your beautiful city to report the football match between your beautiful country and my England tomorrow night,' Green replied. 'You mean you write about football?' she said. 'What a waste of a life!' 'Maybe,' Green said. 'But most of us waste our lives, yet in football I see ballet and movement, I hear music and see a stage play. You might like ballet, *Les Sylphides* for instance. You might love music, Beethoven's Fifth perhaps, and you know the last word to be spoken. You might like a Shakespeare play and you know all of it. Football contains for me all these elements of art. And you never know the ending. It can be different every time.' Winterbottom loved the exchange. He would have liked to have said something similar. After the match, with Spain winning 3-0, Green, an inveterate drinker, was back at the Anglo-Hispana Club and met the lady again. 'I see what you mean,' she said. 'I enjoyed it thoroughly.' Green asked her what she did. 'I am the ballet mistress of Antonio's Dance Ensemble,' she said. His point was well made.

Billy Wright made way for a new captain, Blackburn's Ronnie Clayton, in 1960 as Winterbottom switched from England's traditional 'WM' formation to his preferred 4-4-2, the formation which Alf Ramsey used to win the World Cup six years later. Clayton, an industrious and stylish wing half, lasted only five matches before the increasingly peevish Johnny Haynes was given the captaincy. The 1960/61 season was a stimulating time for English football and Winterbottom particularly. He believed 4-4-2 was ideally suited to the abilities of this new crop of players and Bill Nicholson, his former helper, produced arguably the finest club side of all time in Britain – Tottenham Hotspur, the first 'double' winners in the modern era. On 26 October England defeated a strong Spanish team 4-2 on a sodden Wembley pitch with Tottenham's bustling Bobby Smith scoring twice. The following spring Smith added two more in the 9-3 obliteration of Scotland on the same pitch. Mexico were then swamped 8-0. The omens were good for the World Cup.

The competition was scheduled for Argentina and with their large stadiums and passionate supporters they were firm favourites. But in May

1960 Chile was devastated by earthquakes. More than 5,000 people died and thousands more were left homeless. Carlos Dittborn, the Chilean FA president told FIFA, 'We have nothing. We must have the World Cup.' FIFA relented and the poor Chileans were delighted. Sadly, Dittborn died from a heart attack at the age of forty-one, a month before it kicked off.

An imposing National Stadium was erected under the Andes mountains but two other venues were totally inadequate and England were based at Rancagua, the worst of the two. Rancagua was a small town inland from Santiago, 8,000 feet above sea level. Jimmy Armfield, the articulate, organ-playing, pipe-smoking Blackpool right-back who had replaced Howe, wrote in his autobiography:

> Our destination was a tiny village called Coya, home of the Braden Copper Company who owned it and that was our home for the three qualifying matches. How Walter had found the place, I will never know. The only way in and out of Coya was a single-track railway and while these days Rancagua is a ski resort, 42 years ago it was a one-horse town in the middle of nowhere. It wouldn't have had a prayer of being a World Cup venue today. We were housed in little chalets and there was a café, a cinema showing black and white films with the sound track in Spanish and a sort of tenpin bowling alley.

Modern players would have rebelled. Don Howe recalled one redeeming feature:

> It had a great little hospital, very modern. We were larking about on a slope of a mountain covered with huge cacti when someone crashed into a cactus and Alan Hodgkinson, one of the goalkeepers, finished up with a very sharp needle sticking into his big toe. It was good to have a hospital so close because England didn't travel with a doctor in those days.

The Rancagua ground held only 10,000 spectators and, with little atmosphere, the mood of Winterbottom's players worsened when they lost 2-1 to Hungary. Antonio Rattin was among the opposition in the next game, against Argentina, and Armfield recalled: 'One of their players tapped me on the shoulder and when I turned round, he spat into my face. We had to put up with that kind of thing for the full ninety minutes.'

England rallied, winning 3-1 with Bobby Moore outstanding and the mercurial Jimmy Greaves and Bobby Charlton both scoring. In the decisive game, Bulgaria had to win to qualify but they defended throughout and, with England being over-cautious, it was dull viewing in front of only 5,700 fans.

Now Brazil were in the way. There was no Pelé but Garrincha, 'The Little Bird', was the match-winner, his 5ft 7in frame rising to beat Tottenham's Maurice Norman and head the first goal. Later, his fierce free-kick bounced off the chest of goalkeeper Ron Springett to fall conveniently for Vava to make it 2-1. Garrincha also added the third.

Winterbottom brought in another innovation. He asked two of his more talkative players to speak to the press afterwards and Armfield told the writers, 'We were disgraced. We got some valuable experience and we will be better prepared in 1966.' He was right.

The drab, goal-less draw against colourless Bulgaria was followed by the 3-1 defeat against Brazil in Vina Del Mar and that turned out to be Winterbottom's last match in charge. On the way back home, the southern-based players flew to London with the official party. The six from the north went on their own, stopping overnight in New York. 'For all the FA knew,' said Armfield, 'we could have been touring the USA for weeks.' Winterbottom and Rous had made detailed plans for the FA's centenary in 1963 but a few months earlier Rous was asked by a leading figure in FIFA, Harry Cavan of Northern Ireland, to be the body's president. Rous was sixty-six and past retirement age but was fit and healthy and intimated he would be agreeable. He had to give up his £3,000 a year salary at the FA – the new job drew no salary. He was duly installed as an amateur. Winterbottom had spent sixteen years running both the national side and the coaching scheme and when Rous asked him if he was interested in becoming the FA secretary, he said yes. There were seventy applicants and a virulent press campaign derided another candidate, Denis Follows, the secretary of the British Airline Pilots' Association. Rous wrote in his book:

Walter had an enviable international reputation, was acceptable at all levels of the game, was brilliant administratively and was a forward thinker of sound but original judgement. However, there were those who felt our relationship was a handicap. Some told me they were certain to vote for Walter, though now they changed their minds saying they wouldn't be dictated to by the Press. Many of them were incensed, particularly by a Sunday newspaper article which said 'Follows is plump, red of face, a nail-biter, horn-rimmed spectacled and nobody's fool.' That offensive comment may well have been a vital factor in giving Denis an overwhelmingly majority over Walter by 50-20.

Follows had plenty of support because he was the FA treasurer for some years. But everyone who understood the game knew that Winterbottom was the far better man. Follows was later knighted. He was a nice, efficient, civil servant-type man. Football went downhill when Winterbottom departed, with no fanfares, to become general secretary of the Central Council of Physical Recreation and, later, director of the Sports Council. His contribution to British sport was exceptional and his knighthood in 1978 when he retired was richly deserved.

Jimmy Greaves said of him, 'If I wanted a manager who'd make friends it would be Walter. If I wanted a winning team, I'd take Alf Ramsey.' Alan Hardaker, the former Naval Commander who was secretary of the Football League when he dominated it for more than twenty years, said, 'Walter was a dedicated theorist but lacking the kind of background and steel the job demands. He was never quite a part of the earthy world of the professional football.' Hundreds of managers, coaches and disciples of Winterbottom would vehemently disagree.

Many great men are not accepted and this was another example. The next day after Winterbottom's obituary appeared in the *Daily Telegraph* Jimmy Hill, one of his leading disciples, penned this angry letter:

Sir Walter Winterbottom, charming man that he was, would already have forgiven the compiler of your somewhat misleading obituary. To suggest that he could not communicate, let alone inspire professional players, is nonsense. If there were those who could not understand his theories, they were in a measly minority.

During the fifties he was well ahead of his time. The fact that Stan Matthews, Tom Finney, Bobby Charlton and Jimmy Greaves were under him and an ignorant, unqualified selection committee above him, illustrated just how far collectively we had fallen behind more sophisticated countries.

Nearly everyone then believed that good players were born and not made. The Hungarians hit such complacency for 6-3 at Wembley. Walter's England, still unappreciated by some, slowly narrowed the professional gap by continuing to lead those who controlled the professional game at Lancaster Gate out of their power-struck wilderness. Ron Greenwood, Bill Nicholson, Don Revie, and even Brian Clough, made their own successful way with their own personalities and ambition, but all learnt something from Walter.

The real sadness for English football is that the councillors failed to do justice to Walter's enormous contribution. In electing Denis Follows, they virtually eliminated England's best football brain for years from continuing to serve English football.

So there!

Walter, loved by so many, died at the Royal Invernia Hospital in Guildford on 16 February 2002 at the age of eighty-nine. His wife Ann — it was an idyllic, happy marriage — and two daughters survived him and one son died. One who knew the real truth, former Football League secretary Graham Kelly, said:

> This charming man whose thirst for knowledge could never be slaked, was surfing the internet right up to the end. If you could market the football know-how passing through the church gates at his funeral next Friday, you would make a fortune.

WW never worried about money. He just loved football, and people.

ALF RAMSEY

1962–1974

Inasmuch as… Alf was a Winner

P 113   W 68   D 28   L 17   60%

Alf Ramsey wasn't a disciple of Walter Winterbottom. He wasn't even an FA coach. But he brought the qualities which Winterbottom lacked: his intense will to win, his singularity, his stubborness, his determination and his hardness. It was as if the six-man FA panel wanted to rid all vestige of amateurism from the ranks of would-be candidates fostered by the scholarly Winterbottom and instead choose a real, tough professional. Ramsey was a player's man who won their respect and that was his greatest strength. Winterbottom was essentially an establishment man, although he had a good relationship with the players too. While Winterbottom was always loquacious and matey, Ramsey was more guarded in his words away from the training pitch and the dressing room, so much so that one critic Max Marquis, author of a controversial book about him entitled *Anatomy of a Football Manager*, claimed he was 'inarticulate'.

No, he wasn't inarticulate. Sometimes he used a delaying device, employing phrases like 'inasmuch as' or 'in respect of' before he came out with the more meaningful words. When he completed the sentence he would stop and wait for the next question. He was never frightened to say 'no comment', like his friend and colleague Bill Nicholson. Too many England managers have talked too much and found themselves in trouble. Graham Taylor was the most talkative and Bobby Robson, Don Revie, Kevin Keegan and Walter Winterbottom were not far behind. One of the many failures at the FA was not appointing a press advisor who had a thorough background in national newspapers and understood the dangers of 'red-top' journalism. Red-top newspapers are the ones who take chances on stories and embellish them, like *The Sun*, the *Daily Mirror* and the *Daily Star*. One false sentence from an harassed England manager can make the front page, as Glenn Hoddle knows to his cost.

The only appointee at the FA who had the right qualities was Colin Gibson, the former *Sunday Telegraph* and *Daily Mail* sports editor. Within a short time he was forced to resign over the Faria Alam affair. It wasn't his fault that the FA and their lawyers wanted Mark Palios to be retained as chief executive and Sven-Goran Eriksson out. But the plot to discredit Eriksson backfired and Palios and Gibson went. Eriksson stayed.

Ramsey hardly ever came out with anything quotable and the only other one of the ten full-time managers who followed his example was Eriksson. In his twelve years as England manager Ramsey slipped just twice, the first occasion being his forecast about the outcome of the 1966 tournament and the second his ill-advised words about the Argentinians, when he compared them to animals.

Was he serious about England winning, putting immense pressure on himself? After he was appointed, he told Tony Garnett, the sports editor of the *Eastern Daily Times*, 'England will win the World Cup.' Asked at a press conference shortly afterwards if he meant it, he replied:

> I say it again: I think England will win the World Cup in 1966. We have the ability, strength, character, and, perhaps above all, players with the right temperament. Such thoughts must be put to the public, and particularly to the players, so that confidence can be built up.

Later this smallish, gnome-like man privately admitted he had gone too far, not in expressing his thoughts to the players but in announcing them to the public in general. Arthur Rowe, his mentor at Tottenham, said, 'It was no cheap, throwaway phrase. He meant it.' It made headlines around the world and Ramsey was criticised for spreading too much expectation, the virus which these days is still rampant in English football. After England's victory in the final at Wembley he never once said, 'I told you so.' That said plenty about his character. He wasn't an egoist.

His criticism of the Argentinians was distorted by some newspapers and used against him. Ramsey wasn't calling Antonio Rattin, the captain, and his players 'animals'. What he actually said, in a television interview, was, 'I have been a little disappointed that the behaviour of some players in this competition reminded me of animals.' A good PR aide on the FA staff would have put that right within minutes but the controversy will never die.

Like Winterbottom, Ramsey was misunderstood by many people and his immense contributions were underplayed. He was a great man, like Winterbottom – indeed, these two remain the outstanding figures in English football, staying the longest time in charge, winning the most matches and setting the best example in maintaining standards on and off the pitch. Ramsey was given a false image. Words like 'obtuse', 'strange', 'obsessional', 'secretive', 'moody', 'complex', 'contradictory' and 'rude' were applied to him yet his friends knew him as a kindly, amusing and self-deprecatory man with a smile. Back home in Ipswich – his wife Lady Victoria still lives in the same house, having now been there more than forty years – he was the real Alf Ramsey, not the one he showed to the inquiring public. He would sooner jump into the river Orwell than pose as a celebrity. He was an ordinary man, with humble beginnings, who made good.

A lot of small, insignificant things were built into big issues to denigrate him, like did he have elocution lessons? This story kept appearing over the years and though Ramsey refused to comment, he did say to his friends that it didn't happen. But if he went to elocution lessons so what? Today's managers are often tutored by press advisors or more intelligent agents. They are taught to say the right things. He wasn't born a Cockney speaking the Cockney 'Gor Blimey' accent. Many players who grew up with him poked fun at him when they met him in his England blazer. Chelsea's Allan Harris, brother of Ron 'Chopper' Harris, recounted an encounter with him at Millwall's old Den where the Queen's English comes out rather differently than in the London gentlemen's clubs. 'Why are you talking so posh?' he asked an embarrassed Ramsey before he made his excuses and left.

Ramsey came from Dagenham, a depressed overspill town off the Thames Estuary. A lot of words were written about his age. Did he lop off two years to advance his career when he joined Tottenham from Southampton in 1949 at the age of twenty-nine? He was born on 22 January 1920 but for many years his birth date was given as the same day in 1922. It was 1967 before his real date was published in *Debrett's*.

Alfred Ernest Ramsey was born at 5 Parrish Cottages, Dagenham. His father Herbert Henry Ramsey was a hay and straw dealer and his mother, Florence, was a housewife looking after four sons, Albert, Len, Cyril and Alfred, in straitened financial circumstances. In his book *Talking Football*, published in 1952, he claimed he was born in 1922 and his father ran a smallholding.

My brothers and I lived for the open air from the moment I could toddle. The meadow at the back of our cottage was our playground. For hours every day I learnt how to kick, head and control a ball, starting with a tennis ball and it is true to say that we found all our pleasure this way. We were happy in the country and I was fourteen before I attended a cinema, a jungle story starring Jack Halt.

He never lost his enthusiasm for a certain type of film. Before internationals, he often took the whole England squad to watch adventure films, cowboy films and James Bond films.

At seven Ramsey was chosen for the junior side at Becontree Heath School and his brother Len, who owned a pair of boots, told him he needed to buy a pair himself.

With the help of a kitchen knife I extracted eleven pennies from my money box. I realised it wasn't enough money so Len went to his mother for help. I handed my eleven pennies to my mother and next day I was given my first pair. 'They only cost 4s 11d,' said mother. I couldn't have been prouder than when I put them on and strutted around the dining room, only to be pulled up by my father. 'Go careful on the lino, Alf,' he said. 'Those studs will mark it.'

We used to walk four miles a day to school and all four of us made the journey kicking our ball around. We agreed that the one who kicked the ball into the ditch would have to retrieve it and rather foolishly I made that mistake, taking off my shoes and socks and wading in, out of my depth, and afterwards I was confined to bed with a severe cold. That cold taught me a lesson. It impressed upon me the need for accurate passing. Practice makes perfect.

As England manager he insisted on accuracy when passing the ball. 'Treat the ball like a jewel,' he said. 'Never lose it.' By the age of nine he was captain of the school and later he was picked for Dagenham Schools against West Ham. The game took place on the famous Spotted Dog ground and the captain of the West Ham team was Benny Fenton of Charlton Athletic, who later became manager of Millwall, brother of Ted, the former West Ham manager.

As he was about to leave school his parents asked him what he would like to do. 'Be a grocer,' he said. So he started out as an errand boy for the local Co-op store.

> Every day I'd cycle my way around Dagenham [incidentally, Terry Venables lived not far away] taking to customers their various needs. My wage was twelve shillings a week and out of that I gave my mother ten shillings, putting a shilling in my saving box and keeping the other shilling for pocket money.

For two years he worked every Saturday afternoon and his football suffered. But for the unfortunately named Edward Grimme, manager of his local sweet shop, Alf might well have been lost to the game. Mr Grimme called up a few former players, all around the age of sixteen, including Ramsey, to a meeting above his shop with the purpose of forming a new team. 'What a happy club it proved to be!' recalled Ramsey. 'They were among the most valuable football lessons in my life.'

The East End of London was a fertile breeding ground for promising young footballers and hundreds of part-time scouts scoured the public pitches looking for talent. To the amazement of Ramsey, and also that of his colleagues, he was tapped by a Mr Ned Liddell, a representative of Portsmouth FC, the First Division club that had held the FA Cup throughout the war after winning the trophy in 1939. Ramsey was now playing at centre half, despite being only 5ft 8½ins. At 12st 8lbs he admitted that 'I was rather bulky.' Mr Liddell called him over after the game and said, 'Let's go into a quiet corner of the field where we can talk without being disturbed.' Alf must have seen stars in his eyes. That night he signed amateur forms.

Alas, he heard no more. On 24 June 1940 he was called up into the Army and sent off on his first long train journey, to Truro, rising rapidly to the rank of Sergeant in an anti-aircraft unit. He was whisked round several other camps, finishing up at Barton Stacey in Hampshire. Not being in the front line, he was able to play plenty of football and was soon picked for an Army side against Southampton in a pre-season match in 1944. 'I'd never played against professionals,' he said. 'It was bewildering.' Saints won 10-1. Six days later his CO called him in and said Southampton wanted him to play again. 'Have you ever considered becoming a professional footballer?' asked the

Colonel. 'No sir,' said Ramsey. 'I've never given it a thought because I don't think I'm good enough. But I'll give it a try.' He later recalled, 'those who know me will tell you I'm a quiet fellow who never shows emotion but [as he left the office] I did a little tap-dance with delight.'

He was signed in a London-bound train after the club treasurer forgot to give him his £10 signing-on fee. Asked what his expenses were, he said, 'Tuppence ha'penny.' 'Are you sure?' asked the club chairman. 'What about a taxi?' 'No,' said Ramsey, 'that's what I spent.' He was scrupulous about money and later admitted, 'I earn the maximum of £1,000 a year and think I am well paid.' His starting wage was £2 a week and his best friend at Southampton was Ted Bates, the man who became manager and president of the club over the course of his long, happy and distinguished life. Ramsey knew him as 'Teddie'. For six months in 1946 Sergeant Ramsey was transferred to Palestine and skippered the Palestine Services XI.

Back at the homely Dell, he spent many fruitful hours with Sid Cann, the reserve-team coach. Cann had played right-back for Manchester City and Charlton and he told Ramsey he ought to be a right-back, not a centre half. He painted out a football pitch on the dressing room floor and showed the art of defending. It was like a university crash course from an enthusiastic professor. Another player, Alf Freeman, performed the same task, passing on his knowledge in long walks in the Hampshire countryside. This rarely happens today, especially with foreign players. They hardly exchange any words with the coaches because they arrive as the finished product. Home-grown talent is squeezed out to the detriment of the England side – Ramsey would have been a powerful voice against this globalisation of the game. Some of his critics described him as xenophobic and they were probably right. He wasn't keen on Argentinians and Scots, in particular.

The day that changed his life in footballing terms was the one when he played against Sam Barkas, the Manchester City right-back, who was thirteen years older. 'It proved to be the greatest day in my football life,' said Alf. 'He was the first defender I'd seen who could pass like a great forward, like Alex James. I found a man upon whom I was determined to try to mould my style.' He spent hours working on kicking and running and was always in bed by ten, exhausted, with ten hours of sleep ahead of him.

The other day that changed his life was when he met Victoria, a beautiful brunette who was married to a businessman in Southampton. They fell in love and, after the divorce, Alf and Victoria embarked on a wonderful love story which was to last fifty years. They went to Bournemouth on their honeymoon and she shared his love of vaudeville acts in seaside theatres. Victoria's devoted, loving support was invaluable and she proved to be the ideal partner. She called him Alfred and he called her Vic.

On the field, Alf's football had improved since the 1947/48 season when he was picked for the England trip to Italy and Switzerland. He was told to report to the Great Western Hotel, next to Paddington Station, and sat in a leather chair for hours watching the stars like Matthews, Wright and company go by. Thinking that he might not be needed, he saw a man approaching who turned out to be the England trainer Jimmy Trotter. 'Are you Alf Ramsey?' asked Trotter. 'Yes,' said Alf. 'I was getting worried. I wondered whether I was good enough.'

He was picked for the 'B' international and impressed and the following year he made an excellent debut for the senior side in the 6-0 win over Switzerland. He was entranced by Walter Winterbottom's ninety-minute 'pow hows' as he called them. Alf recalled:

> It left a lasting impression. Realising that he had chosen the best men for the job, he did not waste time trying to sell ideas to footballers who have proved themselves. Rather he acted as chairman, calling for ideas from the floor. He was a splendid speaker and he blended our ideas and picked out the chinks in our opponents' armour and suggested ways to take advantage of them.

Unlike many of his teammates, Ramsey wasn't a big drinker and soon gave up smoking in the Army, saying, 'It affected my wind.' He drank an occasional short, a gin and tonic or a brandy. If there was anything to celebrate, he was happy to join in the festivities. He was a gambler for a while, backing the greyhounds when he joined Tottenham. One of his colleagues, Eddie Baily, asked how much he'd won after a meeting and he said, 'Mind your own business!'

Southampton were touring Brazil and he flew off to Rio himself to join up with them. On arrival he found himself being interviewed by a English-speaking journalist. 'It struck me next day that my reporter friend had written considerably more than I had said to him in the course of our brief talk,' he said. It was a lesson he never forgot. Keep it short.

Ramsey came under the influence of another remarkable teacher, Arthur Rowe, when he signed for Tottenham for £21,000 on 15 May 1949. Rowe was born a short distance from White Hart Lane and had played for Spurs as a centre half. He spoke Cockney although he wasn't born within the sound of Bow bells and he was a very persuasive, friendly coach who introduced a style of play which was christened 'push and run'. 'It came from the kids' way of kicking balls against walls and pavement kerbs and collecting the return,' said Rowe. It was the basis of Tottenham's glory days before the full bloom emerged a decade later under Bill Nicholson. Rowe told his players: 'Put good football before results. Do that and the results will come.' Ramsey could be a prickly character but he appreciated Rowe's approach. He said, 'The chief never criticised us and his purpose was to help the players.' When Ramsey took over with England he did the same, speaking in a quiet, firm tone of voice, without shouting and swearing. On the rare occasions he swore, he used the words with effect. He meant them. Many managers use the F-word in every sentence and it ceases to ruffle players.

After England's 4-2 win against Czecholovakia in Bratislava in 1963 the players asked if they could go out drinking afterwards. Jimmy Greaves and Bobby Moore were the ringleaders and Alf said, 'Gentlemen, if some of you want a f——ing beer you can have one at the hotel.' Back at the hotel the person to buy the first round was Ramsey. Greaves, who had a number of differences with him, said in his autobiography *Greavsie*:

> Alf and I got on very well even though our attitudes to football were different. Alf was very technically minded and believed in the importance of tactical variations and gameplans. I still went out and played off the cuff. His public image was of a taciturn and stoic man but he was great company and a ready wit. He liked a drink and the players had a few long sessions with him after matches when he would drop the veneer a little and let himself go. He had a good sense of humour and a lot of warmth and charm.

In his six years at Tottenham, Victoria saw nearly all of his games at White Hart Lane and, to his surprise, his mother had his Second and First Division championship-winning medals for the 1949/50 and 1950/51 seasons engraved and presented to him. Florence doted on him and he once said, 'I love my mother's meat pies and puddings. They cannot be beaten.' Ramsey was often involved with coincidences. In 1950 he was training with the England squad at Whitley Bay when Walter Winterbottom told him that

Billy Wright was injured, shook him by the hand and said, 'Congratulations, you're the new captain.' Ramsey recalled, 'When I was with Southampton we were training at Whitley Bay and Bill Ellerington, the captain, dropped out and I took over. It's a small world.'

His climb to leadership now reached another phase when he was asked to make the speech after the banquet following England's 2-2 draw against Yugoslavia, his first speech of his life. Bill Eckersley wrote a lively speech for him but Alf ignored the jokey Lancastrian's effort and read out a boring one. There was a match in which Stanley Matthews was about to pick up Ramsey's pass when the England manager-to-be shouted, 'Hold it, Stanley!' One of the players said, 'You've taken a liberty with Stan, mate!'

By 1954 the sensitive Rowe had already had a breakdown. He had another, and left. He still worked as a consultant until his seventies but was to die from Alzheimer's, the same complaint Ramsey would later suffer from. Jimmy Anderson, who spent fifty years at Tottenham, took over but he was ineffectual. He signed Danny Blanchflower and the loquacious Irishman soon took charge on the field. Most of Anderson's ageing team were heavy smokers. They were running out of puff.

Ramsey was left out the following year and, now thirty-five, he was looking for a managerial position. Someone told John Cobbold, the Old Etonian chairman of Ipswich FC, that Ramsey was a good man. Cobbold rang the Tottenham secretary and later recalled, 'We got permission to speak to him and after a bit of humming and hawing he agreed to join us.' Ramsey had no experience and both parties were taking a huge gamble. Ramsey was on a low salary and the conditions were primitive. The offices had been built by the Army during the First World War and Ramsey's office sprung a leak and buckets had to be used to catch the rainwater. There was one communal bath and the water was heated by a delapidated, coke-fired boiler outside the window. One wife of a key player kept coming in to see Ramsey to complain and on one occasion he heard her voice in the corridor, got up from his seat and jumped out of the window, sliding down the coke and making off.

Cobbold spent a lot of time making fun at Ramsey's expense, calling him 'Old Stoneface' and telling him to 'bugger off!' But he admired his professionalism, his expertise and his determination to succeed. According to the club secretary David Rose, Ramsey never wasted words: 'I'd say something to get the conversation going, like, "I thought so and so had a good game" and he would reply, "Oh, do you think so? I didn't think so." He did that to cut me off.'

The new manager made a poor start, losing his first game. No Ipswich manager had done that before. But from twenty-fourth place in the Third Division, he took the side to the title in 1956/57, only his second season, with the team scoring 101 goals. In the club's first six seasons under Ramsey Ipswich rose from the bottom of the Third Division to earn promotion to the top flight in 1960/61 as the club celebrated its twenty-fifth anniversary. The next season the team won the First Division championship, outdoing Tottenham, and the Cobbolds – John and his brother Patrick, who were successive chairmen – arranged a swish celebratory dinner at the Savoy Hotel. Ramsey rose to speak and as he droned on, a voice kept interrupting, shouting from behind a curtain, 'C'mon Ramsey, stop boring everyone', 'Enough's enough Alfie' and other insulting comments. It came from the disguised voice of John Cobbold.

Ramsey's team, valued around £25,000 as against the £250,000 of Tottenham, had won, outwitting the other contenders with a simple plan, using two withdrawn wingers, Roy Stephenson on the right and Jimmy Leadbetter on the left, to supply two high-scoring strikers, Ted 'Cannonball' Phillips and Ray Crawford. Ipswich won both of their League games against Spurs and afterwards their manager Bill Nicholson admitted he had been too careless. 'We should have given them more respect,' he said.

Ted Phillips said, 'Alf was the best I worked with and most people would say the same. He won the World Cup for England, no one else. He knew the game inside out and spoke sense.' Asked if Ramsey ever lost his temper, he said, 'No, never. Once Kenny Malcolm threw a boot at him and he carried on as though nothing happened.' Phillips had a habit of turning a hosepipe on the players and once he soaked Ramsey's suit; another player, Irishman Dermot Curtis, recalled, 'Alf was amazing. He took his tie off, said nothing and walked out to his car. He was soaked through but he drove off as though nothing happened.'

In 1962 Ipswich were still in the goals, except they were going in the wrong end, and with no money and a time of strife looming, Ramsey was angling for a new post. Winterbottom's hopes of becoming the FA secretary in succession to Stanley Rous were ended by a plot from within, headed by

Professor Sir Harold Thompson, the Oxford University chemistry expert. An insider who worked at the FA at the time said:

> Tommy, as we called him, was a horrible, arrogant and clever man who was universally disliked. He called everyone by your surname and he wielded enormous power in the council. There were murmurs about trying to get him out but they couldn't topple him.

Ramsey wasn't a prime candidate to take over as England manager. Burnley captain Jimmy Adamson was the first choice but he turned it down, saying he didn't have the necessary experience. Ron Greenwood was in the same position. 'Too soon for me,' he said. Nicholson should have been a candidate. He had worked under Winterbottom for years as coach of the Under-23 squad and knew England's best players better than anyone. But the new FA chairman Graham Doggart, the former Cambridge University player and England international from the renowned sporting family, approached John Cobbold on 1 October and the Ipswich chairman welcomed the invitation. 'I don't want him to go but England's need is greater than ours,' he said with a hee-haw series of chuckles. Doggart was a county cricketer with Middlesex and a man of integrity and moral strength – the kind of man the FA needs today – but sadly he collapsed and died at the FA annual meeting a few months later. Chelsea chairman Joe Mears, also much respected, succeeded him before he too died suddenly, on the England tour to Scandinavia just before the World Cup started.

Ramsey now knew he was in a strong position and he insisted on being given full control over selection of players. Doggart agreed after two weeks of discussion. A provision was that members of the FA council were allowed to 'assess' players – not that Ramsey would take any notice of their views. Ramsey was to make another major, overdue change, appointing a team doctor. The appointee was Dr Alan Bass, born in Leeds, based in Harley Street. He was Arsenal's team doctor and was extremely popular with the players and the officials. In Chile, the Sheffield Wednesday centre half Peter Swan became seriously ill after being given the wrong treatment, emphasising the need for a full-time doctor.

Ramsey didn't want the other half of Winterbottom's job, head of coaching, so the job was given to Allen Wade, a lecturer in PE at Loughborough

College and a former Notts County player. Ramsey was offered the manager's job, at a salary of £2,000 a year, and accepted. 'He never made a fortune,' said the FA man. 'He was only getting £5,000 when he was sacked in 1974 and I'd be surprised if they paid him more than six months' money as compensation.' There were fifty-six people employed by the FA, all poorly paid, compared to the present 250, most of whom are well paid.

In the autumn of 1962 Ramsey was adamant that the news should be delayed by a day. It wasn't the first time the FA were kept waiting by Alf. When he was sacked he wanted a much longer delay, for 'personal reasons'. Right the way through his working career, he always had the last word. His first game in charge, in Paris, was a disaster. Ron Springett, the goalkeeper who had problems sighting the ball from distance, made several mistakes as England were crushed 5-2 by a skilful French team. There was hardly any adverse comment. But the critics started up after the Scots won 2-1 at Wembley two months later, complaining that Jimmy Melia wasn't good enough and shouldn't have played. Ramsey began building a new side to develop his World Cup challenge. He started from the back, introducing Gordon Banks in place of Springett as his first move.

Ray Wilson was brought in at left-back and England's 2-1 victory over a Rest of the World side in a match celebrating the FA's centenary signalled to the other sixty-nine World Cup entrants that Alf's England were rising to the top strata again. Jimmy Greaves, who scored the winner in the eighty-seventh minute, said, 'That was a great game of football, with the supporters and press alike all in agreement.' England played thirty-six internationals between 1963 and the start of the World Cup and lost only four, with Greaves, the greatest finisher England has produced, scoring 21 goals in 24 of the matches. But, as he admitted in his book *Greavsie*, 'Though I felt very much part of the England set-up the fickle of fate was to ruin it for me.' By this time Greaves was having problems with drink but it was a tackle from a French defender named Joseph Bonnel which put him out of the competition at the halfway stage.

Ramsey knew the formation he wanted and identified the players to fit it, summoning new parts for the jigsaw: George Cohen, Nobby Stiles, Jack Charlton and latecomers Alan Ball, Geoff Hurst and Martin Peters. Earlier, Ramsey had rung Ron Greenwood and said, 'This boy Peters can't play!' He got that one wrong. Peters was the stealth man in the side, the man who Greenwood said 'was ten years ahead of his time'. Ramsey was also slated for not having wingers but he had three in his World Cup squad and they were all given a chance – John Connelly, Terry Paine and Ian Callaghan made one appearance each in the first half of the tournament.

When he discarded them, he revived memories of his deep-lying wingers Stephenson and Leadbetter at Ipswich by using Ball and Peters as workhorses who wouldn't give the ball away easily. They were team men, not flair players whose form was likely to fluctuate alarmingly. Ramsey was even suspicious of Greaves, who was laid out with hepatitis in the build-up. When the Tottenham striker had his leg sheared open by a reckless tackle from the Frenchman Bonnel, an injury which required fourteen stitches, the manager didn't put any pressure on him to regain his place, preferring the all-round qualities and physical strength of Hurst. Ramsey once told Jack Charlton, 'It's not so much picking the best eleven players but the most suitable players to fill complementary jobs.'

Bobby Moore shared a room with Greaves at the Hendon Hall Hotel not far from Wembley but both men might have failed to keep their places in the squad for reasons other than footballing ability. In the previous two years Ramsey's relationship with Moore was sometimes strained. Moore and Greaves were big drinkers and before leaving for a game in Portugal they persuaded some other players, including another big drinker, the late Johnny Byrne, and moderate drinkers Banks, George Eastham, Bobby Charlton and Ray Wilson to break the team's curfew. When the offenders returned to their rooms and started to get into their beds they saw their passports lying on their pillows. The next day Ramsey called them in and said:

> You can count yourself lucky to be standing here right now. If there had been enough players for this squad, I would have sent you all home. Gentlemen, may I for the first and last time remind you of your responsibilities as members of the England team. All I hope is that you have learned your lesson and will not behave in such an irrational and irresponsible manner again. Gentlemen, the matter is now closed.

It was a brilliant managerial decision. Nothing emerged into the newspapers until much later. Once or twice Moore strayed again – but without the same results because by that time he was irreplaceable. Moore loved a drink but those who knew him well never saw him really in a drunken state. He was renowned for his tidiness and always had his own iron in hotel rooms.

But for injury, Jimmy Armfield could have been England's captain holding up the Jules Rimet trophy in 1966, not the incomparable Moore. The virtuous and well-respected Armfield skippered the side on thirteen successive occasions until he was injured in 1964 and Moore took over. By the World Cup he was fit again and was included in the twenty-two-man squad but failed to start a game. He had a wonderful relationship with Ramsey and was the only player to attend his funeral in 1999 outside of the players that appeared in the final. In his autobiography he wrote:

> He had real steel. He was a player's man par excellence and believed that players were the only people who really knew about professional football. He never had much time for directors and made no attempt to ingratiate himself with officialdom, the media people or people on the periphery of the game. He was unflinchingly loyal to the players and would always defend them in public, taking the criticism himself; nor would he criticise individual players in front of the others. In return, the players gave him total loyalty.
>
> He was intensely patriotic and believed our football was the best in the world. At times, he would resort to near jingoism saying things like, 'This lot don't like the English, you know. So let's go out there and show them what real football is all about.' This call to arms was applied to many of our opponents, particularly the Scots and Germans. He never sought personal glory. He wanted to win for England and his players. He knew exactly what kind of players he wanted. He didn't want showboaters as we call them today.

The theft of the World Cup, later found by 'Pickles' the mongrel from Norwood, provoked many laughs and the whole nation was behind the team when the first match kicked off at a tarted-up Wembley, which had 10,000 unfilled seats. The opponents were Uruguay and their players seemed to be reluctant to cross the halfway line in a dour game which ended 0-0. Five days later an overawed Mexico side turned up impersonating the Uruguayans and England won a comfortable 2-0 victory, with the champagne moment coming from a Bobby Charlton thirty-yarder.

England's third game made up for the lack of controversy and drama in General Ramsey's advance (when he was at Tottenham, Ramsey was nicknamed 'The General'). A pedestrian France were well beaten 2–0 but the short-sighted Nobby Stiles, Ramsey's enforcer, chopped down Jacques Simon with an awful challenge, causing uproar on the French bench. FIFA officials called for disciplinary action and the FA advised Ramsey to leave Stiles out for the next game as punishment and keep the peace. Ramsey told them, 'If he goes, I go.' The FA backed down. The untidy Stiles, with no teeth in the front of his upper jaw, was probably the most popular member of the squad. He shared a room with the immaculately tidy Alan Ball and, as a Catholic, he used to steal out before breakfast to pray at his local church.

Adidas, the boot supplier, paid each player £1,000 in cash for using their boots, which was the same amount the players received later for winning the tournament – except the second sum was subject to tax and with Ball admitting he qualified for the highest bracket of tax, he had to hand eighty per cent back to the Exchequer. The players were given £2 a day 'on condition that it shouldn't be considered as a precedent,' said the FA. Luck went England's way in a weak Group One and Ramsey had to admonish his players for their uninspired performance against the French. But he showed a flash of humour in the tunnel outside the dressing room when a journalist said to him, 'Does this avenge the Battle of Hastings?' He thought for a moment and said, 'When was the Battle of Hastings?'

England's quarter-final against Argentina was one of the most shameful episodes in international football. Ramsey had roused his players with pre-match exhortations to 'beat this lot' but the fault lay entirely with the Argentinians, who were guilty of bodychecking, punching, arguing, shirt pulling, play acting and kicking. FIFA said in their report, 'They brought the game into grave disrepute by their flagrant breaches of the Laws and disregard for discipline and good order.' Their surly captain Antonio Rattin was at the heart of all that was wrong. He was a tall, arrogant figure who wanted to run the game with his own rules. The diminutive German referee Rudolph Kreitlin eventually ordered him off for persistent dissent and he refused to go. It took eight minutes to talk him into leaving, with the FIFA official, England's Ken Aston, who stood at 6ft 4ins tall, being the only man to confront him eye to eye.

There is a famous picture of Ramsey stopping George Cohen from exchanging his shirt with an opponent at the end and in a television interview Ramsey brought up the word 'animals' which caused such a furore around the world. Thirteen minutes from time Hurst's glancing near-post header from Peters' cross – a tactic pioneered by Ron Greenwood – gave England the victory and a place in the semi-final against Portugal, the team that had kicked Pelé out of the tournament.

Ramsey didn't agree but the critics billed it as Bobby Charlton *v.* Eusebio. Portugal's Mozambique-born striker was to finish up as top scorer in the competition with nine goals. In Portugal he sometimes scored goals with powerful shots from the halfway line and his strength and power was immense. Eusebio, who barely looks any older today, scored from a late penalty but Charlton scored both goals in England's enthralling 2-1 triumph, the second a spectacular long-range shot. Today's pictures are far better than those of the 1960s, and far more plentiful, but that picture of Eusebio leaving the pitch with his shirt pulled up to wipe away his tears tells a story without any need for accompanying words.

Saturday 30 July 1966 goes down as the greatest day in English football history – England 4, West Germany 2 after extra time. It was the most dramatic World Cup final of all, perhaps better than the one in 1954 when Germany won 3-2 over Hungary. One often-recalled moment was the sight of Ramsey sitting on the bench, glum faced, as the final whistle went and everyone was on their feet and screaming their delight. But that was him. His early life, his Army life and, later, his life in professional football all taught him to keep his emotions in check.

On the morning of the World Cup final Ramsey had already made up his mind about the Greaves issue and Greaves knew it. After getting up and showering, Greaves started packing at the team hotel. 'What's happening?' asked Moore, his room mate. 'It's all up with me,' he said. 'I'm off.' His great friend implored him to stay on after the game 'to have a few bevvies'. But when the post-match ceremonies were performed he picked up his bag and went home and got drunk. Twenty-five years later he was still feeling the pain, turning down the invitation to attend the anniversary dinner.

Before the 2006 World Cup Jack Charlton came up with a very illuminating story about Ramsey. Interviewed by a German TV company, he said, 'Alf never spoke to the team in the dressing room before matches and it was the same at Wembley in the final. He preferred to sit next to you and give you his instructions. He said to me, "Get tight on their centre forward and don't let him turn." I said, "Does that mean I can kick him?" He said, "Do what is necessary." In the Leeds lingo that was licence to kill!'

In his pre-match talk Ramsey gave his usual rundown on every opponent to each player. 'You know what to do,' he said. 'Win it and you will.' Harold Shepherdson, the much-loved trainer, told the players, 'Play for Alf' – and they did. Although it was a sunny day there were a few showers and it helped the excitement, with players on both sides making mistakes, except for the peerless Moore who laid on the third goal of Hurst's hat-trick, the first ever scored in a final. The perpetual debate over Hurst's second, a shot that came down close to the line and was deemed to have crossed by Russian linesman Tofik Bakhramov, will never end. Was it an act of revenge by a Russian who recognised that millions of his countrymen died at the hands of German soldiers? We will never know. There were calls for line judges or technological aids then but forty years on little has changed. Helmut Schoen, the respected and much-liked German manager, who spoke good English, admitted later that he made a tactical mistake by asking Franz Beckenbauer, his best attacking midfielder, to mark Bobby Charlton. These two great players cancelled each other out.

In the dressing room after the match, the stone floor was awash with champagne and some of the players were on their way to being tipsy when they emerged to board the coach for the drive through packed streets to the banquet. It was held at the Royal Garden Hotel in Kensington High Street, a hundred yards away from the offices of Associated Newspapers, owners of the *Daily Mail*. When the players were ushered into the main dining room they realised that the FA had organised a separate dinner downstairs for their wives. The ladies' gifts were… pairs of scissors! These days David Beckham and Gary Neville wouldn't have tolerated a separate meal. The players' presents from a grateful FA were suits, ties and briefcases. The next morning Ramsey first raised the subject of bonuses, a sum of £22,000 coming from the FA for winning. Moore was the first to say, '£1,000 a man irrespective of who played in the side.' Ramsey agreed. It was a short meeting, no agents being around in those days.

The popular Moore was voted Player of the Tournament and it was tragic that he was the first of the twenty-two to die, from cancer in 1993. He was awarded the OBE soon after the final, the only player to be awarded at the time. The others were honoured at various later dates. Ramsey was made a Knight of the Realm, the first man from Dagenham to be honoured, and he was proud to accept.

After a short holiday, Ramsey was back working in his office at the new building in Lancaster Gate. What do England managers do between internationals? Someone on the same floor as Alf revealed:

> Not a lot really. Alf used to read his letters and dictated replies to the sensible ones. Then he'd call one or two managers and then go off for lunch, often with a journalist whom he trusted. He was back for tea and after a couple of things to attend to, like appointments, he walked round the corner to the nearby Lancaster Gate underground station, caught the Central Line to Liverpool Station and went back to Ipswich by train. He rarely travelled first class in his early days.

The older players like Cohen, Wilson, Jack Charlton and Stiles were injured or not fit for another World Cup campaign and Greaves wasn't going to make himself available unless he was given a starting place. A press campaign was launched calling for Greaves to be recalled. 'I am being crucified because I am not selecting Greaves yet he told me he does not want to play for England,' said Ramsey. That wasn't quite accurate. At twenty-nine Greaves was still the kingpin in the penalty area and Francis Lee and Jeff Astle, who played in the 1970 World Cup, weren't in his class. Greaves didn't want to be sitting on the bench 6,000 feet above sea level.

In the European Championships England lost 1-0 to Yugoslavia in a nasty semi-final game in Florence with Alan Mullery, who replaced Stiles, becoming the first England player to be sent off, a minute from time. However, in the remaining nineteen matches up to the start of the Mexico World Cup England lost only once, going down 2-1 to Brazil in Rio de Janeiro. The FA mandarins were content with the way the team was going, but not its PR. On a three-match summer tour to Mexico City (a dull 0-0), Montevideo (won 2-1) and Rio in 1969, Ramsey's indifference towards Mexican journalists was causing concern. After the goalless draw against Mexico Ramsey missed a good chance to ingratiate himself and his team to the local press, ready for the real action a year later. But instead of expressing his pleasure about his visit, he launched a critical analysis of what had gone wrong: a band playing through the night outside the team's hotel, no motorcycle escort to take the team to the stadium and local people booing and jeering England. By the time of the World Cup Finals, one newspaper was describing England's squad as 'a team of thieves and drunks'.

The drinking reference was from the arrival of Astle at the airport when he had taken a drink or two to calm his nerves. But the major setback came after a warm-up game in Bogota two weeks before the World Cup kick-off when a shop girl named Clara Padilla, working in a small jewellery boutique in the Tequendama Hotel where England had just booked in, reported that a bracelet worth £625 had been stolen. Asked to name the culprit – the two Bobbys, Moore and Charlton had been browsing at the time – she implicated England's captain. Bobby Moore's renowned calmness came to the fore and he insisted that he was innocent. Apparently 'fingering' famous people and accusing them of phantom thefts was common at the time in Bogota and Helmut Schoen, the German manager, told Ramsey later that one of his players had had a similar experience. The England squad flew off to Mexico with Moore still detained but a witness who failed to appear won him his release and when he arrived back at the team hotel in Mexico City later the whole squad lined up to cheer him.

Ramsey asked for new, quieter rooms in Guadalajara but it made no difference. Several people in the group had to take sleeping tablets as the bands and hooters blared out below. With the temperature, which soared to 100°F, and the 6,000ft altitude sapping the energy of the players, diets were carefully checked; no salads, no ice cream and only bottled water could be drunk. That didn't prevent Gordon Banks going down with a stomach upset the day before the big game against West Germany. England survived a mauling from the aggressive Romanians in their opening game in Guadalajara, Geoff Hurst's goal clinching the win without too many worries.

Brazil were next, in the same sweltering stadium. Ramsey made an unusual pre-match speech. 'Would you give gold away?' he asked his players. The Bogota bracelet was still in everyone's mind. What was he on about? Before anyone spoke, he said, 'Well, the ball is gold today. Don't give it away and you will defeat these Brazilians. If you give it away in this heat you might not get it back.' Both sides passed and passed and passed and some people, including Bobby Charlton, said it was the most technically correct match ever played. Old films captured the quality of the passing but the contest needed more action in the penalty areas. There were highlights, including the incredible save by Gordon Banks to deny Pelé's downward header, Alan Mullery's limpet-like marking of the world's best player and the miss of the tournament by substitute Jeff Astle.

Ramsey rested four stars for the Czechoslovakia game – some of the Czechs had been suspended for not trying – and England got through by an Allan Clarke penalty. There was little threat from the Czechs. Now it was off to Leon, a city higher, dustier and scruffier than Guadalajara. The West Germans had been based there for their group games, having spent only two weeks preparing in Mexico compared to England's four. Possibly this had given them an advantage. Banks was unable to play and Chelsea's Peter Bonetti was promoted to his place. In the aftermath of the inquests, the likeable Bonetti was the man who took most of the flak. After Mullery and Peters gave England what seemed to be an unassailable 2-0 lead, 'The Cat' dived over a low cross-shot from Franz Beckenbauer, which went in. At that point Bobby Charlton was replaced and that was to be his last appearance, his 106th. 'We'd hit the wall,' said Alan Ball. Colin Bell, a player with immense stamina, took over. It was a sensible decision.

Ramsey made another substitution, Norman Hunter for Martin Peters, and that was harder to understand. Hunter for the injured left-back Keith Newton would have made more sense. Uwe Seeler scrambled the equaliser and, as England's players wilted, Gerd Muller volleyed the winner from three yards in extra time. There were tears in the England dressing room and no one spoke for a while. Ramsey briefly praised his men and looked to the floor. His players looked as deathlike as Banks back in his hotel room. It was another twelve years before England were back in a World Cup Finals.

The next day the team travelled back to Mexico to catch the homeward flight and there was some relief in the coach. Tommy Wright, one of the reserves, sat sobbing in his seat and Ramsey put his arm round him to console him. 'There's no beer left on the bus,' said Scouser Wright.

In *The Official History of the FA*, Bryon Butler wrote:

> There were no reproaches from the FA. Ramsey reported that England's players had done everything he had asked, and given the same challenge, he would pick the same players and play the same way. His position in the late '70s was still strong.

Two years later his squad were dumped out of the quarter-finals of the European Championships, losing to the same opposition, the Germans, 3-1 at Wembley and drawing 0-0 in Berlin two weeks later. The strident criticism mounted from all quarters and the message was clear: England must qualify for the 1974 World Cup in Germany. Poland, one of the more committed Eastern European sides, stood in their path. Alan Ball, now a senior player, lost his temper when Martin Peters was badly fouled and grabbed the assailant by the throat and pulled him down. Ball was duly sent off and Poland won 2-0 in Chorzow.

The home game against Poland took place on 17 October 1973 and Ramsey told his players after the 1-1 draw which put England out, 'The gods were against you.' He was absolutely right. England had thirty-nine shots at Jan Tomaszewski, the possessed Polish goalkeeper, and only one beat him, a penalty from Allan Clarke. The shot count was 39-2, the corner count 26-3. In the fifty-seventh minute the ball was being played down the right in front of the Royal Box when the intimidating Norman Hunter, preferred to Bobby Moore, foolishly tried to stamp on the ball instead of knocking it away. It fell in front of Gadocha, who ran on and crossed for Jan Domarski's shot to beat Peter Shilton. Should Shilton have stopped it? He said he was temporarily unsighted by Emlyn Hughes. So, for the sight of Hughes, we lost an empire. Hunter thought Shilton was the culprit but said, 'Like an idiot, I said it was my fault.'

Mick Channon, who played forty-six times for England, played in that match and later he said:

> Alf admitted to me that he made a mistake leaving me out of the game in Poland, which was big of him. You got the impression that Alf didn't give a damn for the press and all he was interested in were his players. There was no doubt that his contempt for the media got him sacked.

It was a flukey result but no one took that into account. Ramsey was in the dock and a bombardment from Fleet Street panicked the FA into discussing his future. New FA secretary Ted Croker said, 'I was amazed at the virulence of the campaign against him and I felt sorry for him.' On Guy Fawkes Night, when he could well have been burnt at the stake, the FA gave him unanimous backing. And we all know what that means. Within a month Italy came to Wembley and won 1-0 and the hounds were unleashed.

On St Valentine's Day, the FA reconvened and the amiable Dr Andrew Stephen, the chairman, said Ramsey wanted a new contract and more money but he thought he should be replaced by a younger man. Ramsey was fifty-three after all. One senior member brought up Ramsey's ill-advised handling of the press. 'It needs to be improved,' he said. It was too late, of course. The vice-chairman, the odious Professor Sir Harold Thompson, backed Dr Stephen. 'He must go,' he said. Two months later the dismissal was ratified and a stunned Ramsey said, 'Can the news be delayed until 1 May?' They allowed him that but not much more.

He told friends, 'They didn't really give a reason.' And he didn't give his own explanation to his friend from Ipswich, Ted Phillips. The two men travelled back on the train to Ipswich on the day of his sacking and Ramsey offered to buy him a whisky. 'What's going on?' asked Phillips. Ramsey laughed. Then he bought another round and when Phillips got off at Colchester he was picked up by his wife Margaret. 'Did you see the front page of the paper?' she asked. She held up the evening newspaper with a front page headline reading 'Alf Ramsey Sacked'. You would think he could have told his old mate but that was Alf.

Dr Neil Phillips, the England doctor, told a revealing and poignant story about some expensive dinner mats. These were commissioned by the FA as presents after winning the World Cup:

> Alf and his staff heard about them and someone found them in a garage covered with dust. Denis Follows, the FA secretary, said, 'They are aerial photos of the venues of England's games.' Alf said, 'We'd like to have some for my staff.' But Follows said they were only for the councillors. It always rankled with Alf.

Before the Northern Ireland *v.* England game in 1969 someone telephoned the police, possibly from the IRA, and said Ramsey was going to be assassinated. There wasn't enough time to search the stadium so the officer in charge came into the dressing room to talk to Ramsey about what was to be done, whether they would abandon the match or go ahead with it. Neil Phillips said, 'Alf replied that he was going to lead out the team as usual, with Harold Shepherdson on one side and Les Cocker on the other to protect him. That caused a big laugh.' The game went ahead.

Ramsey almost went in purdah, rarely emerging, after his sacking. He was manager of Birmingham for five months, a director for longer, but it didn't work out. Increasingly bitter, he put his name to critical articles in the *Daily Mirror* and upset his near neighbour Bobby Robson, who lived half a mile away in the same road. He rejected Robson's overtures, once refusing an offer from Robson to drive him home from Stamford Bridge. He said in his most haughty voice, 'I arrived here by train and will return by train.' He played golf every week, rather badly, and he and three friends used to play for the right to pay for tea back in the bar. He didn't win too often.

Alf Ramsey died of Alzheimer's on 28 April 1999. Most of his boys, the World Cup winners, turned up, with Bobby Charlton and George Cohen giving addresses. Geoff Hurst said later, 'I was disappointed not to see more people from the footballing establishment.' They were ashamed, that's why.

DON REVIE

1974–1977

The Man Who Loved Football,
His Family and Money

P 29   W 14   D 8   L 7   48%

This is where things went wrong. Lamentably, the FA failed to do what most clubs do when they sack their manager – they didn't line up another suitable candidate. Ramsey's dismissal gave them plenty of time to find one but they procrastinated and finally asked Joe Mercer, the Coventry City general manager, to take over as caretaker manager until they found the right man. Joe was fifty-nine and a few years earlier had had a stroke. 'I'm only standing in,' he insisted. 'I'm too old for all that hassle.'

But there was little criticism directed his way in the summer of 1974 when his brief stewardship lasted just seven matches, with only one – against the Scots – resulting in defeat. Mercer, born in Ellesmere Port in 1914, soon brought smiles back to English football. If there was a contest for the happiest man in football at that time he would have won it easily. He typified the best of Scouse humour and when he arrived at Lancaster Gate to discuss matters with his new bosses a receptionist asked him, 'Do you have an appointment?' 'Yes, for seven matches,' he said. Peter Shilton said of him:

> Everyone loved him. He had a banana grin, bandy legs and a heart bigger than his head. He saw reporters as friends who were there to help him get his message across. He wanted to play with a swagger but some of his team talks were woolly. Sometimes we took the field not knowing who had been nominated as penalty takers.

Joe's jolly style of management was briefly interrupted when Kevin Keegan was arrested for allegedly standing on a conveyor belt in Belgrade Airport during the summer tour to Germany, Bulgaria and Yugoslavia. Keegan claimed he had been beaten up after being frogmarched to a detention room. There was a team meeting that night and the players were ready to go home until Mercer, who was hampered by a sore back, said:

> Listen lads, the only way you can show these people up is to get out there and give their team a bloody good hiding. We can go home, no problems. But Kevin won't be able to come with us. He'll probably have to stay behind and answer charges. The only way we'll get him out is by sticking together and answering them on the field. It's their country off the field but they can't stop us on it.

The players accepted his sensible advice and Keegan headed the equaliser in a 2-2 draw, with Malcolm Macdonald shooting wide on his own in the final minute. That was Mercer's final game in charge and the search was on for a permanent manager.

Gordon Jago, who was manager of QPR, Gordon Milne (Coventry) and the late Jimmy Bloomfield (Leicester) were interviewed. They were highly qualified, successful coaches and very likeable men but the feeling in the council chamber at the FA was that they were all lightweight. More advertisements for the England manager's job were placed in the newspapers but the FA could have saved the outlay.

Shortly afterwards Don Revie rang Ted Croker's private line in the FA secretary's office and said, 'I am very interested in the job.' The path had been cleared by a football journalist named Tom Holley, who spoke to both parties in private. In those days managers relied on journalists to find their next job without upsetting the authorities. Revie built up a cadre of friendly journalists which provided him with plenty of good PR throughout his career.

Croker, son of a policeman, a professional footballer for a brief time at Charlton, a successful businessman and one of the few RAF pilots to survive an aircraft crash on the Pennines, wasn't well versed in these behind-the-scenes machinations and had only been appointed secretary nine months earlier. He was very excited. Revie was the outstanding club manager of the day with three Manager of the Year awards and eight major trophies in his thirteen years with Leeds. When Croker told his chairman, chain-smoking Scots doctor Sir Andrew Stephen, his boss was equally excited. They sent a three-man delegation to Leeds to speak to Revie – Croker, Stephen and Dick Wragg, the chairman of the FA International Committee – and it was a brief meeting. They conceded almost every point to Revie except rearranging the football calendar to suit England and not the clubs. To say that they threw themselves at the feet of the Leeds manager wouldn't be an exaggeration. Revie was duly appointed with universal approval, or so it seemed, and they had a lot of time to regret their hasty and ill-advised decision.

Leeds wanted a large sum, higher than the current transfer fee for a player, as compensation but the next day, doubtless after Revie told them he was going anyway, they changed their minds. Croker said of him, 'he was a man of strong personality.' That could be transposed to 'getting his own way' and he usually did. In the background there were a number of shady transactions and events which someone on the FA should have known of and warned the decision makers about – for Revie was in many ways a crook, a devious man who cheated in order to become a winner and stay one. He was also a paradox. Those who knew him well looked on him as a friendly, cuddly man who was much loved by those who worked with him. When he left Elland Road many of the staff cried, particularly the lady members of staff. He never forgot anyone's birthday and if someone was ill, he always sent flowers. His empire at Leeds was compared to the Mafia with him in the leading role. The directors left everything to him and rarely raised objections.

Nicknaming him 'Don Readies', as some people did, was valid because he grew up in a time when players were paid 'readies', inducements which were never declared on any tax forms. Players moved from club to club to pick up brown envelopes full of cash and the word 'bung' came into common parlance. In his brilliant book *Don Revie, Portrait of a Footballing Enigma* Andrew Mourant wrote that it was significant that his name was an anagram for *envie d'or*, 'love of gold'. Yet when he died on 26 May 1989 from motor neurone disease in desperately sad circumstances at the comparatively young age of sixty-one, he left just £67,786 in his UK estate.

Alan Ball told a revealing story in his latest autobiography about the time when he was at Blackpool and the big clubs wanted his services. One day a Yorkshire voice came on the line and said Revie wanted to sign him for Leeds. The unknown man arranged a meeting with Ball on the Saddleworth moors to put Revie's case to him. Ball said:

I suspected that it wouldn't be the end of the matter but I was not prepared for what happened next. About ten days later, there was a knock on the front door. Lesley, my late wife, answered it. It was a dark, rainy night and there was a man on the doorstep. He gave her an envelope and said, 'This is for Alan.' Lesley took the envelope and we counted out £100 in notes. It happened almost every Friday and all the man would say was, 'no names, no pack drill, here is an investment.' I kept it for a long time.

Soon afterwards, he signed for Everton, not Leeds. In 1979 Ball was fined £3,000 for breaching the regulations after admitting the facts but Revie never appeared before a similar FA commission. He denied having played any part in the Ball incidents and by then had sued the *Daily Mirror* for libel on other more serious matters, ostensibly to prevent any further comment in the public domain.

The *Mirror* had made a number of allegations against Revie over fixing matches but none reached the courts. The most serious one was about an alleged £500 bribe offered to the highly reputable manager Bob Stokoe of Bury. 'I remember the situation very clearly,' said the late Stokoe, who managed Sunderland when they beat Leeds 1-0 in the 1973 FA Cup final. Stokoe's joy at the end of the game was graphically captured by photographs and TV footage as he charged onto the pitch with his arms aloft. It was his way of celebrating a memorable triumph over a cheat and liar. He said, 'He offered me £500 to take it easy. There were no witnesses. I said no. And when I said no, he asked me if he could approach my players. I said under no circumstances and reported it to my chairman.'

Another newspaper, the *Sunday People*, claimed that three players were approached and offered various sums, up to £1,000, to take a dive in the final League match of the 1971/72 season against Wolves. Leeds had already scraped to a 1-0 victory over Arsenal in the centenary FA Cup final and two days later they needed to beat Wolves at Molineux to win the double. They lost 2-1 in front of 53,379 fans with Revie moaning about two penalty appeals which went against his players. Mike O'Grady, who used to play for Leeds, was supposed to have been contacted about the bribes through a third party. He denied everything. The FA investigated and failed to find creditable witnesses and the case collapsed.

Frank McLintock, Arsenal's double-winning captain, waited nearly forty years to reveal his account of the way Revie tried to bribe him before an Arsenal *v.* Leeds match at Highbury on 7 May 1968. In his book *True Grit* he wrote:

> Don whispered, 'You and Barbara should have a nice holiday this summer. You could go anywhere in the world you wanted as a guest of Leeds United. Just take it easy out there tonight.' I lost my rag and shouted, 'You come up to me and ask me to take it easy. Are you f——ing crazy?'

McLintock scored in Arsenal's 4-3 win and said, 'There was no ambiguity about what Don had said. He was a flawed man in flawed times.'

Revie used to put pressure on referees, often leaving friendly notes in the officials' room at football clubs. Once he wrote to Ray Tinkler, the referee who booked Billy Bremner in a game against Northampton, and pleaded to him to cancel the booking because Bremner would be banned. The FA charged Revie with misconduct and censured him. Years later, Bremner's name was brought into another alleged corruption charge concerning the Leeds goalkeeper Gary Sprake, who denied everything. Bremner eventually won £100,000 in libel damages.

Revie was a master of gamesmanship, seeking every advantage, fair or otherwise, to benefit his own side. Norman Burtenshaw, one of the tougher referees of the previous generation, said:

> He took everything to the limit. If Leeds were winning in the second half, their players took turns to go down injured, breaking the rhythm of the game to frustrate the other side. Les Cocker, his trainer, used to race out there shouting 'lie down' and out came the contents of his bag. It took a lot of time to pack it away again. In one game he was so upset about an incident that he punched an opposing player in the face and put him down for a count!
>
> There was a strange case in 1972 when I was due to appear at a personal hearing asked for by Allan Clarke. It was not long before the FA Cup semi-final against Birmingham and if Clarke had lost his appeal he could have missed the match through suspension. An official from the League rang me and asked me to take the Fourth Division game between Hartlepool and Southport on the same day. I said I had to attend the Clarke hearing. The

official told me to ring the FA and get it cancelled and I did that. I realised then that the Hartlepool *v.* Southport match was the only game on that night. So why me? There were eighty referees available and it was a 352-mile trip for me. Clarke duly played in the semi-final and later withdrew his appeal. I got the impression that this particular official, who is dead, was in the pocket of Revie. And that wasn't the only case of its time.

The disciplinary record of Revie's Leeds side was the worst in the Football League and one season the club was fined £3,000 by the FA. Revie responded by staging a PR exercise – getting his players to kick balls into the crowd and to hand their sock tags to supporters as a goodwill gesture.

He tried every subterfuge to win concessions from the Football League over dates of fixtures to suit his club. Alan Hardaker, the belligerent and respected League secretary, hated him and the two men carried out a vendetta against each other, inflicting an immense amount of damage to English football. When Revie was appointed England manager Hardaker rang Croker and said, 'You're off your head appointing him.' Peter Croker, a long-serving defender with Charlton, warned his brother Ted that he was making a big mistake. Four years later most people realised it was a calamitous mistake. One word explained it: expediency.

Revie's successful record as a club manager persuaded everyone to take him on as England's third full-time manager, irrespective of his disciplinary excesses. These days top managers must have coaching qualifications and Ted Croker said after the affair ended:

It was a surprise to discover that Revie was only a holder of our preliminary certificate and not the full badge. That made a mockery of our coaching system. We wanted the coaching side to be brought closer together with the international side and with Revie not being an FA coach, the gulf between the two was as great as ever. I was also disappointed at the lack of coaching experience of people whom Revie appointed, including Gordon Banks and George Eastham, both extremely nice and personable men but lacking the necessary experience. Within six months I realised Hardaker was probably right. Revie had the ruthlessness to succeed at club level but different qualities were needed at international level. He didn't have them.

Professor Sir Harold Thompson was a powerful figure in the FA for more than two decades and in 1976 he succeeded Sir Andrew Stephen as chairman. In a short period he acted as an appointer and supporter of Revie but would become his chief prosecutor and judge in the disciplinary case two years later. The son of a Yorkshire colliery manager, Thompson was a forceful, abrasive man who was knighted for his work as an international scientist, particularly in China. He played a prominent part in the sacking of Alf Ramsey, insisting that the FA had financial problems brought on by the failure to qualify for the World Cup in 1974. He wanted a new start under a younger, more enthusiastic manager who could handle the press. He backed Revie's candidature from the start despite his strong links with the amateur game before the amateur/professional distinction was abolished in 1974. He had played centre half for Oxford University in the late 1920s and founded Pegasus, an amateur side taken from the best players at Oxford and Cambridge universities.

One former Pegasus player said, 'The trouble with "Tommy" was that he was an expert on amateur football but knew little about the professional game.' When Alan Ball was charged with misconduct over the £100 weekly bungs in 1978 he asked Ball at the hearing 'what does your father do?' Alan Ball senior played professional football for fifteen years and managed seven clubs. Thompson's elevation to the top at the FA was one of the worst appointments since the organisation was founded in 1863. So how did he do it? 'First, his intellect,' said the ex-Pegasus man, continuing:

> He was brighter than the others and he was a very convincing, and persuasive speaker. Most of the others were small men, mostly nice guys, without that gift. In the Revie High Court case Judge Cantley described him as 'an honourable man' which he was to a certain degree.
>
> But many of his colleagues knew about his reputation for groping young ladies. There was one incident on a flight back from an England trip when he was caught putting up his hand up the skirt of a stewardess and the crew wanted to get him taken to court but it was hushed up.

Journalists at the back of the plane were told about it but none of them wrote the story. These days it would have been on the front pages. Thompson would have been kicked out of the FA.

When Revie was appointed he kept his home in Leeds and moved to a temporary home in Putney. It was a convenient journey to Lancaster Gate. He got on well with Dr Stephen but Thompson kept questioning him about his expenses and other irksome matters. The relations between the two men were soon strained. Thompson addressed him by his surname from the start and when Revie said, 'Can you please call me Don?' the pompous Thompson responded, 'When I get to know you better, Revie, I will call you Don.' Revie is alleged to have responded by saying, 'When I get to know you better, Thompson, I will call you Sir Harold.' Thompson never got to know Revie well and he wasn't the only one.

Revie grew up in Middlesbrough, close to Ayresome Park, and was always called by his first name, or a nickname. Donald George Revie was born on 10 July 1927 in poor, humble circumstances. His father was a joiner and was often unemployed and his mother, who died of cancer when he was twelve, used to take in washing for five shillings a week, walking four miles to deliver it. His tough upbringing brought just one relief, his love for the rag ball which he started kicking about in the near-deserted streets. His hero was George Camsell, the Middlesbrough centre forward who, in the year Revie was born, scored 59 goals in 37 matches. A friend, George Tinsley, was the first in his group to own a football and Revie spent hours kicking it against walls, mastering his skills.

He wasn't the first footballer from this background who developed a habit of hoarding his wealth when he finally graduated to the top of his chosen profession. Footballers know their career could be ended with one kick and that, without any training or capability for a second career, they could be plunged back into poverty for the rest of their lives. It explains why corruption still lingers on in the game, fuelled by the activities of unscrupulous agents and some managers. In France in 2005 police and tax investigators raided the offices of many football agents, starting an overdue clean-up operation. The English FA should have initiated a similar campaign but it was a year before an inquiry was set up. By this time the game was dominated by a few powerful men who ran the big Premiership clubs, some of whom dealt with unscrupulous agents.

Revie was a bright pupil in school, capable of going on to matriculation standard, but at fourteen he was forced to work as an apprentice bricklayer. He spent long days building walls and the rest of his time advancing his footballing education. His skills blossomed and three years later he signed for Leicester City. He had some outstanding mentors, including the former Leicester and England midfield player Sep Smith. 'I worked him so hard that he often burst into tears,' said Smith. It showed the emotional side of Revie. Even when he was England manager, his eyes could still well up with a tear or two. Anyone who has lost his mother before time, or someone close, will know that feeling.

Revie was building a reputation for bad luck and it dogged him through his life. He challenged Tottenham midfield player Ronnie Burgess in a home game and was carried off, screaming with pain. The X-rays showed three breaks in the ankle and the new Leicester manager John Duncan gave him encouragement, saying, 'It's 1,000 to one against you playing again but I'm confident you will be the one to do it.' His understanding manager proved to be right and in 1949 he married Duncan's niece Elsie, a Scots school-teacher from Lochgelly. It was the start of a forty-year love story. A strong personality in her own right, she played a star role in the family, advising and helping him and finishing up as president of Leeds United. She died in March 2005 at the age of seventy-seven. Leeds manager Kevin Blackwell said, 'She was the mother figure of Leeds United.' Revie named his son Duncan after the manager and, asked about the boy's footballing prospects, he replied, 'He's too slow.' It was a very close, and protective, family. When he took charge at Leeds, he brought that family approach to Elland Road and it was one of the reasons for his success. He tried to copy it with England but it didn't work.

A second serious injury kept him out of the 1949 FA Cup final when he was struck a fearful blow in the nose, leaving him close to death after a dramatic eight-hour taxi ride back from Plymouth. A doctor told him he was an hour from death. Most managers are superstitious and Revie was one of the most obsessive. Among his phobias were the colour green and ornamental elephants, while rituals included taking the same route to the dugout before a match and wearing his 'lucky' blue suit. One season he wore a mohair suit that was falling to bits and the zip of which had broken. He still used it, using a safety pin. He also had an obsession with birds, which he thought brought bad luck. That was why he removed the peacock from the Leeds badge.

His key playing years were spent with Manchester City between 1951 and 1956 when the innovative style of the team was based on the 'Revie Plan'. He added plenty of input but the original idea came from Les McDowall, the manager who had studied the methods of the Hungarians. Revie wore the number 9 shirt and played in midfield, confusing opponents and spectators alike. The plan was based on intelligent passing movements with the emphasis on keeping possession, rather like the methods now used by Jose Mourinho at Chelsea. Most clubs used the long ball at that time and for a while Revie feared he might be bypassed. Soon he was conducting a magnificent orchestra. In 1955 he was presented with his first of six caps for England and at the end of the season he was voted Footballer of the Year. But there was a reverse at the end of the season when the injured Jimmy Meadows went off in the 1955 FA Cup final and ten-man City went down to Newcastle by three goals to one. Asked about the prospect of substitutes being adopted, he said it wouldn't be a good idea. Strange! He was one of the first managers to use substitutes for tactical reasons.

There was an incident the following season that revealed his stubbornness and loyalty to his wife. He claimed he hadn't been on holiday in six years and was intending to have a short break at Blackpool during Elsie's holiday period. McDowall said he could go but would have to commute to Maine Road for training every day. Revie refused and went on holiday. When he returned, he was suspended and fined. If he believed in something, he would stick to it, backed by Elsie. He departed for Sunderland and in 1958 he signed for Leeds. In his nineteen years as a player he scored 110 goals from 515 League and cup matches. He was a fine, industrious player but not a great one. He was a thinker, a schemer and a planner but not a genius. He was suspicious of highly talented, individualistic players and among those jettisoned by him as England manager were Alan Ball, Frank Worthington, Stan Bowles and Malcolm Macdonald.

He took over as player-manager of Leeds in March 1961 and his first signing was Albert Johanneson, the black South African winger who died almost in the gutter. Revie often spoke to his players about how to conserve their wealth and not squander it and he used the example of Johanneson's unfortunate downfall. Few managers had been bold enough to sign a black player before that time.

He insisted on wearing suits and ties and the players were fined for all kinds of minor offences. 'We were dour, physical, over aggressive – you name it and it was said or written about us,' said Norman Hunter in his book *Biting Talk*, continuing:

The Gaffer used to come in with the cuttings to show us. 'Look what they're writing about you,' he said. 'We'll show 'em.' He was brilliant. His attention to detail was amazing but what made him such a great manager was that he could always get the very best out of his players. He'd tell us 'You'll make it' and though we knew we weren't fit, we still played. I went through five seasons without missing a game. Les Cocker used to give me painkilling injections and I would get out there. The Gaffer liked to play the same team.

We bent the rules to suit us and today that wouldn't be tolerated. I made my presence felt with some hefty tackles but never went in with the intention to hurt anyone. I was a bit of a softy really.

What Hunter was actually saying was that Revie preached intimidation on the field. The Leeds *v*. Chelsea matches were fine illustrations of this with Hunter *v*. Chopper Harris top of the bill. With England, these tactics couldn't have been used.

Before departing Elland Road on his journey south to take up the England job, Revie made sure the journalists and commentators were well disposed towards him by providing drinks and sandwiches for the first time before press conferences. 'He came over as your favourite uncle,' said a senior journalist. 'He remembered your name and was always matey – well, at the start.' He asked the FA for a mass meeting of present and future England players so he could spell out his plans. Croker was surprised because the number of players was eighty-one. These days there wouldn't be as many as that playing in the Premiership who would be available for selection for England. The gathering was held in a hotel in Manchester and Revie told the players to have an early night but many of them were smirking. 'We'd been playing in a League game and that's the time when we normally let our hair down,' said Mick Channon. 'You can imagine, it was like meeting old friends you don't normally see socially except at the odd annual dinner. I am not saying that everyone got paralytic but I'll bet the landlords and club owners of Manchester did a roaring trade that night.'

Revie told the players next morning that they were responsible for the game's image and they should coach boys without payment. He said, 'you should get down on your knees every night and thank God you are doing something you love and are well paid for it.' The players' appearance money was £60 a man and that had been kept at that level for many years.

The players played for their pride, not money. Now he announced that the rewards were upped to £200 for a win and £100 for a draw. He said he appointed an agent to handle the commercial spin-offs for the players and his name was Harry Swales, an old friend. The England strip was now supplied by Admiral, with a new design featuring brighter colours. The alarm bells were ringing. 'Is Revie making money from the deal?' asked one commentator.

One of the most controversial parts of the new Revie plan was to introduce dossiers on opponents. Revie also provided games, like bingo, carpet putting and cards to occupy the minds of the players. Revie acted as the banker at these games, with Kevin Keegan helping him. On one occasion Channon took £250 from them in a putting competition when he was 25-1 in the betting. Revie encouraged his players to play cards for money, often joining in himself. Of the dossiers, Channon said, in his book *Man on the Run*:

> Most of the players didn't bother to read their dossiers and Dave Clement told me he still couldn't understand his after reading it six times. These dossiers really became an obsession with some who would take it too seriously and start believing they were facing some kind of supermen. It was different at Leeds where players grew up with his habits and many wouldn't have known any different.

Before his first game in charge, against Czechoslovakia in the European Championships at Wembley in October 1974, Revie added another gimmick, the playing of 'Land of Hope and Glory' before the kick-off. Song sheets were issued to the 84,000 crowd and Trevor Brooking, who came on as a substitute that day, said:

> The basis of his appeal was patriotism. We were going to do it for the fans and the country. We had our own song within the camp – 'It's a Grand Old Team to Play for' – and Revie tried to create the togetherness he had built up at Leeds. In the end, and this was possibly why he failed, he tried too hard.

England won joyously, two late goals boosting the final score to 3-0. The Germans were beaten 2-0, Cyprus were beaten twice, the home countries were overcome and in his first year, Revie was unbeaten. The reaction of the media was still supportive as the journalists munched their salmon sandwiches at England's VIP headquarters in deepest Hertfordshire. Hardly anyone criticised the constant changes in personnel. At Leeds Revie insisted on fielding the same side. Now it was the opposite with England. 'We had the impression he didn't know what was his best side,' said Croker. 'He would see a player having a good game and he'd be in.' In just over three years he capped twenty-nine newcomers and only once in his twenty-nine games fielded an unchanged side. He called up fifty-two players and was well on the way to capping all the eighty-one in the inaugural players' meeting. There were some odd names among them, including Steve Whitworth, Ian Gillard, Dave Clement, Mick Doyle, Phil Boyer, Tony Towers and Dave Thomas, none of whom were international standard. Three came from QPR and someone suggested he selected them because he lived round the corner from Loftus Road.

Revie's man management was being questioned. He dropped Emlyn Hughes when he was at his peak, at the age of twenty-seven, only to change his mind. Then he slung out the chirpy Ball, who never forgave him. The first Ball knew about it was when his wife took a call from a journalist who said, 'Alan has been dropped.' The official letter from the FA, signed by Revie's secretary, arrived the following morning. Before the 2-2 draw against Wales at Wembley, Keegan was summarily axed and responded by packing his bags and going home. Revie promptly changed his mind and apologised. The Troubles were at their height and there had been discussion about whether England should play their previous fixture, against Northern Ireland in Belfast. Croker had received a threatening message, supposedly from the IRA, about Keegan as the team assembled. Revie spoke against the idea of going to Belfast but the advice of the security experts was to go ahead. The decision was left to Keegan, and he wanted to play. So for him to be dropped for the next game against Wales was seen as a terrible insult to the bravest player in England's squad. As the team coach was about to drive away from Windsor Park there was a loud explosion nearby. The coach sped off to the airport and everyone was relieved to make it back to England.

Keegan was excellent in the 5-1 win over the Scots at Wembley but was overshadowed by the performance of new skipper Gerry Francis, who scored twice. Revie persuaded the FA to put up handsome rewards for winning the European Championships, £5,000 a man to win the trophy and bonuses for reaching the last eight and last four. Hardaker said, 'Money, money, money.' Revie replied, 'Football is a short career.' The bounty disappeared in the fog at Bratislava in October 1975. The kick-off was put back for twenty-four hours and on the next day England lost their first game under Revie, 2-1 at the hands of the eventual champions Czechoslovakia.

Suddenly, everything was going downhill for Revie and his dissatisfied players. The critics condemned his defensive way of playing, his lack of adventure. Every time a player was seen out drinking it made the headlines. Ball was one of the ringleaders when some senior players came back to the hotel well after the 10.30 p.m. curfew and he thought later that that was a reason why he was dumped. Sir Harold was continually harping on about what was going wrong and Revie looked a haunted man. Channon said, 'By this time he was a very nervous man. You could see that in him, he was sweating. I don't think he could trust anyone. He thought everyone was going to do him. Caps were dished out far too readily. You have to say he was losing control.' Revie was taking sleeping tablets. And some of his players were also taking them.

His bad luck continued when skipper Gerry Francis, his best defender Roy McFarland and Colin Bell, his outstanding midfield player, missed the whole of the 1976/77 season including the watershed match against Italy in Rome in November 1976. He had to make six changes, whereas Italy featured seven players from one club, Juventus, and it wasn't a surprise that a supine England side lost 2-0. A few months later another watershed hove into view, the arrival of Johan Cruyff and his Dutch team at Wembley. Before the kick-off, Cruyff rang Croker and asked what the crowd would be. 'I was taken aback,' said Croker. 'He wanted to work out the bonuses and that explained why they played so well.' Revie's men were almost drowned as the waters converged. It was a rare example of a great player winning a game almost on his own with Cruyff controlling the game in every square yard of the pitch. England were relieved to only lose 2-0. Howls went up from all sides. Revie told his friends that the pressure was affecting his family. It was time to go. England beat Italy 2-0 at home but Italy's wins over Finland guaranteed them a place in the World Cup Finals at the expense of England.

In the spring of 1976 a senior official of the United Arab Emirates FA heard about Revie's disquiet over his job and contacted him. The Arabs wanted

Revie as their national manager. It would be a less pressured job. The Scots had beaten England 2-1 at Wembley and the tirade of abuse mounted. Revie was supposed to be in Helsinki to watch the Finland *v*. Italy game. Instead, he flew to Dubai to discuss terms. But was Revie the UAE's first choice? According to Bobby Campbell, the former Portsmouth, QPR, Chelsea and Fulham manager, he was the man heading the wanted list, not Revie:

> Someone rang me from the UAE and offered me a fortune. I must say I fancied it but I'd just joined Fulham as their new manager and I had just signed my contract so I kept my word and stayed at Craven Cottage. They eventually signed Revie and Revie's deal was concluded in a car park at Leicester City Football Club. Amazing!

In the summer of 1977 England went on a tour to Brazil, Argentina and Uruguay. Revie was still in charge. All three matches were drawn but the real contest took place in a hotel room in Buenos Aires, a city which was almost under martial law, when Revie told Dick Wragg, the pipe-smoking chairman of the FA International Committee, that he was resigning. He wanted £55,000 compensation for the final two years of his contract. He was quitting 'in the best interests of the team', he said, arguing, 'All the press lads used to say that if I hadn't banged the drum to get people into Wembley then things would have been bad. And I brought a lot of money from sponsorships.'

Wragg was flabbergasted and so were his colleagues. Revie's demands were angrily rejected and the meeting soon broke up. Afterwards Croker said, 'We thought that was the end of it.' On the evening of 11 July sports reporters from the national newspapers rang Croker and chairman Thompson to ask them to comment on Revie's resignation 'because of pressure on his wife and family'. Revie had sold his story to the *Daily Mail* for a fee of around £30,000 excluding extras, without having the courtesy to tell his bosses first. Next morning there was outrage, not just among the footballing public but in the rival newspaper offices. Revie was called 'a traitor and a scoundrel'. It was reported that Revie flew to Dubai in disguise. Revie denied that but admitted he was wearing a cap and sunglasses. In the 40°C Dubai summer he would have needed sunglasses. He flew to Switzerland with his loyal friend and colleague Les Cocker, and then to Athens before going on to Dubai. But at Athens airport he was spotted by a *Daily Mail* reader who rang the sports desk in London. An executive thanked him for the tip and said the *Mail* were publishing the story and asked him not to ring any other newspaper. The scoop of the decade was nearly blown.

Revie signed a four-year contract worth £340,000 and he also received a signing-on fee of £100,000 and huge sums in expenses. Jeff Powell, who was a close friend, quoted him in the *Mail*:

> I sat down with Elsie one night and we agreed that the job was no longer worth the aggravation. It was bringing too much heartache to those nearest to us. Nearly everyone in the country seems to want me out and I am giving them what they want. I know people will accuse me of running away and it sickens me that I cannot finish the job.

There was no mention of the demand for £55,000.

'I was deceived; we all were,' said Croker. 'He should have been castrated,' said Stokoe. His leading critic, Brian Clough, said, 'What a despicable way to go.' In 1972 Revie had cleverly arranged a nine-year deal with Leeds to be paid £10,000 a year for attending four board meetings every twelve months. After Clough took over as manager of Leeds, where he lasted just forty-four days, he said, 'I soon found out all about his so-called family. It had more in keeping with the Mafia than Mothercare. He hadn't really left at all. He was down every corridor, round every corner, and in every cupboard.'

The FA condemned Revie's treachery and charged him with four offences: setting a bad example, acting deceitfully, debasing his official position, negotiating a new post when his full attention should have been given to the national team's cause and damaging the image of football and the FA. Revie's lawyers said they did not accept that the FA had any jurisdiction over him and he would not attend the hearing. The FA countered, saying that he would be suspended from any involvement with football under the FA until he appeared.

A year later, with the lawyers totting up huge bills, Revie's advisors gave the go-ahead for the postponed case. Croker told Thompson not to preside at the hearing on 18 December 1978 because his presence would be prejudical to the case. Thompson ignored his advice and his decision proved very costly to the FA. Appearing for Revie, Gilbert Gray QC kicked off with a series of spectacular goals. He claimed that Thompson, who was quoted as saying, 'The recent events have been quite disgraceful and Revie has behaved very badly,' was unfit to sit in judgement because he was biased. The FA commission rejected Gray's submission and banned Revie from English football for ten years. Some people thought it should be a life ban. Others thought it was harsh.

But Revie's lawyer knew he was backing a winner and applied to the High Court for the verdict to be overturned. English football's most publicised court case opened in November 1979 and it lasted eighteen days. Elsie accompanied Revie to the High Court from their hotel and she said, 'Every taxi driver was on Don's side. None of them asked us for the fare and everyone wished us luck.' Judge Cantley, who obviously disliked Revie, quashed the ten-year ban on the question of bias. In his hostile, two-hour summing-up he said:

> You held the highest post of its kind in English professional football and you published and presented to the public a sensational and notorious example of disloyalty, breach of duty, discourtesy and selfishness. Your conduct brought English professional football, at a high level, into disrepute.

Mr Gray asked for Revie's costs and said, 'It is apparent, if I may say so, that there may not be a great deal of warmth moving to Mr Revie from any direction.' Cantley replied, 'I haven't exhibited any more than I can help.' He ordered Revie to pay two-thirds of his own costs. The FA was ordered to pay the other third to Revie, as well as their own costs, which eventually totalled £141,000. Both sides lost heavily and it was like the Battle of Jutland in the First World War, with both navies limping back to dock with little ammunition left.

With absolute power, Revie did a good job in establishing a creditable international squad in the UAE in the next three years. His friend Lord Harewood, a former president of Leeds United, said:

> He used to take the players away before matches, the idea being to keep them away from their wives. Yet on match days the players still seemed exhausted. What he hadn't twigged was that some of them were quite as happy to pop into each others' beds as they were into the bed with their wives. Don was naïve in some ways and he was not a man of the world in sexual relations.

Revie was sacked by the Arabs in 1980 and this time he didn't sue anyone. Surprisingly, in view of the harshness of the conditions in the Middle East and the reluctance of his wife to stay on, he went on to manage First Division club Al Nasr in the UAE and then Al-Al FC in Cairo. In 1984 he was back in England and at fifty-seven he was wanted by the detestable Jim Gregory, chairman of QPR, as manager. The two men soon fell out over money and that was the end of Revie's footballing career. He had a property in Marbella, played golf at Wentworth, next to another of his properties and finished up living in Kinross, Perthshire, not far from Elsie's birthplace. In 1986 he was still playing good golf – occasional rounds under 80 – until a year later when he discovered he was suffering from the incurable motor neurone disease, a slow process where the body switches off to inevitable death. He died in Murrayfield Hospital, Edinburgh on 26 May 1989, Matt Busby's eightieth birthday.

For all his flaws, he didn't deserve that cruel finale. He was only sixtyone. He was a man who wanted to be loved – and he was by many. His family, and those in the Leeds family, were there at his funeral but no one from the FA hierarchy. A bottle of his favourite drink, cognac, lay on his coffin but there wasn't too much to celebrate.

RON GREENWOOD

1977–1982

*A Decent Man Whose Luck
Went Against Him*

| P 55 | W 33 | D 12 | L 10 | 60% |

On a hot summer's day in July 1977 FA chairman Professor Sir Harold Thompson was sitting with Ron Greenwood in the basement in Whites Hotel, the same hotel where Ashley Cole was tapped-up by Chelsea in 2005, when he came out with a phrase which was used a quarter of a century later in another, more shocking, context. He said, 'Everyone is being roasted', referring to the abrupt defection of Don Revie.

These days 'being roasted' would more likely refer to a girl having sex with overpaid footballers in a five-star hotel but that is not to say Thompson's words were wrong at the time. He said to Greenwood, 'The image of the game is all wrong. We need a firm, stable hand immediately and we are wondering if you could take over as caretaker manager of England for a while.'

Seventeen years before, Walter Winterbottom had asked Greenwood if he was interested in taking the England job and he thought it was too soon. Now it was an ideal time. He was fifty-five and was looked upon as the equivalent to a professor in football, with a worldwide reputation. After giving the job to the wrong man, Don Revie, the FA wanted a decent man who took the opposite approach, a Corinthian with high values. Greenwood soon accepted the invitation and wrote later, 'It occurred to me that I was the only man available.'

Greenwood had little respect for Revie and his way of playing the game. He described an incident when Revie, during his spell as England boss, arranged meetings with top managers:

My turn came and Revie opened the conversation by saying, 'We've never really talked, have we?' 'I don't know why not,' I replied. 'I'll tell you,' said

Don. 'Remember when you [West Ham United] beat us 7-0, well we were demoralised but I still went into your dressing room afterwards to congratulate you. You were over by the radiator and I came over and said, 'Marvellous. Miraculous. What a game you played.' And you looked at me and all you said was, 'Thank you very much.' I felt snubbed and I went back to our dressing room and told my players, 'We'll never lose to that bloody man's team ever again.'

The meeting at Whites Hotel was held below stairs because Thompson wanted privacy. Greenwood turned up at the FA offices to see him and Thompson was almost paranoid about being spotted by journalists. 'We'd better get out of here and find somewhere quiet,' he said. The two men walked round the corner to the nearby hotel in Bayswater Road, overlooking Hyde Park and, without going to the expense of hiring a room, Thompson walked through the ground floor and, hearing workmen banging around, he pointed to the stairs to the basement. The two men sat down in the basement, almost deafened. 'We're going to advertise the job, so no promises,' said Thompson. 'See what you can do.'

Greenwood had spent sixteen years running West Ham's finishing school, producing cultured and exciting football played by intelligent, thinking players. Upton Park was THE place to watch quality football in the South. The other place was at Anfield. The fans stood and sat close to the action and the atmosphere was vibrant, almost electric. The leading football journalists of the day loved sitting in the cramped press box and, after matches, Greenwood used to invite them into his office to talk football. It was like having a professor teach them. He didn't lecture them. He engaged them into a two-way exchange of views. One recalled:

We learned a fantastic amount. Most people thought he was an egghead, high in the sky over the ordinary man. But he never talked above anyone. It was a simple game, he used to say, by people with footballing brains. It's about getting your two against the other team's one, it's about space and how to use it and showing self-discipline. We could talk half an hour about a single pass from Bobby Moore or a near-post header from Geoff Hurst. He taught us to appreciate technique and style.

His secretary would bring out the cream cakes, tea and wine and it was often past eight o'clock before the talk ended. He loved a cream cake. And no one in his office ever broke a confidence.

Under his paternal leadership, West Ham won two FA Cup finals and the 1965 European Cup-Winners' Cup, Greenwood's greatest achievement was to provide three players – Moore, Geoff Hurst and Martin Peters – key to England's 1966 World Cup success. However, by 1974 he was losing enthusiasm. He was sickened by the 'professionalism' of people like Revie and their cohorts, calling them 'cheats'. Hooliganism was rampant and football grounds were like concentration camps, players were campaigning for freedom of contract and clubs were in severe financial difficulties. Winterbottom said, 'Ron was always angry when he saw ruthless and brutal aggression getting the better of skill. He deplored the spread of negative football and was disenchanted by the modern obsession with money.'

Greenwood persuaded his directors, the Cearns family and chairman Reg Pratt, to let his assistant John Lyall take charge of the first team and become general manager. He kept in the background and the day after West Ham beat Fulham 2-0 in the 1975 FA Cup final he missed the celebrations and went off for a walk on Brighton promenade with his loving wife Lucy. He needed to rekindle his enthusiasm and it came when he accompanied Winterbottom on a trip to the first World Youth Championship in Tunisia in 1977 as a member of FIFA's technical committee. 'I thoroughly enjoyed it,' he said. 'I saw some marvellous youngsters in action, full of skill and adventure and I drew great hope from them.' Working with FIFA he was mixing with the best of the international coaches who admired his work and passion for the game. Thompson's invitation came at just the right time. 'I could feel the fire rising in me again,' he said. 'I hoped my ideas might be suited to the international game and I was going to help restore faith and dignity in our game and prove to the world we could play a bit.'

A month before Greenwood's appointment, the FA decided to appoint their first press officer. Most other countries had one, including Germany, and their PR was vastly superior to England's. Ted Croker put forward the name of Glen Kirton, a thirty-year-old language graduate who had no experience of the newspapers, radio or television. 'Sir Harold was against the idea,' said Kirton, 'not because of my lack of media experience but because he didn't think he needed one.' A more experienced press officer would have saved the FA a lot of trouble over the Revie affair. Kirton, an open, friendly young man, who struck up a good relationship with Greenwood, was soon plunged into a succession of crises. He was so far down the list of officials that he wasn't accredited for the European Championships and when he was, there was no room allocated for him in Italy. He had to accept an offer from a helpful English journalist.

Greenwood was born at Worsthorne, a small village three miles north of Burnley, on 11 November 1921 and came from humble beginnings. His father Sam, a painter and decorator and a useful footballer, was described by his son as 'a kind and sympathetic man who did not anger easily'. The description could fit both father and son. His mother Ivy left their terraced house at 6.30 a.m. to work in a mill and the family was so short of money that their son had to wear wooden clogs. The only time he wore proper shoes was to attend Sunday school and he played for the Sunday school league, wearing out his second-hand boots at a fast rate. As the cotton industry declined work was harder to find and when he was ten his father set up home in Alperton, not far from the newly built Wembley Stadium. It was a brave decision. 'Our house had a real luxury,' he said. 'It had a bathroom.'

Like Revie, he left school at fourteen, starting an apprenticeship with a sign-writing company owned by a Lancastrian. 'I worked at Wembley, Olympia and Earls Court, which meant I enjoyed a free seat for much of the best sport and entertainment in Britain,' he said. 'One of my jobs was writing out the team changes for the cup finals at Wembley, including the 1938 FA Cup final when Preston's George Mutch scored from the penalty spot in extra time.' He was supposed to be kicking off in the final of the Middlesex Youth final at 6.30 p.m. and had to run the three miles home to collect his gear before going to the ground. He finished on the winning side to make it a memorable day for a seventeen-year-old.

He started at left-back before moving to centre half, where he was playing when he joined Chelsea at the start of the Second World War. He made his debut for the reserves a year later and an Aldershot side which included an all-international half-back line of Joe Mercer, Stan Cullis and Cliff Britton was beaten 6-0. Billy Birrell, Chelsea's Scots manager, told the other players, 'That boy Greenwood has the best football brain I've ever encountered' and he wasn't far wrong.

In 1940 his father was an air raid warden and when an unexploded bomb landed in the garden of a nearby house he advised the people living in it to evacuate. He offered to let them stay in his house and that was how Ron met his wife Lucy. They were married when he was nineteen and he said, 'It was the best match of my life.' When he became a manager, he always advised his players to get married at a young age like him. 'It gives you a stable background, someone to go home to and forget your worries,' he said. Ted Croker said of him:

> Working with young people can keep a person young and Ron Greenwood always struck me as a person who carried his age remarkably well. He had this boyish look about him, possibly from a contented mind. Lucy was a tremendous support to him over the years and I am sure a happy family background contributed to his success in life. He didn't smoke and did everything in moderation.

When the Greenwoods' son was born in 1951 they christened him Neil Franklin after the great England centre half.

The first six England managers, Winterbottom, Ramsey, Revie, Greenwood, Bobby Robson and Graham Taylor, followed the same path – married young to have happy marriages. Glenn Hoddle married young but the marriage didn't last and he has since married a second time. Terry Venables married young before the marriage was annulled and his second marriage has been a great success. Kevin Keegan is happily married, taking the total of successful marriages to seven, and as for Sven-Goran Eriksson – well, he was married for twenty-three years but he has been a ladies' man most of his life. He is the first England manager to have a comedy written about him, a play called *A Play in Swedish, English and Italian.* All about the life and loves of Sven, it played in the Royal Dramatic Theatre in Stockholm.

Greenwood joined the RAF and was stationed in Maghera in Northern Ireland where he played for Belfast Celtic. Later he was posted to Lissett, near Hull and came under the influence of Bradford City's manager Alan 'Bomber' Brown, a fitness fanatic and a strict disciplinarian who went on to manage a number of clubs. One player he admired at Bradford was Len Shackleton, who could put backspin on the ball so it came back to him like a boomerang.

Ron had three years with Brentford and his interest in coaching started when the manager, Jackie Goodwin, invited him to meet Walter

Winterbottom, who had started his coaching courses at Lilleshall. 'Walter gripped us with his ideas,' he said. 'They taught us how to teach but, more than that, they seemed to take us right inside the game. There were new subtleties to think about, new dimensions to work on, new experiments to be tried. The touchpaper had been well and truly lit.'

He coached Oxford University for three years and was appointed coach to the Middlesex FA. His playing career lasted almost twenty years and some of his best years came when playing in west London, for Chelsea, when he qualified for a championship medal when they won the First Division title in 1954/55, and for Fulham, where he played alongside Bobby Robson. The closest he came to playing for England was being selected for a 'B' international. Lucy sometimes complained about him coaching in the afternoons and evenings and he would reply, 'If I'm going to ensure a future, I've got to start working now.' Footballers didn't earn enough and the most determined ones took up coaching. Now they are earning too much and only a handful, like Teddy Sheringham, Stuart Pearce and Iain Dowie, have gone on to gain senior coaching licences.

An incident at Wembley Stadium on 25 November 1953, Coronation year, opened Greenwood's eyes to a style of football he hadn't seen before. As Billy Wright, England's captain, and Ferenc Puskas, the captain of Hungary, went to the centre circle to toss up for ends at the start of the England *v*. Hungary friendly, Puskas flicked the ball into the air, caught it with his instep and dropped it on the centre spot. In his book *Yours Sincerely* Greenwood wrote, 'A million kids now do the same [perhaps not now in these Playstation times!] in their backyards and nobody then had seen it done in the centre circle at Wembley. We all sat up and took notice.'

England were outclassed by the Hungarians and the score of 6-3 didn't reflect what actually happened. England's players were annihilated. Greenwood said:

The Hungarians' game was simple, quick, intelligent and adaptable. It was an exercise in wit and movement. The ball was used with respect but it was made to do most of the work. I felt this was the way football would go, how it would develop naturally, but somehow the British way persisted. Perhaps I was waiting for someone to show me the way. It was as if someone had removed scales from my eyes. All my basic ideas on the game suddenly came together.

Back at Stamford Bridge, Chelsea's popular manager Ted Drake called his players, including Greenwood, together to tell them he wanted them to play that way. His next instruction was, 'Get out there and do twenty laps of the pitch.' 'Not very constructive,' reflected Greenwood. At a later coaching meeting with Gustav Sebes, the Hungarian coach, Sebes told him, 'The English player always stops the ball. He never lets it run.' Greenwood believed that stopping the ball when it was not needed was a bad fault and taught Trevor Brooking how to let it run. Even today, few English players can do this well. And many can't 'weight' their passes; they whack the ball instead. 'You should treat the ball as a friend,' taught Greenwood. 'Caress it, not drive it.'

Coaching was still in its infancy and only now has it been accepted, mainly because of the influx of foreign coaches who have qualified for the UEFA top licence. Greenwood started at the bottom, coaching the under-fourteens at the Ealing Grammar School, and moved up the scale via Eastbourne United, Oxford University, Walthamstow Avenue and Arsenal and acting as manager of the England Youth and Under-23 squads before becoming manager of West Ham (1961–1977). He had just been awarded his FA full badge when he was appointed coach at Oxford University and when he arrived he heard of the daunting reputation of Professor Sir Harold Thompson, who was based at Oxford. One of the players warned him, 'Don't let Tommy try and dominate you.' At a practice session Thompson turned up and said, 'What are they playing at?' implying that something was wrong. Greenwood said, 'Mr Thompson, I am the coach; they're doing what I've asked them to do.' After that they were good friends and that friendship led to his appointment to the top job in English football twenty-three years later.

When Greenwood moved on to coach Eastbourne he said, 'I learned humility.' In his mid-thirties he was mixing and coaching the best young players in the country, including the England Youth squad members like Jimmy Greaves and Bobby Charlton. One defining meeting was with a blond, Adonis-type centre half playing for London Grammar Schools against Glasgow Grammar Schools, by the name of Bobby Moore. It was his introduction to his favourite, and best, captain. He said to him, 'I thought you were brilliant and I'd like you to captain our side.' Never over-expansive in words, Moore said, 'That suits me fine.'

RON GREENWOOD

Greenwood's long apprenticeship took him to Highbury as coach in 1958 and his revolutionary ideas transformed the minds of the more intelligent Arsenal players, if not the manager George Swindin, who demoted him to the reserves. The former Arsenal goalkeeper was a self-publicist with whom Greenwood didn't really get on and it taught him a lesson in how to deal with publicity. The loquacious Swindin regularly upset the players with his comments in the press. It convinced Greenwood that being cautious in front of the press is the better way. He was being considered to take over as manager at Arsenal before Swindin arrived but by then he was in charge of the England Under-23 squad, working with some of the finest talents in England. 'Mixing with foreign coaches was invaluable,' he said.

At West Ham he had a job for life. He was in charge on the playing side without too many interruptions from the decent, honourable men who served on the board of directors. But when Thompson rang Reg Pratt, the West Ham chairman, for permission to speak with him about the England job, the directors gave their blessing. John Lyall, groomed by Greenwood, was ready to take full control at Upton Park and Greenwood, who had been general manager in his final three years, wanted to use his vast experience to help English football and change its course towards a better future. Only seven managers applied for Revie's old job and forty others, mainly from outside the game, also applied. It was indicative that few people had the right qualifications and that still applies now.

Greenwood's first initiative as caretaker manager was to visit Anfield, the place that had produced more England internationals than anywhere else at that time. He wanted medal-winning players who understood each other's game and he chose six from Liverpool for his first selection, for a match against Switzerland. It didn't work in a frustrating 0-0 draw. Five Liverpool players stayed in for his second game, against Luxembourg, and again there was a poor response, a laboured 2-0 win against amateurs. Greenwood always believed in wingers and against Italy he picked two in Steve Coppell and Peter Barnes and, in front of a 90,000 crowd, the more adventurous line-up worked – 2-0 to England was the final score, with Brooking making the first for Keegan and Keegan laying on the second for Brooking. These two gifted players of different styles and attitude – Keegan was all action and made himself into a very fine all-round player; Brooking was immensely strong and skilled but rather languid when it came to running

85

– were the fulcrum of Greenwood's England team in the next four-and-a-half years. At the end they just failed to come up to the finishing line in the 1982 World Cup in Spain when he needed them most. If they had been fit in the final game England may well have qualified for the final stage and who knows what would have happened. 'What a pair!' said the admiring Greenwood. 'They cooked up goals for England that suggested telepathy.'

England still had a chance of making the 1978 tournament in Argentina after beating Italy but with Italy beating Luxembourg 3-0 in Rome, England were out on goal difference. The FA may well have already decided on Greenwood as the full-time manager but they insisted on interviewing six candidates: Greenwood, Brian Clough, Lawrie McMenemy, Bobby Robson and Charles Hughes and Allen Wade, the FA's national coach and director of coaching respectively. Each man was spoken to for forty-five minutes at the meeting at Lancaster Gate on 4 December 1977. Croker reckoned that the charismatic Clough was better than anyone, including Bob Paisley and Bill Shankly, but his lack of diplomacy ruled him out, although his interview was impressive and Thompson warmed to him. Clough recalled:

> I was totally comfortable, even though I never like the formal occasion. I didn't relish sharing the same room with Thompson, now dead and gone. He was a stroppy, know-all bugger who in my view knew nothing about my game. If he was such a brilliant mathematician, he figured it wrong when the FA got rid of Alf Ramsey. I was wary of the mad professor and I could sense that he was wary of me. There were twelve of the FA people in the room, including Sir Matt Busby, Bert Millichip whom I upset, Peter Swales, who voted for me and Dick Wragg, the old blusterer from Bramall Lane.

Clough was the nation's favourite for the job but, with the exception of Swales, the other members of the panel were sceptical of his handling of star players, and also his press relations. He said:

> The entire bloody interview process was a sham and a sop to the public. They gave it to the manager who couldn't make up his mind which should be the very first name on his teamsheet. Ron Greenwood didn't know who was the best goalkeeper. What chance has he got of coming up with the right

combination all the way through to 11? Don't get me wrong – Ron was an accomplished manager, highly respected within the game among fellow professionals and in Europe.

Clough 'tapped-up' Bobby Moore when Greenwood was still at Upton Park and later rang Greenwood saying, 'Can I buy Bobby Moore?' 'No chance,' said Greenwood.

Greenwood heard the news that he had won the vote to carry on as England manager in a peculiar way. He had just had lunch with Lucy in their favourite restaurant in Alfriston, Sussex and was sitting in his car when the news came from his car radio that he was the man. It was another example of the poor management of the FA at that time. Someone should have rung him before the news was released. One of Greenwood's best ideas was to urge the FA to appoint a chain of command and the FA agreed to nine more appointments: Bill Taylor and Geoff Hurst as coaches to help him with the senior side; Bobby Robson as manager of the 'B' side with Don Howe as coach; Dave Sexton as manager of the Under-21s with Terry Venables as coach; Clough, Peter Taylor and the FA's Ken Burton as joint managers of the Youth team. Except for Peter Taylor, they were all Winterbottom graduates from the coaching scheme. At a meeting in Manchester, he asked them all to write down the next England side and none of them agreed with Greenwood's. Significantly, Clough refused to write down his XI.

The Clough-Taylor experiment soon blew up. Their first trip was to Las Palmas and Clough soon upset the FA officials, who almost outnumbered the players. Clough ordered the official interpreter off the team coach because she was smoking. 'I don't care,' he said. 'She's got a fag on. Get her off.' Frank O'Gorman, a surgeon from Sheffield who was on the FA council, came into the dressing room at half-time and Clough told him to 'f— off'. All of the embarrassing incidents on the trip were fully reported back home by two experienced northern football journalists who had a close relationship with Clough. The unfortunate Burton resigned, telling Greenwood, 'I can't put up with that, I'm sorry.' The joint managers lasted a year before resigning. Clough summed up his experience with the FA selectors saying, 'They rejected me because they were scared stiff. They wanted a diplomat and I wasn't one. It was the worst decision they ever made.'

Greenwood relished the next two friendlies: West Germany in Munich and Brazil at Wembley, both World Cup winners of recent vintage. England lost 2-1 in the snow and a depleted side held Brazil 1-1. Emlyn Hughes went into a rage at the end of the game at Munich and charged up to the referee, upbraiding him over a disputed goal. Fortunately there was no disciplinary follow-up.

Greenwood derived great satisfaction from beating the Hungarians 4-1 at Wembley before they left for the 1978 World Cup in Argentina. Sebes, their coach, said to Sir Stanley Rous, the honorary president of FIFA, 'England played like Hungary at their best.' Greenwood thought Trevor Francis the star of the night. It was one of the happiest periods of his managerial life and with only 3 defeats in the team's 29 matches under his stewardship, 20 of which were won, England were in good shape ahead of the 1980 European Championships. They qualified by dropping only one point in a group comprising Bulgaria, Denmark, Northern Ireland and Eire. Eight players played in 6 of the 8 matches, some contrast with Revie's chopping and changing. Keegan and Brooking, who shared a room, were the heartbeat of the team.

Viscount Montgomery, the Second World War general, who was the most popular of Britain's wartime generals, once told Greenwood, 'Any leader has to have luck in his rucksack' and he admitted he had plenty. But in the weeks before the European Championships Greenwood was running short of it. Trevor Francis snapped an Achilles tendon and Kevin Keegan started the tournament suffering from acute tiredness after his exertions with Hamburg. These had been the team's most potent attackers but their lack of fitness was not the reason why England failed. According to Greenwood, writing in 1984:

> The tournament was dull, wretchedly supported and undermined by television. The dangers of live television coverage were spelt out in big letters during that Italian summer and this is a fundamental problem for football. I agree that television gives the game an interesting extra dimension and generates valuable income. But there is a very fine balance to be maintained – for where television is given its head it can take over and destroy. Football is a spectator sport, not a television entertainment where we all put our feet up, watch a replay or two and become instant experts. Great performances are never given in empty theatres.

That balance has not yet achieved. Near saturation of televised football has affected attendances throughout Europe, except in England where public interest is still high, buoyed by immense press exposure. (Those who criticise the excesses of the media often ignore its advantages – its free publicity to the sport. The men in charge, particularly the England team manager, have to stay on their saddles on the bucking bronco and hold on. Only Terry Venables of the ten managers has managed to do it; he fell because of his dubious business activities, not because he fell out with the press.)

Before the tournament, Greenwood practised his belief that grown men should be treated as adults and he encouraged them to continue their normal relaxations, including gambling and going off to the local pub. He allowed their racing experts to hire a helicopter from their team headquarters at the West Park Lodge Hotel in Hertfordshire to take them to Epsom for the Derby. Harold Wilson had started the habit of putting himself before the cameras with the England football squad to court support and Margaret Thatcher did the same in 1980. She invited the squad to 10 Downing Street for a cocktail party and as they posed for a photograph outside she showed that she had a sense of humour, and also a grasp of the subject, when a photographer produced a football and said, 'You'll be heading that ball unless you are careful.' She replied, 'I think Trevor Brooking does that, doesn't he?' Brooking had just won the FA Cup for West Ham with only the fourth headed goal of his long career.

By Prime Minister standards, it was one of the happiest photographs ever taken on the steps of 10 Downing Street. Keegan, hands in pocket and roaring with laughter, was on Mrs Thatcher's right, Brooking was at her shoulder and the late Emlyn Hughes, also convulsed with laughter, was on the left with Martin Peters, Glenn Hoddle, Fred Street, Phil Thompson and others. Brooking reckoned that the period of 1977-1980 was the happiest of Greenwood's life. He said:

> If he had a weakness, it was in handling players, or man management, at club level. Not every player in a club responds the same way to the manager and during his sixteen years at Upton Park he had problems with one or two players. At club level it is not easy for the manager to move dissident players out quickly. With the national side, discipline presents fewer problems because the manager is working with dedicated players – otherwise they

would not have got where they are in the game. Dropping a player acts as the best kind of deterrent to indiscipline. In my experience, no one abused the privilege of being allowed out, something that Don Revie would never let happen. Ron believed in self-discipline.

The 1980 tournament was described as 'leaden, negative and lacking in outstanding players' and few disagreed. It was compressed into twelve days and crowd trouble soon erupted. England were stationed in Asti, an hour outside Turin, and their squad was insulated against the problems of an army of 9,000 England fans in the old city. Belgium, Italy and Spain were their opponents and a win in the opening game was vital. Greenwood had watched the Belgians in five previous matches and their coach Guy Thys hadn't used the offside trap but once the game started he adopted this frustrating tactic. Tony Woodcock had the ball in the net only to have the attempt ruled out for offside. Then Ray Wilkins, his game rather unfairly compared to the actions of a crab by some critics, including Ron Atkinson, beat the offside trap and scored.

Deplorable defending allowed the erratic Jan Ceulemans to equalise and suddenly fighting broke out among a section of English supporters, mainly stripped to the waist with Union Jacks draped round their shoulders, on a corner at that end of the ground. The Italian police retaliated, using their batons and overreacting by firing tear gas. Soon the yellow-black smoke began spreading downwards toward the pitch. Ray Clemence started wiping his eyes and, realising the problem, Greenwood strode up to the match adjudicator and said, 'Our goalkeeper is having difficulty seeing, can the referee stop the game and come over to discuss what we should do?' The UEFA man failed to respond and Greenwood asked him, 'What is going to happen if a goal is put past our goalkeeper because he can't see?' 'It would count,' said the man. Greenwood said, 'In that case, don't you think the game should be stopped until the smoke has cleared?' To his surprise, the adjudicator signalled to the referee to stop play. The match was suspended for five minutes while Clemence and other England players were given treatment for sore eyes. When it resumed, the players were looking at the trouble spots in the crowd rather than at the ball and the match finished 1–1 – a terrible start. This was England's first game in a final tournament for ten years and Greenwood, finally losing composure, said angrily in a BBC TV interview with the late Mike Murphy, 'In ten minutes these imbeciles have ruined it for us. They should be put on a boat and halfway across someone should pull out the plug.' Mrs Thatcher was in Venice at an EU conference and when she heard she said, 'This is a disgraceful embarrassment.' Harold Thompson called them 'sewer rats' and UEFA imposed a fine of £7,500 on the English FA, a lenient sentence.

England, Belgium and Turin have all been at the heart of hooliganism in Europe. England gave the word hooliganism (taken from an Irish family in the Elephant and Castle in the early nineteenth century) to the world and Italy has seen some of the worst examples of it. The Belgians have been almost guiltless but the Heysel Stadium disaster in 1985, with thirty-nine dead at the European Cup final between Liverpool and Juventus, was the third-worst disaster after Hillsborough and Bradford. England's players shared Greenwood's anger as they had an after-match meal back at their hotel. Their thoughts were about that, not football.

England's next game was against Italy three days later in the same Communale Stadium and, with 60,000 spectators packed in, everyone was understandably worried about further disturbances. More than 1,500 policemen were on duty – but there were no arrests. Greenwood left out Liverpool's centre forward David Johnson, a clever player who could finish with accuracy, and brought in the Nottingham Forest striker Gary Birtles, a much less skilful performer. It was a gamble and it failed. In his autobiography, Greenwood blamed Kevin Keegan for the only goal, scored by Marco Tardelli. 'The deeper Kevin dropped back the more Tardelli, his marker, pushed up,' he wrote. 'He was constantly in a position to threaten us and that happened.'

Keegan was always asked for autographs or interviews and he usually obliged. Before the match, two national newspaper photographers turned up with an attractive girl and asked Glen Kirton if she could pose for a picture with Keegan. Kirton agreed and when the picture was about to be taken, she pulled up her skirt. Greenwood said, 'It was a put-up job.' Keegan's gullibility was shown up again before the third and final England game, against Spain in Naples, which they won 2-1 although they were on the way out of the tournament. Keegan said in an interview that he felt the Italians always seemed to get a little help from referees and there were embarrassing headlines announcing 'Keegan accuses referees'. Greenwood used nineteen of his twenty-two players, a sign that he didn't know his best team. 'You have nothing to be ashamed about,' he told them.

He was upset about the hooliganism and also about the way he was criticised by the ITV panel. Experts like Malcolm Allison, Derek Dougan, Brian Clough and others were pioneering the idea of a panel of former players and managers who were encouraged to express themselves in an extravagant manner. The victim, of course, was the England manager and Greenwood – and particularly his wife – took exception to some of the comments. Croker said in his book *And the Next Voice You Will Hear is...*

> He suffered from it but was a master of disguising his feelings. One of the few times I saw him really annoyed was when he had been criticised or misinterpreted in the press. That was his one weakness, if it could be called a weakness, he tended to be over-sensitive in the face of criticism.
>
> We accept that people in public positions must expect to be criticised but no one likes to be faulted, whether it is the head of a big company, the prime minister, or the national football manager. It is said that people in powerful positions eventually get used to it but I don't think they do. Those who criticise, that is the press and the media people, are often just as sensitive as those they attack. There are as many, if not more, writs for libel from press people than from public figures. None of us really likes being told we are wrong and the manager of the national football team is told by more people than most. It needs a strong personality to withstand such criticism.

Greenwood was called 'Reverend Ron' by some of the players and as a believer he needed all his strongest qualities to survive the next few months. England had a reasonable draw for qualifying for the World Cup in Spain in 1982 and their opponents were Romania, Hungary, Switzerland and Norway, none of them world-beaters. After beating Norway 4-0 at Wembley his team won only 1 of their next 8 matches, the worst run in England's footballing history. For decades England had never lost at Wembley. Now they had a dismal sequence of lost, drew, lost, drew, lost, with the losses coming against Spain, Brazil and Scotland and, as a very superstitious man, Greenwood attributed that to the absence of his wife Lucy. She went to most of his internationals games at Wembley and had never watched England lose. After this, he insisted that she had to be present.

The PR started becoming personal with *The Sun* outdoing its rival the *Daily Mirror* with more and more damning headlines like 'For God's Sake, Ron, Pack Up'. 'People were looking on me as though I had committed some crime,' he said. 'I was hurt and I had a feeling of shame.' Another defeat, 2-1 in Basle, led to more abuse. Pot-bellied hooligans wearing T-shirts with the words 'Battle of Turin' resumed the hooligan war, smashing up the centre of Basle and then turning on the football stadium. Greenwood felt sick to the bottom of his stomach. He had been thinking of quitting and within a minute or two of the final whistle he decided to retire from the game. Two days later, he told Dick Wragg, his immediate boss, and Croker, that he was going to resign. He was almost sixty and it was time to enjoy his life. 'Don't be daft,' said Wragg. They decided to keep the news quiet until after the second game on the summer tour of 1981, against Hungary in Budapest.

England's squad stayed in a huge, regal hotel on the banks of the Danube and Greenwood shut himself in his room, cutting himself off from the usual chatter before matches. He was one of the few who thought England would win. Brooking, the man closest to him, felt it could be his night because the Nep Stadium was one of the biggest grounds in the world, with a beautiful playing surface. He scored two goals in a 3-1 triumph which turned the headlines upside down. Now they were heroes instead of clowns. 'I never struck a ball better,' said Brooking. His shot arrowed straight to the angle of the post and bar and lodged against the top of a stanchion. Hilkka, his Finnish wife, watching at their home in Brentwood with his parents, said, 'I had to look twice at the screen to make sure it was Trevor.' It was their eleventh wedding anniversary and out came the champagne.

The result didn't change the manager's decision. The journalists were taken aback by his brief summing-up. 'I'd like to thank you for your support over the years,' he said. 'Our win was a good one, well deserved, and it's given me great pleasure to beat the Hungarians. I don't want to answer any questions. Thank you.' None of them realised the real meaning of his words.

At the front of the Boeing 737 on the flight back to Luton, on Whit Sunday, Greenwood pulled the curtains across to give some privacy as he told the players that it was his last game in charge. He looked emotional and the players were stunned. 'You're out of order,' said Keegan. Mick Mills said,

'If you retire, I'll never speak to you again.' The journalists sitting further back down the plane knew nothing of the drama as they finished their final drinks. On the ground, the players were still in groups discussing what should now happen as they waited for their luggage. Wragg was going to make the announcement inside the main hall. Suddenly Greenwood, almost overcome by the emotion of the players' reaction, told the squad, 'Okay then. I'll tell Mr Wragg I won't resign. I'll give it until after the World Cup.' They chorused, 'Great!' Greenwood gave the news to Wragg, who said, 'I was going to have another go to change your mind but you've saved me the trouble!'

Historically, September is a bad time for England footballers and on the ninth of that month another catastrophe struck Greenwood, causing him to regret being talked out of retirement. The game was at Oslo's Ullevaal Stadium and Norway's 2–1 win provoked a furious reaction, far worse than the one at Basle. 'I felt like public enemy number one,' said Greenwood. Bjorn Minge, Norway's loudest and brashest radio commentator, came out with the immortal words which will always be replayed at the right times:

> We are the best in the world. We have beaten England – Lord Nelson, Lord Beaverbrook, Sir Winston Churchill, Sir Anthony Eden, Clement Attlee, Henry Cooper, Lady Diana, Maggie Thatcher, can you hear me? Maggie Thatcher, your boys took a helluva beating!

But with Switzerland unexpectedly faltering, England just needed to draw with Hungary in their final game at Wembley in November. They won, and Greenwood told the players, 'We have been given the kiss of life.' Lucy was there, high in the stands. She had still to see England lose at Wembley.

It was twelve years since England had reached the World Cup Finals and their emergence was dogged by major political considerations. The Falklands War was still raging and though the FA wanted to continue, a majority of letter writers called for withdrawal. When HMS *Sheffield* was sunk the mood swung further against going ahead. If the *Hermes* or the *Invincible* went down the FA would have to pull out. Fortunately the war ended the day after England's inaugural game, an uplifting 3–1 win over a high-quality French side.

Security worries were heightened by the threat from Eta, the Basque separatist group that was still killing innocent people. The England squad were based eight miles outside Bilbao, where the Eta commanders were mainly based. The FA had chosen a hotel called Las Tamarises, which had an excellent wine cellar but was close to an unattractive beach and a chemical works a mile away. One night Ted Croker and several of his colleagues were woken at 4 a.m. in the Lezama training camp before the French game with headaches caused by the changing wind directing sulphurous fumes into the building. At the main hotel they were often woken by the sounds of armed Spanish police officers tramping around on the roof. Sixteen marksmen were on duty round the clock.

One of Greenwood's ideas was to send an England side to Bilbao to play in a friendly in the St Mames Stadium in March to win local support. It was well received and the FA's new security officer Les Walker, a former Metropolitan Police commander who had been in charge of the 1981 Brixton riots, was the ideal man to cope with the English hooligans, aided by Spanish police whose reputation preceded them. In an area of terrorism they acted first, not waiting to ask questions.

There was another innovation, less welcome, the arrival of 'the rotters'. Kirton explained:

> With hooliganism rearing its head, the newspapers sent news reporters to follow England as well as the usual sports journalists. They were known as 'the rottweilers'. Their job was to dig out tasty stories for the front pages and some of them were pretty upsetting. A few months earlier a bright photographer took a picture of a dead dog on the beach near the hotel and it was sold round Fleet Street with captions like 'Greenwood's Footballers on Dead Dog Beach'. No one mentioned that the beach had been cleaned up weeks before. Then there was the case of the 'ballet dancers'. Someone rang us and said it would be a good idea to invite a London ballet group to meet the players for some pictures and we agreed. They turned out to be topless dancers and the pictures weren't what they seemed.
>
> But I got on well with the 'rotters'. They had a job to do and most times they put over their copy in an acceptable manner, only to be jazzed up by people back at the newspaper offices with exaggerated headlines. In my nineteen years with the FA no journalist really turned me over. Ron didn't like what appeared but you had to grin and bear it. At the end of the tournament, the regular journalists chipped in to pay for an expensive watch for

Ron when he retired, with an engraved message of thanks. Ron also got on well with the sports writers, although one or two papers used to annoy him. But there was one who got up his nose, the freelance Andrew Warshaw. He used to keep asking infuriating questions, like about his cream cake consumption!

Another smart move to win over the locals in Bilbao was when Greenwood invited along an old playing opponent, Ronnie Allen, the former West Bromwich Albion and England forward who once managed Atletico Bilbao. Ronnie spoke Spanish and was used as an interpreter and advisor. Allen possessed a fiery temper, as one journalist recalled:

> The game was West Ham v. West Brom when Ronnie was the Albion man-ager and just before the end Billy Bonds upended Willie Johnston with a very aggressive tackle right in front of the dugout. Bonds might have been sent off but the referee didn't even book him. Outside the dressing room we asked Ronnie about it and he was dismissive. But we knew he might come up with something meaty eventually and Brian Woolnough, who was with *The Sun* at the time, chased him out to the car park and asked for his opinion. Brian came back and told us that Allen had said, 'Bonds behaved like a gorilla.'
>
> Most of the papers used headlines like 'Bonzo the Gorilla.' A few weeks later I was at The Dell, Southampton's old ground, and I saw Allen coming out of the Albion dressing room screaming and shouting at me about that story. He completely lost it. The next time I saw him was when I was queu-ing at the passport check on the way to Bilbao. Right behind me there was Allen. I feared the worst but he stuck out a hand and said, 'How are you old friend?' He also proved to be an excellent diplomat in Bilbao.

Two days before the France game Ned Barrett, the British consul-general, rang at 9 a.m. to remind Croker that the British party was expected at 12.30 for a reception at the town hall to meet the Mayor. Croker knew nothing about it. He rang Greenwood and the manager said he didn't know about it either and the players had been invited to lunch at a golf club. Croker, Greenwood and Geoff Hurst went to the reception and it led to head-lines about England snubbing the Mayor of Bilbao. Roger Heywood of the

Daily Telegraph had two mistakes in his story, which was, as one FA council man said, a rare case of a 'rotter' behaving like one.

Despite all the problems with adverse publicity, England's players enjoyed their short stay in the Basque country. Bryan Robson started it, scoring in twenty-seven seconds in the game against France, which was played at a temperature of 100°F, forcing the shirt manufacturers to come up with a more suitable shirt for the next game against Czechoslovkia. Now wearing aertex shirts, England won an unappetising encounter 2-0 to top their group. Both Keegan and Brooking, who were unfit when they arrived, were still short of fitness and Greenwood was worried about Keegan's hyperactivity. Kirton said, 'One day he wanted to play me at tennis and it was two-thirty in the morning before we finished.' Keegan kept complaining about the state of his back, although the team doctor Vernon Edwards told Greenwood that in his view there was nothing wrong with it.

Keegan came to Greenwood with an astonishing request. 'I'm still not right,' he said. 'I've got a specialist in Hamburg who treated my back. Do you think I ought to see him?' Greenwood said, 'Well, it's pointless you staying in Spain if you don't think you'll be fit.' So he agreed to this bizarre plan. It was almost midnight. 'How are you going to Hamburg?' asked Greenwood. 'I'll drive to Madrid and catch a flight,' said Keegan. He went to the girl at reception and asked for a car. 'I can lend mine,' she said. It was a Mini, a two-seater of old vintage and it was penned in the garage by dustbins. 'The refuse people collect rubbish at 1 a.m.,' she said. After waiting for the refuse men, Keegan set off, alone, on the 250-mile drive. The next day the press wanted to know where he was and Greenwood kept saying, 'He's visiting his specialist.' Which was true, except that he was in Hamburg. Four days later, Keegan turned up and declared himself fit.

England's performance level dropped in the 1-0 defeat of Kuwait, being caught offside no less than twenty times to the annoyance of Greenwood. He must have been tempted to recall both Brooking and Keegan. He didn't, mainly because if either of them broke down it would ruin his chances in the latter stages. His caution was understandable but in hindsight he should have brought them on in the final minutes in the 0-0 against West Germany in the Bernabeu. The other results went against England yet again and they now needed to beat the hosts Spain by two goals or more to qualify for the semi-final. Spain were out but their fiery players played for pride and the result was another totally frustrating 0-0. Greenwood sent on Brooking and Keegan twenty-seven minutes from time and each of them missed comparatively easy chances. There were tears in the away dressing room as Greenwood said, 'You've done your best. None of you have let your country down. Things just didn't go for you.' As the team coach drove off, a brick was hurled into a window, narrowly missing Greenwood and his coach Don Howe. It was the first time in the tournament that there was no police escort. Losers don't normally have protection, only the winners.

It wasn't a memorable tournament and the final reflected the dissatisfaction of the footballing public around the world. A rejuvenated Italy, inspired by a reborn Paulo Rossi, beat West Germany 3-1 in a match littered with fouls that mainly went unpunished. After he arrived home, Greenwood, essentially a private man, told the FA that he didn't want his private telephone numbers to be passed on. 'He wanted to be left alone,' the official said. As General Douglas MacArthur said, 'Old soldiers never die, they fade away.' The General was eighty-four when he died. Ron died at the same age, in February 2006, and his family requested a private funeral. There was no minute's silence at the football grounds, unlike George Best who had several, but before the England v. Uruguay friendly on 1 March the FA relented. On the day that Peter Osgood, one of the flair players Greenwood had given only four caps to, died at the age of fifty-nine from a heart attack, they gave the order for a minute's silence for these two very different but much-admired men. It was totally respected.

BOBBY ROBSON

1982–1990

A Man of Passion Who Nearly Made it

| P 95 | W 47 | D 29 | L 19 | 49% |

The FA already had a successor to Greenwood: Bobby Robson, who had been appointed as England 'B' manager by Greenwood four years earlier. In the Blair years an appointment of that type would reek of cronyism but that wasn't the case then. Walter Winterbottom's enthusiasm for coaching spawned a group of similarly-minded coaches and Don Howe, one of his disciples, persuaded Robson to sign up for a coaching course at Lilleshall when they shared hotel rooms while playing for West Bromwich Albion. Greenwood had been one of the first to graduate from these coaching courses and Robson, who achieved his FA full badge in 1961, came from the next batch, so a kind of evolution produced England's fifth full-time manager. It was a sensible way of conducting the affairs of the England squad.

As part of Robson's further education while he was still a player, Allen Wade, a former FA director of coaching, advised him to take up part-time coaching and he fixed him up with a post at Oxford University. Greenwood had held the same position a decade earlier. Robson used to drive to Oxford from his home in Worcester Park in his Morris Minor on Tuesdays and Thursdays and the fee of two guineas per session, plus mileage money, earned him useful cash to help bring up a family of three sons, all of whom went to public schools. He also coached an amateur side near his home two nights a week and, having to lecture intelligent young men, particularly at Oxford, he soon became adept in speaking in public. His generation of successful managers and coaches mainly came up that way. Today's obscenely overpaid players don't have the same motivation, which is why there are so many foreign coaches now moving into English football.

The hyperactive Robson – he is still that way in his early seventies, according to Don Howe – married Elsie, a nurse at St Stephen's Hospital in London in 1955. She was eighteen when he first met her near Durham, where they now live. She often jokes about his two marriages – one to her and the other to football. She has been a magnificently loyal supporter of a man who has dedicated his life to football.

In 1977 the FA had had six candidates lined up to succeed the disgraced Revie. Now, five years later, there was just one. Greenwood told the new FA chairman Bert Millichip, later Sir Bert, a solicitor and former club cricketer in West Bromwich, that the FA would be wasting their money advertising the job and drawing up a short list. Robson was out on his own, he said, and Millichip too was good friends with him. When Robson played for West Bromwich Albion he arranged the purchase of his house at Handsworth. The well-liked Millichip and some of his colleagues met and soon approved Greenwood's recommendation. He rang Patrick Cobbold, the Ipswich chairman who succeeded his brother John, a victim of cancer in 1986, and asked the club's permission to let Robson talk to him.

Cobbold said, 'He will leave here only for the England job. I want him to stay but it will be up to him.' Patrick Cobbold, an Old Etonian like his brother, had a wickedly funny sense of humour, and he promptly rang Robson and said, 'We've decided to give you another ten-year contract on more money.' Robson said he still wanted to take the England job. 'What about doubling up jobs?' said Cobbold. 'You can manage Ipswich and England at the same time. What about it?' Robson had to laugh.

Just before the start of the 1982 World Cup Robson had a meeting with the FA's senior officials at Lancaster Gate and another at the Chiltern Hotel in Luton before the England squad flew to Bilbao. One of the difficulties was Robson's salary. It was £72,000 compared to the £65,500 offered by the FA. 'I like the sound of the job but I don't like your terms,' he told Ted Croker. Later the FA increased his stipend, eventually up to £80,000, well below the salaries of half-a-dozen First Division managers. It showed Robson's keenness to take the job.

In his thirteen years at Ipswich Robson turned a rundown, impoverished club based in a small town of 110,000 inhabitants into the second most successful club in the country after Liverpool. He founded an academy at Portman Road which produced more than a dozen international players, more than Greenwood produced from West Ham, and, with the aid of the Cobbolds, he balanced the books. David Rose, who served the club as secretary for forty-four years, found it much easier to work with him than with Alf Ramsey. 'Bobby was always keen to chat and he virtually ran the club, even down to the number of toilet rolls we needed,' he said. 'Alf didn't want to chat. He would say, "Oh really," and carry on with his work.'

John Cobbold was unsure of appointing Robson in 1969 as a successor to Bill McGarry, the former England midfielder who was one of the toughest disciplinarians in the game. When McGarry, who died in Namibia in 2005, left to go back to Wolverhampton, a building company was called in to repair the doors and walls he had kicked in anger. Robson had been sacked by Fulham's chairman Sir Eric Miller after only nine months at Craven Cottage and when he was told the news he burst into tears. Miller was a crook and soon afterwards he shot himself in the head to end his life.

Robson was living near the Beatles in Ripley, Surrey, and with school fees looming and himself out of work for three months, queuing up for his dole money, he was in despair until his friend Dave Sexton, then Chelsea manager, offered him some part-time scouting. His first job was to cover an Ipswich game at Portman Road and Murray Sangster, one of the Ipswich directors, said to him, 'Are you Bobby Robson?' When he said yes, Sangster told him about McGarry's resignation. Robson promptly wrote a letter of application. Without a bit of luck, and a kind act by an old friend, Robson's brief managerial career might have ended.

John Cobbold's first choices all turned him down and he told some of his drinking friends 'Christ, we're down to Robson. We're going to give the job to Mickey Mouse!' At his interview, Robson won the Cobbolds over with his passion and enthusiasm and use of language – not the kind of words McGarry used. He got the job without a contract but Cobbold told him, 'You will have two years.' Robson called the hard-drinking Cobbold brothers, nephews of former Prime Minister Harold Macmillan 'Mr John' and 'Mr Patrick'. He said:

> I was a teetotaller when I started but they used to invite me to the directors' room and I started drinking, sweet sherry and then going on to the harder stuff. They were unique people. Posh really with their tweeds and check suits who went shooting with the toffs, including Harold Macmillan and their

friends. If we lost, Mr John used to ring me and invite Elsie and me to lunch to cheer us up. After we won he didn't invite us out but he would open a bottle of champagne.

John Cobbold, the funnier of the two comedic chairmen, said:

There is no truth to the rumour that Bobby runs Ipswich Town. On the contrary, I am a ruthless dictator. I ring him every morning and say, 'What's on your mind, Bob?' He tells me everything and then I bark out my orders. They are the same every day. They are: 'Right, carry on!'

Early in Robson's reign George Best scored a hat-trick to humble his unpretentious team. There were cries of 'Robson out!' The next day the Cobbolds called a board meeting. Robson was apprehensive when he turned up. Mr John opened the proceedings, saying:

Gentlemen, the first business of the day is to officially record the minutes of the apologies of this board to the manager for the behaviour of our supporters last night. Agreed? Fine, but if it occurs in this ground again, I will resign, forthwith. Right, on to the next business.

It took three years before Robson earned the confidence of a sceptical crowd but the criticism, including in the local press, proved to be good training for his next post, as England manager.

In another incident one of his players who didn't rate him, Irishman Tommy Carroll, ripped down the teamsheet, provoking a fist fight – Carroll and his Scots colleague Bill Baxter ranged up against Robson and his Welsh assistant Cyril Lea. The Robson–Lea pair, with intervention from another player, Geoff Hammond, won the contest and Robson's courage and honesty soon convinced the Cobbolds that they had made the right decision. He was like Brian Clough in one respect: he insisted on sportsmanship and fair play. 'It's not worth getting suspended,' he told his players. When he took England to the semi-final of the 1990 World Cup England was the proud holder of FIFA's Fair Play Award.

Half of England's ten full-time managers – Ramsey, Revie, Greenwood, Robson and Venables – came from poor circumstances, with the first four coming from grinding poverty between the two world wars. It didn't mean they had unhappy childhoods. With their deep love of football to inspire them, the support of a loving, close Christian family and their determination to become successful, they all reached the top. Robson's background was particularly grim. He was born on 18 February 1933 in a two-bedroom terraced house in Sacriston, County Durham. His father, Philip, was a coal miner; a non-drinker and non-smoker who never missed a shift in his fifty-one years down the pit. Robson was the fourth of five brothers born between 1925 and 1939, all born at home. Four slept in two double beds and their father cut their hair and repaired their shoes to save money.

There was no bathroom and the whole family had to use a single tin bath which was brought in from being hung up on the outhouse door. The outside toilet had no light or heating. They used a torch. The parents were Methodists and Philip was a strict disciplinarian before the cane was banned. Once, when the future England manager came home an hour late, his father took his belt off to beat him on his backside. Their weekly treat was a tuppenny ice cream each and their outlet was playing football and cricket in the street. They were nicknamed 'the netties', houses with outside lavatories. When Bobby was fourteen months old, the driver of lorry delivering lemonade, the staple drink at home, accidentally drove into him. 'It was a lucky escape, apparently,' he said years later.

He failed his eleven-plus and the headmaster at the Waterhouses Modern Intermediate School which he attended, a three-mile walk away from his home, banned organised football. Bobby said, 'I think that helped me because I spent more time working on skills. That is where so many youngsters fall down today. They are thrust into competitive games at too early an age before they have a chance to pick up the basics.'

Approaching his seventeenth birthday his skills had developed so quickly that eight clubs wanted to sign him, including local side Newcastle United. His father saved up enough money to take him to occasional matches at St James's Park. Fulham eventually won the race, causing Bobby's mother to worry about him living so far away. She didn't need to worry. The Fulham chairman was Tommy Trinder, one of the most famous comedians in the country, and the club was more like a music hall than a football club. One of the biggest laughs came when Robson and Johnny Haynes failed their national service medical for defective ears. Robson earned the nickname 'Cloth Ears'. Jimmy Hill and Ron Greenwood were in the same side and both were inspirational figures. Most of the players played snooker in the afternoons, although Greenwood always went home. They were at Wembley in 1953 when the Hungarians beat England 6-3 to open the curtains to let in the light.

Robson, now under the influence of Winterbottom, was capped twenty times. He was an industrious, skilful player, similar in style to today's Frank Lampard. He had six years at Fulham, then another six at West Bromwich Albion before returning to Craven Cottage. He was appointed manager of Vancouver Whitecaps only to learn that Ferenc Puskas was in the job and it was the unhappiest period of his life. He was back home waiting for a call until Sexton intervened and his Ipswich career lasted thirteen mainly happy and successful years. Clough said, 'Robert [he always called him Robert] had a job for life at Portman Road but I wished him good luck at the FA, he'll need it.' Seven clubs offered him bigger salaries, including Barcelona, but he stayed at Ipswich. Now, however, he had to take the next step.

The 1980s were the worst time in English football, with brutal deaths, fighting, wanton damage to towns and cities around Europe, drunkenness and crude, inexplicable behaviour. Robson did well to survive. Standards fell, especially on the back pages of a number of newspapers. His determination and character carried him through and these qualities were still in abundance later in his sixties when he twice contracted cancer; he won both battles and still kept working. The pressure was enormous. Only an exceptional man would have stuck it out.

He first found himself at the forefront of the 'hooligan war' on 11 March 1978 when dozens of Ipswich supporters were injured by bricks, seats and other missiles at Millwall's Den, innocent victims of the club's so called 'F Troop' and others. 'It was the worst I ever saw,' said Robson. In the tiny Millwall boardroom later the directors of both clubs condemned the outrage and, caught up in the mood of anger and frustration, Robson said, 'I would turn the flame-throwers on them.' Someone working for television was in the room, heard that and rang the BBC. Sitting at home in Bentley, near Ipswich, at 10 p.m. Robson was horrified to hear Jimmy Hill repeating the inflammatory comment on *Match of the Day*. But there were millions of people at that time who felt that there should be some retribution taken against the troublemakers. A situation that saw outbreaks of hooliganism in Basle, Luxembourg and Turin deepened with the major disasters of Heysel, Bradford and Hillsborough – 190 people were battered and crushed or burnt to death and 800 injured. The public had turned against the national sport. Nastiness pervaded on the field, directors encouraged dishonesty and corruption in a bid to win at all costs and the newspapers were full of vitriolic articles.

It needed a good scout to lead them out of the jungle. Like at Ipswich, Robson started badly and the press soon jumped on him. Being a nice guy, he tried to explain why matches were being lost but they didn't want explanations, only good results. An abrasive type like a Clough or an Alex Ferguson could ride through press conferences and if they didn't like the hassle, they could get up and go. They conducted conferences on their terms, whereas many of Robson's conferences were dominated by the floor. He needed the aggression of a Thatcher or a Jim Callaghan to maintain order and sanity.

Another reason why Robson, now carrying the title of national coach alongside his managerial post, attracted so much hostility from the critics was his friendship with Charles Hughes, the bespectacled, donnish-looking assistant coach who first joined the FA staff in 1964. Hughes, a rather dogmatic man, had a spell of success as manager of the England amateur side unmatched by the senior England managers and his methods were based on direct football. He claimed statistics showed that ninety per cent of goals came from five passes or fewer and many League managers believed in the long ball game practised by clubs like Watford and Wimbledon. He also said that seventy-five per cent of goals came from crosses and, his most derided suggestion, that the key to winning was POMO, the 'possibility of maximum opportunity'. In US sport they love this approach. In England, they hate it. But the POMO theory has proved successful. Rather than the traditional near-post crosses from wide positions, Jose Mourinho's studies of the best European sides showed that the killer pass that inevitably leads to goals is the one pulled back towards the edge of the penalty area from the by-line. And in his spell with England, Sven-Goran Eriksson finally convinced his players that POMO works, although he didn't dare use the dreaded word. Robson said of Hughes in his autobiography:

> He was a very able person and I got on well with him and stood up for him in front of his critics. Unfortunately he didn't have a good relationship with

the public or the press but if they had known him as I did they would have liked him. Of course he was not always right but then who is?

The most opprobrium directed at Robson followed his decision to leave Kevin Keegan out of his first game as England manager, against Denmark in Copenhagen in the first qualifying match for the European Championships. He thought Keegan, who used up more energy than almost any other player in that era, was past his best at the age of thirty-one but an angry Keegan disagreed and vowed he would never play international football again. Keegan kept his word and it led to a nasty, longstanding feud.

Robson later admitted he should have spoken to Keegan in person instead of giving out the news through the media. Keegan was European Footballer of the Year in 1978 and 1979, he had 63 caps, an OBE and countless other honours but he only ever managed twenty-seven minutes of action in World Cup Finals tournaments. With his worldwide reputation, Robson should have thanked him for his services and it would have been good PR. Greenwood said of him, 'He was the most modern of modern footballers' and he was the first English footballer to make a big business out of his profession. He also made a lot of money from the press, mainly from News International Ltd who owned *The Sun*, the *News of the World* and the *Sunday Times*, and these newspapers gave successive England managers, including Keegan when he was later in charge, more unfair criticism than the rest of the newspapers put together. Like modern footballers, too many managers are avaricious, taking money from newspapers they know have served them badly in another way. They don't really need the money. It should be about integrity and self-esteem, not about building up their already swollen bank accounts.

Still steaming with indignation about his exclusion from the England side, Keegan gave an interview to a *Sun* journalist which lambasted Robson under sensational headlines. Robson said, 'If I was wrong in not giving him a call then he was equally wrong in not confronting me personally before he went to the media.' He wrote a letter to him, via the then Newcastle manager Arthur Cox, and it was several years before the two men started speaking again. It was a silly spat which could have been avoided.

Because of Robson's enthusiastic way of talking for a long time before reaching a conclusion, most of the critics thought he was indecisive but Peter Shilton, whom he preferred to Ray Clemence after Greenwood had alternated the two goalkeepers, said, 'I didn't think he was. He was positive and strong. He wasn't afraid to speak his mind and his man management was very good.' Some of his players called him 'Mogadon', the man who put everyone to sleep, and it stuck.

Shilton was one of the best players when Jesper Olsen equalised for Denmark in Copenhagen to make it 2-2 near the end. Robson, who had treated his father and some of his relatives on the trip, thought it was a reasonable debut. But the press didn't agree. Denmark had never beaten England. They expected more. Four points were taken from Greece, nine goals were put past the amateurs of Luxembourg and two more against Hungary. Robson desperately needed a victory against the Danes at Wembley on 21 September 1983. He picked three of his old boys, Ipswich Town's Terry Butcher and Russell Osman at the back and Paul Mariner up front. It was a dreadful game, with Denmark's Allan Simonsen, of Charlton Athletic, scoring the only goal from the penalty spot.

Robson described as it as his blackest day and he was booed and jeered off. Some of the writers were cruel, almost savage, even though England were still in with a chance of qualifying. One headline branded him 'a plonker'. Half the nation was being fed with this type of insult, supplied by the top-selling red-top newspapers, *The Sun* and the *Mirror*, which were in vicious competition. Nigel Clarke, working for the *Daily Mirror*, was asked what he would do with Robson. He said, 'I will fry him.' Robson said:

> I was working in a very hostile atmosphere. There was a war between these two papers and I caught the brunt of it. Even the President of the United States wouldn't have been treated like this, or any politician. I thought, 'Do I have to put up with this?'

But he did, and he persevered and won through.

After the disaster against the Danes, England rallied, beating Hungary 3-0 and Luxembourg 4-0. The main street in the principality was smashed up by English louts, forcing the FA to pay compensation. With the Danes still winning, England's goal tally of 23 for, 3 against, with just one defeat, was not enough. England were out.

He had to go through more purgatory when the evolving England side lost three games in a row, a 2-0 defeat by France in Paris and a humiliating

1–0 loss to Wales at Wrexham being followed by a 2–0 reverse at Wembley to the USSR. As he strode off on the downward-sloping concrete driveway to the Wembley dressing rooms he looked up at the contorted faces of a number of spectators above who were trying to spit on him. They were also chanting 'Robson out! Robson out!' Beer from plastic cups – glasses and bottles were banned by this time – was jerked in his direction and he admitted that he felt like crying, 'not for myself but for my eighty-one-year-old dad who travelled down to the game by train like he usually did on his own. Fortunately he had left to catch the tube to King's Cross so he didn't see it.'

Dick Wragg, the avuncular chairman of the FA's international committee, assured him that the FA were backing him and he gave a rueful smile. His mood improved when a representative of Barcelona approached him with an offer to take charge of the Spanish club, for the third time. The money was several times higher than his salary at the FA and it could have been an easy way out but instead he recommended Terry Venables, the Queens Park Rangers manager. Venables led Barça to the Spanish championship the following season for the first time in eleven years.

In the summer of 1984 England were scheduled to tour Brazil, Uruguay and Chile and Robson's old coaching friend Jimmy Hill advised him to cancel the tour in a live television programme. 'How can I?' he asked. 'I wouldn't dream of it.' One of Robson's endearing habits is to say 'I'll show 'em' or the equivalent. He had nineteen of his players unavailable and he promoted three young players: Mark Hateley from Second Division Portsmouth, whom he kept calling 'Tony' in mistake for his father, and two new wingers in Watford's twenty-year-old John Barnes, a protégé of Graham Taylor, and Stoke's twenty-two-year-old Mark Chamberlain. Robson said, 'My job was on the line and I had to gamble and I gambled on just four experienced players and seven greenhorns.'

The greenhorns beat Brazil 2–0, the greatest upset in South American football since the USA beat England in 1950. Barnes, the laid-back, handsome son of a Jamaican colonel, dribbled through the Brazilian defence a minute from half-time and wrong-footed the goalkeeper to slide in a truly memorable goal, similar to Diego Maradona's second goal against England in the World Cup Finals two years later. Barnes was prematurely hailed as a superstar but he never quite fulfilled everyone's expectations. Between

1983 and 1995 he won 79 caps, enough for some 'experts' to claim he was worthy of being included in England's top twenty all-time internationals in a poll.

Halfway through the second half at the Maracana Stadium Barnes crossed for Hateley to jump to head in the second at the far post. AC Milan were so impressed that they signed 'Tony' for £915,000. Not so long ago Robson was still being labelled a 'plonker' – now he was a hero. But for that amazing turn-up, Robson would have been out. It was England's first win over Brazil and it was Brazil's first defeat at home for twenty-six years. 'It took a big weight off my shoulders,' said Robson. His young team lost 2-0 to Uruguay in Montevideo and drew 0-0 against Chile in Santiago but no one was bothered. On the downside, Robson and his FA colleagues were very angry to hear racist songs and chants delivered by drunk England louts during the flights. On one occasion some English journalists sitting nearby told them to behave themselves. The press weren't all bad. Those same racist supporters travelled to Mexico the following year, 1985, as England played three games there ahead of the 1986 World Cup Finals, which were to be held in Mexico. Robson suspected that they were members of the National Front.

The day after they arrived in Mexico, Robson and his squad were sitting at The Camino Real Hotel in Mexico City when someone switched on a TV to watch the European Cup final between Juventus and Liverpool at the Heysel Stadium only to see a blank screen. One of the players rang home and was told thirty-nine people, mostly Italian, were dead and 400 injured. Robson realised that England might well be thrown out of international football. To everyone's surprise, the next day's England v. Italy match went ahead, the Italians winning 2-1 with the aid, according to Robson, of a biased referee. Not only did the England v. Italy match go ahead, so did the European Cup final itself. Both games should have been cancelled – that they were not provided a further example of how money rules the world's most popular sport.

Millichip and Croker flew back to London and the next day were summoned to 10 Downing Street to face the wrath of Prime Minister Thatcher. Millichip had already withdrawn English clubs from European competitions and UEFA now decided impose a ban of five years. He also wanted a football levy board, similar to racing, as had been recommended by the Chester Report seventeen years previously. Mrs Thatcher quoted the £800,000 transfer fee Everton had paid for Gary Lineker as an example. 'You have to put your house in order yourselves,' she said. She had no sympathy. Croker's suggestion that 'These people are society's problem' provoked a humorous response from the PM. As several of her officials gaped she said, 'Steady the Buffs', meaning a regiment about to charge off. When Croker retired in 1989, after sixteen fraught years in charge, he wasn't knighted. His three predecessors, Denis Follows, Stanley Rous and Frederick Wall, had all received that honour.

Eventually, the England team were reprieved by FIFA and UEFA after considerable lobbying by the FA. If England had been banned Robson would have been out of a job. Now he was able to carry out his plans. The games in Mexico, used to acclimatise at the 6,000ft altitude ahead of the World Cup Finals a year later, were played in a surreal atmosphere. England lost to Mexico 1-0 but beat West Germany 3-0, their first success against the Germans for fifty years.

As England's plans were laid for the thirteenth World Cup Finals there were plenty of scare stories to ruffle Robson's growing confidence. The tournament was originally scheduled for Colombia but they withdrew because of lack of funds. It was either Brazil or Mexico, and Brazil, financially embarrassed, suddenly dropped out, leaving Mexico, whose government was struggling with its worst financial crisis for fifty years. Eight months before the opening day a severe earthquake struck close to the capital, leaving up to 25,000 people dead. None of the proposed World Cup grounds were affected so the tournament went ahead. Because of the demands of television, the matches kicked off in the heat of the day. Bombs were left near the US Embassy and stories were filed back to England claiming that kidnapping was about to break out in this destitute country with high unemployment. The Argentinian fans apparently wanted revenge for defeat in the recent Falklands conflict. None of these stories was true. Only one English supporter was injured and no one was kidnapped or mugged.

The England squad left a month earlier than most of the other countries and for the first time the FA paid for the costs of taking the players' wives and girlfriends to accompany their menfolk to Colorado Springs for more altitude training. Playing two friendlies in Los Angeles and Vancouver helped defray the expenses but Bryan Robson's fall in LA, when his shoulder popped out, proved to be a crucial handicap later. The England party were surprised by the lack of security at Broadmoor Centre in Colorado Springs. The players trained at a US Air Force base where 4,500 officers were trained and from where the US bombing raid on Libya was dispatched a few weeks earlier – yet no one was ever stopped and asked for identification.

Robson and his backroom staff had intricate plans to keep the players happy once the ladies went home. They had brought video equipment and cassettes, tennis and table tennis equipment, volleyballs, cricket bats and balls, Trival Pursuit and other games. They also had thirteen television channels to watch in English. For the first time the squad had a female doctor, Lesley Young. She was recruited because the popular, pipe-smoking Vernon Edwards from Watford, a key man in the outfit, had had a heart attack and later died, eleven days before the first game. It cast gloom over the build-up. 'He was a father figure to the players,' said Robson. 'It was like losing a player.' Another doctor, John Crane from Arsenal, was called in.

Portugal were England's first opponents in the 96°F heat and sixty per cent humidity of Monterrey, a city which was not far above sea level and more amenable than some of the other venues. Perhaps Robson's men had taken too much notice of the reports from the Portuguese press. The Portuguese players threatened to strike over bonuses and their FA asked FIFA for permission to alert twenty-two more players. The consensus was that England would win comfortably. But in a slow-tempo game played on a bumpy pitch, Portugal won 1-0 with Peter Shilton conceding his first World Cup goal in 499 minutes.

England were quartered up the mountains in Saltillo and the FA tried to fill the hotel to keep out any members of the press. Months before, at least thirty press people had booked in, to the annoyance of Robson and Croker. One from the *News of the World* had been deputed to stalk Robson to catch him out with any indiscretions. The night before the second game, against Morocco, Croker returned from a tennis game against Jimmy Hill and, entering a room, he saw a priest standing in the half light. 'What's going on?' he asked. Norman Medhurst, the long-standing physiotherapist said, 'The photographers want a picture of the priest blessing the players' boots.' Croker almost exploded. 'This simply isn't on,' he said. 'I must ask you to leave immediately.' As the outsiders left, he told Medhurst, 'I have to protect the players. We'll all be back to the Don Revie days with all his superstitions. You can imagine how that picture would be captioned!' The same night a number of English fans got into the hotel, which was protected by fifty armed police officers on a twenty-four-hour guard. They were politely ejected.

Robson must have left his luck in his rucksack because everything went wrong. In a match he described as 'a series of misadventures', Bryan Robson, always called 'great' by his namesake, was felled and his shoulder was dislocated again, putting him out of the tournament. Then, just before half-time, Ray Wilkins, already cautioned, disputed an offside decision and threw the ball at Paraguayan referee Gabriel Gonzalez. Out came the red card and Wilkins, normally the calmest player in the squad, had to go. He was unlucky – Gonzalez spoke English. Twenty-four of the thirty-six referees used spoke English, good reason for England's players to refrain from swearing.

'I'll never forget it,' said Wilkins. 'Me, the first England player to be sent off in a World Cup Finals.' FIFA confirmed two days later that he was sent off 'for molesting the referee'. In today's football few players would be left on the field, particularly at Old Trafford. The game ended 0-0 but Robson soon got to work on his exhausted, spiritless players. 'You've kept in it,' he said. 'And we'll get through to the second round, you'll see!'

The next day, sprawled alongside the pool wearing his personal stereo earphones, he looked totally downcast. Croker had brought him the summaries of the London editions. The headlines were damning. One newspaper called for him to be sacked immediately and the half the nation believed he was responsible for the poor start. The following day the newspapers brought more disturbing news - the players had rebelled against his leadership. Bryan Robson had supposedly called for a drastic change in tactics, with four players in midfield. Robson the manager was livid. He told some of the writers, 'If you're going to write stuff like that, that's scandalous. Just don't come near me.' He was furious with the picture of him lying at leisure by the pool when the public were given the impression that he didn't care. The team management had a meeting and discussed whether they should cut off relations with the journalists and the photographers. They laid down new rules, no photographs at the hotel except for a brief staged session by agreement. That seemed to work. A fragile peace was restored.

One person keeping calm was Gary Lineker. He hadn't scored and was still recovering from a damaged wrist in Vancouver. That was his excuse for easing off training. He was never a hard trainer. A useful cricketer who played a few games for the Leicestershire second team, he loved chatting to the press men who shared his love of cricket. Now it was his turn to move to the front of the stage. In the game against Poland, a match which England had to win, he had four shots at goal and three went in. Robson adopted the 4-4-2 system the players wanted and he brought in a clever footballer in Peter Beardsley to partner Lineker. Beardsley provoked some much-needed fun, with his dentures (Beardsley had had twenty-two teeth out when he was sixteen) and his Geordie accent loaded with clichés.

Glenn Hoddle was the next player to excel; his performance against Paraguay in the second round match at the splendid-looking Azteca Stadium in Mexico was outstanding, almost matching that of Shilton, who made two exceptional saves. Croker said of Hoddle, 'He is an extremely modest and likeable young man but I sensed a heightened level of determination about him, as though he knew this would be his year. But I thought he should shoot from longer distances in this rarefied air.' Actually it wasn't so much rarefied as smoggy, polluted air! Lineker, with two, and Beardsley scored the goals.

England discovered their hotel was built next to a four-lane motorway and after three days they booked out and moved to another one next to the airport, which would have been equally noisy except their rooms were soundproofed. They relaxed daily at the English-built, hundred-year-old Reforma Club up a hill, which had a cricket pitch, well used by Lineker and his friends. Pictures of Queen Victoria adorned the walls. Some patriotism was useful because, having reached the quarter-final for the first time since 1970, Robson's players had to prepare themselves to take on Argentina, four years after the end of what was known in South America as the Malvinas War. Politics and sport fused but Robson insisted, 'I am only talking about football, not politics.'

Off the field, the two set of officials appeared to get on well, Croker making friends with Admiral Carlos Lacoste, a former member of the Argentine junta who was a highly regarded FIFA official. 'There is no resentment,' said the Admiral. 'Except against Margaret Thatcher and her Cabinet.' Relations

between Robson's men and the organisers were less friendly. The day before
the game Robson was told his players could only train in flat-soled foot-
wear because the potholed pitch was under repair. On a slippery, renovated
surface that was out of the question so the players had to train at another
ground. Later in the day Robson was incensed to learn that the Argentinians
had trained on the Azteca pitch wearing their studs.

On the day, 114,580 filled the ground. These spectators were to be baffled
by the incident in the fifty-first minute which came to be known as the
'Hand of God' goal. It should be been 'Hand of a cheat'. Diego Maradona
was at his peak, rivalling Pelé from the previous generation as the greatest
all-round attacking player in the history of the game. At 5ft 6ins he could
win matches on his own, and he won this one. Maradona passed to Valdano
and the ball ran loose to Steve Hodge, whose attempted back pass skewed
into the air towards the oncoming Shilton.

England's third and final captain in the campaign – the others, Bryan
Robson and Ray Wilkins, were out of action – started to jump for the
bouncing ball eight yards from goal. Maradona, who was good in the air,
also jumped with his left arm raised. Shilton failed to make contact and the
ball carried on into the empty net. In his latest book he said:

> It was my ball and I flung my right arm, ready to punch it clear. After that,
> my mind was all a fuzzle. I punched thin air. Maradona made contact but
> not with his head. An almighty roar swept down the massed tiers of seats.
> Maradona was bolting across his penalty area, jumping up and punching the
> air with his left hand. It came to me then. That's it! He used his hand.

There were 1,500 journalists sitting in the middle of the second tier and
not many of them were sure of how the goal went in. Nowadays each journalist has a small television monitor in front of him or her or, if not, bigger
sets every few yards. One replay would have been enough to confirm
Maradona's act of bad sportsmanship. Shilton chased after the referee, the
thirty-six-year-old Tunisian Ali Bennaceur but failed to change his mind.
There was no consultation with the Costa Rican linesman. And not many
of England's players joined in the protests. One can imagine what would
happen today! A mass molestation of the official, red cards flourished and
FIFA later reversing the decision. Shilton admitted, 'I hadn't achieved the

ideal height and distance,' a plausible defence for his action, but he should have advanced a few more yards and jumped higher. Maradona, giving away six inches, would have been knocked aside in the accidental collision. 'It shattered us,' said Robson. 'But I had to put on my brave face and not use the decision as an excuse for the 2-1 defeat.'

Four minutes later England's punctured players stood by as Maradona, elbowed earlier in the face by Terry Fenwick, glided past Peter Beardsley, Peter Reid, Fenwick and Terry Butcher to slide in the second goal, one of the greatest solo goals of all time. Lineker headed his sixth goal of the tournament in the eighty-first minute, making him the leading scorer, and six minutes later he should have equalised from a Barnes cross. 'If we'd won I was convinced I would win the World Cup,' said Robson. Instead, skipper Maradona held it aloft – after Argentina beat West Germany 3-2 in an entertaining final – in his left hand, the ungodly hand.

There was an astonishing PR lapse afterwards. Shilton, the chief witness, wasn't interviewed and no interview with him was sought by the press. Maradona was interviewed countless times, insisting that there had been divine intervention. Years later he admitted, 'I did it for my team, for the dead in the Malvinas War, and the survivors and it was a little bit of pick-pocketing of the English.'

Although there was less pressure on Robson after his team were robbed, he still went to Bert Millichip and told him that if they were thinking of replacing him, this would be the ideal time. Millichip ridiculed the idea. Robson voluntereed the idea to appoint an assistant to groom the next manager, with possible candidates including Terry Venables, Steve Coppell and Howard Wilkinson. Peter Swales said, 'There isn't enough work for one, never mind two!'

Still deflated, Robson and his players asked to bring the flight home forward to the next day and they flew via Miami to London carrying 280 pieces of luggage. It should have been 281 to include the box carrying the World Cup. After a holiday, Robson turned his attention to trying to win the European Championship in Germany two years later, a competition in which England have yet to reach a final since it started in 1960. Hopes were raised again by qualifying at the expense of Yugoslavia, Northern Ireland and Turkey with the best record of any nation. 'It was the best period in my time as manager,' said Robson.

He spoke too soon. His overpraised players lost all three games in the Finals, 1-0 to the Republic of Ireland, 3-1 against Holland, the eventual winners, and 3-1 to the USSR. There were plenty of reasons, one being that Lineker had hepatitis. 'It was the worst summer of my life,' said Robson as the abuse piled up. For the second time he offered his resignation to Millichip, who replied, 'We can absorb the pressure, can you?' Robson nodded. 'Then get on with the job Bobby, get us to the World Cup Finals again.' He did, in the best possible manner. The side didn't concede a single goal against Sweden, Poland, nor Albania to reach the Finals in Italy. The roller coaster was moving back to the highest point again and a potentially great talent was emerging, twenty-one-year-old Paul Gascoigne, whom Robson called 'as daft as a brush'. The day after this comment was made the Tottenham star turned up for training with a brush stuck up his sock. No one could argue that he hadn't a great sense of humour – however, it often spilled over into stupidity and embarrassment.

There are few true, natural geniuses in sport but Gazza was one of them, yet the flaws in his character proved to be his downfall. He was so enthusiastic, so hyperactive that he found difficulty in sleeping, going off for long walks into the night. When he eventually went to bed, he always had the light and television still on. He was almost like a mad cat and some of his major injuries were brought on by his own folly.

Robson admitted he held him back 'so when I unleashed him in Italy he would be a tiger'. It didn't quite work out. Born in Gateshead in a council house with a shared bathroom, the twenty-one-year-old was ready to launch his international career in the autumn of 1988. He warmed up with extravagant gestures during the England v. Denmark friendly game at Wembley before Robson brought him on with five minutes to go in front of a worryingly small crowd, numbering only 26,000. In his 1998 book, Robson claimed he gave Gascoigne his debut against Saudi Arabia in another 1-1 draw two months later. But according to Gazza his first international manager got it wrong. He did play in that game though. He was sent on near the end again in place of fellow Geordie and roommate Chris Waddle. 'Give us a goal,' said Robson. 'F——ing hell,' said Gazza, 'you've only given me five minutes.' (The purpose of staging the friendly match was partly to help arms sales to the Saudis but the critics erupted, with one tabloid heading its back page 'Go, For the Love of Allah!') In Albania, stuck in a hotel with no amenities,

Gascoigne spent much of his time collecting up tablets of soap and throwing them out of the window at the chickens outside.

After several severe lectures, Robson picked him for the World Cup squad and the day they were due to fly off to Sardinia Gazza discovered he had left his passport in Newcastle. A friend brought it to London just in time for him to board the flight. FIFA's plan was to quarantine England's supporters away from the mainland, on an island which has a reputation for extracting retribution. With thousands of police officers, spotters and English policemen, there was little misbehaviour, with the Irish, also stationed in Sardinia, setting a wonderful example of drinking to excess and still retaining their dignity.

The day before departure the now-defunct newspaper called *Today* carried a story about Robson's private life, an alleged long-ago dalliance with a woman, and claimed that he had written to every member of the FA international committee offering his resignation. The FA's high command were prepared to issue a denial but Robson and his advisor preferred a press conference at Lancaster Gate. It proved to be a stampede, photographers and reporters shoving equipment into his face, but Robson handled it well. 'It's garbage,' he said. And the FA believed him.

Robson let slip that the FA weren't going to offer him a new contract. The bad publicity was too much for them. But the players still backed him and he convinced them that they had a chance of success in a group which contained Ireland, Holland and Egypt. Robson had already had secret talks with PSV Eindhoven, the club backed by the electronics firm Phillips. He had taken Ipswich to Eindhoven some years ago and had strong links with the officials of the club. Fred Street, the physiotherapist, said:

> I don't know why the FA didn't keep him. The press didn't help. Two weeks before there were headlines saying 'Sack Robson!'
>
> The FA had another manager lined up, irrespective of what happened. They could have looked fools if we had won it – and we came very close. We would have beaten Argentina in the final but for missing those penalties in Turin. They weren't a good side.

The other manager was Graham Taylor, who was in Italy for the whole tournament. For years he had paid for his own trips to attend overseas internationals, particularly featuring England, and he built up a dossier about the world's leading players. He did the necessary homework to put himself top of the FA's shortlist.

Accompanied by their wives and girlfriends, the players stayed in a quiet hotel, Is Morus, thirty miles from Cagliari, which had no distractions, no televisions or radios in the rooms and no visitors. Gazza provided some distractions. Waddle ordered a large, gooey chocolate cake of Brian Johnston class to present to him on behalf of the squad for his twenty-third birthday. As he started to hand it over, he rammed it into his friend's face. 'I love chocolate cake,' said Gazza. At dinner Robson presented him with another cake, with a brush on it. In his book *Gazza* he stated that his month in Sardinia was the happiest of his life. He sounded like a child. 'I always had someone to play with,' he said. 'I didn't have to worry about boring domestic things or me house or girlfriends. I could escape all that and leave my responsibilities behind.' His tragedy was that he never grew up.

The temporary truce with the Press soon ended when an Italian girl employed as a liaison officer for the organising committee was reported as being over-friendly with some of the players. It may have been untrue but the exposure of the 'facts' infuriated Robson and his henchmen. 'Sheer rubbish,' he said. The FA consulted their lawyers. Nothing happened.

The first match in the Sant' Elia Stadium on the waterfront at Cagliari was against Jack Charlton's Ireland and it was like a First Division match at home between two over-physical teams. Bryon Butler described the 1-1 draw brilliantly: 'On a night of lightning, thunder, wind, rain, clacking helicopters and suffocating security, the game presented British football at its lumpish worst, a game of hassle, clout and counter clout.' The press hit out. 'Send them home!' implored one headline.

Holland from the House of Orange presented the next hurdle, and there was the usual conflict between certain factions, led by Ruud Gullit, Marco Van Basten and Jan Wouters. For the first time, Robson used a sweeper, Bryan Robson, and it worked. The players were so excited about the result, a mundane 0-0, that eight of them broke their curfew and went to a pub, bingeing away and arm wrestling with Italians, according to Gascoigne's weighty and revealing book, published in 2004. Police sirens screeched, the players panicked and they ran as fast as possible back to the hotel. Waddle and Gascoigne were fooling around in their room later when

Bryan Robson, the captain, who should have set an example, arrived and challenged Gascoigne: 'Come on you Geordie bastard, you can't take your f—ing drink.' Captain Marvel, as he was called, tried to tip Gazza off his bed and slipped. The side of the bed crashed on Robson's foot, opening up a nasty cut on his big toe. There was so much blood that Waddle called one of the physios. It looked bad and manager Robson was contacted. The angry manager realised that the players had been drinking and when Gascoigne claimed it was an accident, he said, 'I don't believe you. I'll speak to you later.' Captain Marvel flew back home and David Bloomfield, the FA press officer, explained he was suffering from 'a longstanding Achilles tendon problem'. Which was true – but this wasn't as bad as the cut toe. It seemed incredible that these highly paid athletes were unable to maintain self-discipline at the highest point of their careers for just a few weeks. The drinking culture was still in full force. With the arrival of so many overseas players in recent years this habit has declined, but it still exists.

Gascoigne continued his summer madness the next day, racing up to the swimming pool and diving in only to come up complaining of a stubbed toe. Robson was furious. He was furious a lot at that time. The breach with the press worked in his favour though because the journalists were kept away from the players – otherwise one player at least would have leaked the news about Captain Marvel's toe injury. Egypt were third-rate opposition and England proceeded to the second round through Mark Wright's first international goal.

The next venue was the old city of Bologna. Like many Italian cities, it had remained largely untouched through the centuries. To go there was like walking back to the sixteenth century. Instead of cooping their players up in their hotel rooms, making them bored and restless, football managers should arrange meaningful trips on these football expeditions, to show their players another country's culture. On the short flight from Cagliari, Gascoigne asked the pilot to let him take over the controls. The next minute the aircraft lurched and went into a dive.

Belgium, semi-finalists in the 1986 World Cup, were the next team England had to face and they were tough opponents in the expensively renovated Stadio Dall'Ara, first built in 1926. Ceulemans and Scifo struck England's woodwork before David Platt volleyed in Gascoigne's free-kick thirty seconds from the end of extra time. Robson kept his cool throughout.

The word from home was that he was now a hero again. The nation was right behind the boys.

The party flew off to Naples for the quarter-final against Cameroon, one of the best sides out of Africa. Robson sensed that he had a wonderful chance to go right to the final and the players felt the same way. They were looked on as the third favourites for the tournament behind the Italians and the Germans. The squad was happily settled at a discreet hotel in Amalfi, a beautiful town high on a cliff. Everything was ready.

The effervescent Gascoigne was fooling around, still drinking and overeating, and Robson had staff watching over him to keep him in check. In Gascoigne's book he recalls the manager's partiality for making references to the Second World War and how himself and Lineker arranged a sweepstake, the money going to the man who correctly guessed how many minutes would go by in one of Robson's lectures before the war was mentioned. It always brought uproarious laughter.

Robson kept warning his men against complacency but they fell for it and at half-time, when Platt's goal had given them the lead, he told them, 'Carry on like this and we're out.' The Lions of Cameroon were muscular and strong but they were too reckless. Thirty-eight-year-old Roger Milla, the old conman from Reunion Island, was felled by Gascoigne and Kunde equalised. Then Ekeke scored a second. 'They were the biggest team I'd seen,' said Robson. 'And they could play.' Nine minutes from time, Robson realised he could be back in the nasty headlines again.

A minute later Kunde fouled Lineker in the penalty box and the penalty was awarded – England's first in eight years. Lineker, ice cool, converted. Extra time followed and in the last seconds of the first period Lineker was through against goalkeeper Thomas N'Kono when he was again brought down. Asked what he was thinking about prior to taking the kick, Lineker said, 'Actually, my brother in Tenerife and what he would say if I missed.' Suddenly his cool was replaced by anxiety as he ran in and shot straight at where N'kono had been standing. Luckily, the goalkeeper had dived to the side.

At the end the Cameroonians did a lap of honour, enthusiastically cheered by the 55,000 crowd and the England players. They brought colour, glamour and excitement to the tournament. Later Milla said, 'If we had beaten England Africa would have exploded. There could have been deaths. The good Lord knows what He did and I thank Him for stopping us in the quarters. That allowed some calmness.' There was little calmness around England. The nation was out celebrating. History was about to be made.

With a semi-final against West Germany in three days' time, Robson banned alcohol at the Hasta Hotel at Asti twenty miles out but Gascoigne got round it by ordering milkshakes and persuading a barman to switch his drink to Baileys. Robson walked in and asked, 'What's that?' Gascoigne replied, 'It's a milkshake.' 'I'll have one,' Robson said, whereupon Gascoigne managed to snatch a milkshake and hand it to his manager. On the day of the game, 4 July, the players were ordered to rest in their rooms but Gascoigne went to the hotel's tennis courts and talked a couple of American guests into playing a game with him. Robson heard the noise and went off to find him. 'What the f—— are you doing?' he said. He escorted him back to his room, shaking his head.

The day before, Italy had gone out on penalties to a weakened, argumentative Argentinian side in the other semi-final. The Argentinians had scored only five goals to reach the final, the lowest tally ever, and with four players suspended and Maradona in poor form, the winners in Turin were favourites to win the trophy. 'You'll never have a better chance to win glory,' Robson told his players. The semi-final turned out to be the finest game of the tournament, with two physically strong sides playing to their capacity in 90°F heat, even though it was late in the evening.

Paul Parker, the twenty-six-year-old London-born defender who started his career with Fulham, proved to be a pivotal figure in an enthralling and passionate game. Just after half-time a free-kick taken by Andreas Brehme bounced off Parker and over Shilton's head into the net. Ten minutes from time England were facing an undeserved exit until Parker crossed from the right and Lineker, surrounded by three defenders, placed a perfect shot past Bodo Illgner.

Before the game Robson said to Gascoigne, 'You do realise that you will be playing against the best midfielder in the world,' meaning Lothar Matthäus. Gascoigne replied, 'No, Bobby, you've got it wrong. He is.' Gascoigne's apparent arrogance was justified. He did outdo Matthäus, once nutmegging him with a pass through his legs to the glee of the 6,000 English supporters, 1,000 of whom had been treated to free tickets by the FA, at a cost of £40,000. It was hoped that this would reduce the likelihood of hooliganism resulting from fans turning up without tickets.

At full-time, an excitable Robson reminded his players they had survived two penalty shoot-outs. According to Shilton, neither himself nor anyone else had been involved in one before. Players of both sides started tiring in extra time, with strain showing in their sweat-streaked faces. Chris Waddle hit a post and Thomas Berthold did the same. Gascoigne beat two players, knocked the ball too far ahead, and as Berthold got a foot to the ball, he lunged from behind to win the ball back. Berthold collapsed as though 'hit by a sledgehammer' in Gascoigne's words. Brazilian referee Jose Wright, highly praised up until then, pulled out a yellow card. Gascoigne, already having been booked in the tournament, was out of the final, if England were to reach it. Tears streamed down his face, Waddle told him to settle down and Lineker gestured to the bench intimating that he needed more moral support. Gascoigne rallied. 'I'll show 'em,' he told Waddle.

After England lost 4-3 on penalties, Robson was asked if the team had practised them. Not specifically, he said. Some managers like penalty practice but others, like Robson, feel that it is down to temperament and bottle. In the interminably long minutes before the shoot-out started, he decided to leave Gascoigne out of the proceedings. With tears in his eyes, he probably would have missed. Lineker took the first and converted it with ease but some experts queried the idea of letting the best finisher start, suggesting that he might have been better equipped than others to handle the increased pressure of taking a later kick. At 3-3 Stuart Pearce walked purposefully forward to pick the ball up and put it on the penalty spot. He was a good penalty taker, scoring nine out of ten in domestic football. He was renowned for having the hardest shot in England. He came thundering up, his left boot made perfect contact but unfortunately for him – and for his colleagues and the 30 million television viewers at home – his shot hit Illgner's legs and bounced away. Olaf Thon took the next penalty and sent a firm, low shot into the corner to make it 4-3.

Now it was Waddle's turn. From the manic way he ran in, like a fast bowler intent on bowling a fearsome bouncer, many people in the press box suspected he would fail. They were right. The ball sailed high and wide into the night sky. Gascoigne could be seen breaking down in a flood of tears – it was a natural reaction and it won the sympathy of the nation. Matthäus went over to Waddle and hugged him. It showed immense respect for one top professional from another. The distraught Pearce was ordered to take a drug test and, with his body drained of fluids from his exertions and the nervous tension, it was a long time before he was able to produce a urine sample.

Back at the hotel in Asti, a drunken party developed, with some of the players throwing their manager, fully clothed, into the pool. 'It nearly stunned him,' said one. Nigel Kennedy, the violinist who is an Aston Villa fan, was there to help rouse spirits.

There was one matter still to settle – the third *v.* fourth-place match at Bari's magnificent stadium. Hosts Italy won 2-1 in an anti-climatic game memorable for one thing, the final appearance of Peter Shilton in his record 125th international match. At the age of forty, English football's most pro-fessional performer had reached the end. Sadly, like so many great players, he never had success as a manager.

Robson and Lineker stayed on for the final, which turned out to be the worst in the history of the World Cup. The cynical Argentinians put up a disgraceful performance, with Monzon and Dezotti sent off, and the West Germans won 1-0 in the lowest scoring final ever up to that point. England were awarded the Fair Play Award for the fewest fouls, one every 6.79 min-utes, and the fewest cautions, six out of a total 174, and Robson was rightly proud of it. He has always been a sporting man, an honest man, a passionate man. His achievement of taking England to a semi-final on foreign soil must be rated very close to Ramsey's achievement of winning the tourna-ment in 1966. Ramsey did it by teamwork and had just three great players: Bobby Moore, Bobby Charlton and Gordon Banks. Robson also had three: Bryan Robson, who dropped out through injury, Lineker and Shilton. Gascoigne almost attained greatness without ever reaching it. Robson had half the press against him for much of the tournament whereas Ramsey had almost total support.

When the England squad's aircraft landed at Luton's nondescript airport they were astonished to see how many people were there, estimated at up to 100,000. There was a huge banner on a building which read 'England 22, The Press 0'. As Robson said, 'I came from zero to hero.' He was awarded the CBE by the Queen and went off to a more comfortable existence as manager of PSV Eindhoven, a quiet town in the south-east of Holland. As Bryon Butler wrote, 'He left with dignity and with grey hair.'

GRAHAM TAYLOR

1990–1993

Robbed in Rotterdam

| P38 | W18 | D13 | L7 | 47% |

raham Taylor smiled more than any of the other nine full-time England managers put together. He had fewer grey hairs and fewer furrows in his forehead. He exuded self-confidence and calmness but on 12 October 1993 in a hotel in Rotterdam, facing seventy English and Dutch journalists he simply blew up. He used the F-word.

The F-word is commonplace in dressing rooms, on training pitches and even out in the middle of televised games watched by millions. The players use it all the time. But for an England manager to use it, well, it isn't the done thing, as one FA councillor said afterwards. What happened that afternoon was a classic example of how the press can destroy the career of a well-respected international manager.

It was the last press conference before the Holland *v*. England World Cup qualifying match at the Feyenoord Stadium, De Kuip, and England needed to win to go to the Finals in the USA the following summer. Both teams were staying in the same hotel. The journalists were staying there too and that contributed to the explosion. There was too much contact with the players. These days the press are kept well away and when they are invited to go to a conference, procedures follow strict lines – boring questions producing boring, unmeaningful answers.

England had beaten Poland 3-0 at Wembley thirty-six days before the Rotterdam gathering but now Taylor was reticent about his team and the way it would play. Taylor was the most talkative of the England managers and this time he needed to come up with some decent answers. He failed to do it, and it proved his downfall. Rob Shepherd, the correspondent of the short-lived *Today* newspaper, stood up and asked a question about the team. 'I think you are going to play the same way we did in Oslo,' he said. In the words of the *Daily Mail* correspondent Neil Harman, 'The word "Norway" had only to be mentioned for the hackles to rise; for Taylor to cough and splutter – his face reddening – at the idea that the atmospheres in Oslo in June, four months ago, and Rotterdam now were somehow related.'

In June, Taylor admitted he had got it wrong at Oslo when Norway won 2-0 and he was assailed by the massed ranks of the football journalists. A headline in *The Sun* read 'Norse Manure' and there was worse to follow. England had tried to play the long ball game, which was derided by his critics. The idea of playing that way against the Dutch was repulsive, as one commentator reported.

Speaking directly to Shepherd, Taylor said:

This is one of the biggest things that has ever shaken me. I just cannot under-stand this. Everything is up. Yet I come here and I think: bloody hell, what is this? I never expected this. It is astonishing. Come on, rise up. If I saw a face like yours among our players he would be out. Brace yourself, Rob. Put a smile on your face. Don't be so silly.

Shepherd, who once played for West Ham's junior side, persisted with his question. On the field, he was a rugged opponent. He mentioned Oslo again. Instead of taking another question, Taylor continued his protesta-tions, saying: 'This has nothing to do with Oslo. What's the problem pal? Raise yourselves. We are going to win. I don't get these vibes that you say you are getting. I'm staggered about this suggestion.' The Dutch journalists laughed. 'Come on, smile!' exhorted Taylor. Shepherd started to respond again. Taylor went on talking. The proceedings were being televised around the world and they were featured in a Channel 4 documentary later, in which the swear word count was thirty-eight f——s, three c——s, two s——s and an obscured w——.

When the conference broke up, most of the journalists were still laughing and joking. But the headlines the next morning were damning, highlighting Taylor's 'tantrums'. There were already enough problems, like the potential risk of fighting between the rival supporters, to ruffle the confidence in the England camp.

The team Taylor chose had too many unexceptional players, like Carlton Palmer, Gary Pallister, Tony Dorigo, Lee Sharpe and the substitute Andy

Sinton. It lacked a world-class player. Gary Lineker was on his way out, Bryan Robson was finished and only David Seaman and Alan Shearer had real class. The man Taylor really missed was the eccentric, clownish and infuriating Gascoigne. His relationship with him was at the heart of his turbulent three-year reign.

After his impact in Italia '90, Gascoigne should have developed into another George Best, carrying England into the next World Cup. Taylor picked him for the two opening games of his reign, the first a friendly against Hungary, the second a European Championship qualifier against Poland, both wins, but inexplicably dropped him for the next one against Ireland, preferring the pedestrian Gordon Cowans from his former club Aston Villa. Gascoigne claimed that his manager didn't give a reason. Perhaps it was because the game, which ended 1-1, was played under English long ball tactics, unsuited to Gascoigne's style of play. Recalled for the friendly against Cameroon, he was then out for eighteen months after a hernia operation and also damaging his own knee in a crazy tackle in the 1991 FA Cup final. He missed twenty-one international matches as England slipped down the world rankings and out of the European Championships in Sweden.

When he re-emerged, he was picked for the World Cup qualifying game against Norway in October 1992 and his behaviour was such that Taylor finally realised that he would never change his ways. Two days before the match he had a drinking session with Paul Merson, an alcoholic, and the bill was charged to his room. Taylor spoke about his 'refuelling habits' the next day at a press conference. Gascoigne was furious. 'He should have taken me aside first, not just come out with it in public,' he said. One disaster followed the next. A Norwegian television crew asked Gascoigne if he had some words to Norway. 'F—— off, Norway,' he said. He insisted it was a joke. Lawrie McMenemy, Taylor's assistant, tried to talk the television people out of broadcasting the offending word but failed. 'You'll have to excuse him,' joked McMenemy. 'He's got a small vocabulary.' More dreadful headlines followed. The game ended in frustration for England; 1-1 was an appalling result. The return game in Oslo, the game which was headlined 'Norse Manure', was even worse and at half-time Gascoigne lost his temper, shouting and screaming at the other players and also at McMenemy. He was retained against Poland at Wembley, scoring in a 3-0 win, but was unfit for the crucial game in Rotterdam.

1. Walter Winterbottom (second from right) with coach Don Howe and players Ray Wilson (extreme left) and Peter Swan.

2. Bobby Moore gives the Jules Rimet Cup to Alf Ramsey watched by Jimmy Armfield, who would have been England's captain instead of Moore had he been fit.

3. Was this Alf's biggest mistake? With England 2-1 up against the Germans in Mexico in 1970 he substituted the puzzled Bobby Charlton, making his 106th and last appearance for his country, and the Germans went on to win 3-2.

4. Labour Prime Minister Harold Wilson, first premier to exploit the popularity of football and win votes, chatting with Alf Ramsey in 1966. Denis Howell, the best ever Minister of Sport, is in the middle.

5. Joe Mercer soaks up the sun.

6. Don Revie conducting an unusual training routine.

7. The raincoated Danny Blanchflower, manager of Ireland, with the similarly raincoated Ron Greenwood, walking round the track at Wembley.

8. Ron Greenwood feels the heat.

9. Tear gas stops play as Ron Greenwood speaks to his players in the match against Belgium in Turin in 1980.

10. Bobby Robson is consoled by Franz Beckenbauer in Turin after England go out of the 1990 World Cup on a penalty shootout.

11. Bobby Robson makes a point at a press conference in the 1990 World Cup with Glen Kirton, the FA's longest serving press officer, sitting next to him

12. The substituted Gary Lineker trudges off in 1992 as Graham Taylor prepares to face his critics.

13. Graham Taylor upsets the FIFA official during the Holland *v*. England game in Rotterdam.

14. Terry Venables awards Robbie Fowler his first cap – an outsize one.

15. Terry Venables with Bryan Robson. Robson was being groomed as a possible England manager under Venables. What went wrong?

16. Terry Venables consoles Gareth Southgate after the defender's penalty miss in the Euro 96 semi-final shoot-out. Don Howe is on the right.

17. Triumph in Rome. Glenn Hoddle with Paul Gascoigne… before they fell out.

18. Send for Eileen Drewery!

19. Hoddle and his coaching staff of (from left) Ray Clemence, John Gorman and Gary Lewin.

20. Caretaker manager Howard Wilkinson takes charge, briefly, as David Davies, the high-ranking FA official who ghosted Glenn Hoddle's controversial book, calls up another interviewer.

21. Kevin Keegan and Alan Shearer join the new FA president the Duke of York at a charity function to promote the NSPCC.

22. Keegan suffering as another two points are dropped in the game against Bulgaria.

23. Caretaker manager Peter Taylor gives David Beckham the captaincy for the first time.

24. Wilkinson hands over to Sven at Soho Square.

25. Sven and partner
Nancy Dell'Olio watch
a Davis Cup tie between
Great Britain's Tim
Henman and Sweden's
Jonas Bjorkman at
Birmingham.

26. David Beckham with
Sven-Goran Eriksson at
the Jeju Stadium, South
Korea.

27. Who called? Real Madrid, or perhaps the fake sheikh?

Before the game in Oslo Taylor called a team meeting and asked the players to mark themselves out of ten. Ian Wright gave himself ten out of ten. Taylor awarded him eight. He saw it as a light-hearted exercise but Tony Adams thought it was undermining the players' morale. 'That was the time he lost the full backing of the players,' said Adams. Taylor took the squad to train at an air base in private and said he didn't want any details to be passed on to the press, especially his idea of using three centre halves. But Rob Shepherd must have found out.

Dennis Bergkamp, scorer of Holland's first goal in the game at Wembley on 28 April said, 'England weren't the same side when Gascoigne went off injured.' Gascoigne was elbowed in the face by Jan Wouters and his cheek-bone was fractured. The result, 2-2, was a serious setback and McMenemy said, 'We should have won it. We didn't get the rub of the green.' Des Walker, England's quickest defender, made a rare mistake that led to Holland's eighty-seventh-minute penalty. Next morning, facing the assembled journalists, Taylor crooned a few lines from Buddy Holly's 'Raining in my Heart' to sum up his feelings. He never forsook his sense of humour. McMenemy recalled another occasion:

> He loved watching *Coronation Street* and one of his highlights was being invited to their studios in Manchester. Once we were at a meeting at Whites Hotel round the corner from the FA when I had to ring him in his room when I knew he was watching the latest edition. It was a particularly emotional scene in it and I said to him 'you sound as though you're upset.' He said 'I've been shedding a tear or two'.

By the time the second Holland game came round, McMenemy was no longer sitting next to Taylor at press conferences. He was the man who whispered a few words in his ear when things were going wrong. In Taylor's defence, the 2-0 victory by Holland's ageing team in Rotterdam was a travesty of a result. 'We were robbed by the referee,' said McMenemy. 'The ref, Karl Josef Assenmacher, was never given another international after that, which showed what FIFA thought of him. FIFA admitted that he had made two serious mistakes which cost us the game.' Before Holland's captain and sweeper Ronald Koeman scored the first goal from a free-kick in the sixty-second minute, England had been ahead on chances, with Merson hitting the bar. Just before, Koeman had brought David Platt down and the referee had awarded England a free-kick just outside the penalty area. 'I was pulled back,' said Platt. 'It should have been a penalty and Koeman should have gone off. Whether it was a free-kick or a penalty, he had to go.' Koeman, renowned for his straightness, said after the match, 'Yes, I am surprised that I was allowed to stay on. I thought I was about to be shown the red card.'

England's free-kick, taken by Tony Dorigo, was charged down by a Dutch defender within ten yards and the referee should have ordered a retake but didn't. Then, when Holland were awarded a free-kick at the other end, Koeman's free-kick was cleared by an England defender in a similar position and Paul Ince was cautioned for arguing. This time the official pointed to the spot where the first kick was taken and Koeman converted it with a curling shot past David Seaman's grasping fingers.

There was a celebrated picture of Taylor standing face to face with the FIFA representative. He was saying, 'You know we feel cheated, don't you? Even if he doesn't see it as a penalty, he has to go. You know that – and the fella scores from the free-kick. You can't say anything, I know that. You see, at the end of the day, I get the sack now.' Turning to the approaching moustachioed assistant referee he said, 'I was just saying to your colleague, the referee's got me the sack. Thank him ever so much for that, won't you.' Taylor said in a television interview the next day, 'If anyone tells me that was fair and consistent refereeing we are living in a different world. This match wasn't about team changes [he had made five] or formations, it was about incidents.' Tony Adams said, 'It was one of the cruellest nights of my career. I missed a header and Bergkamp latched onto it and shot past Seaman. Game over, as was Graham's management of England.'

A month later Taylor resigned. England needed to beat San Marino in their final game by a huge number of goals and rely on Holland failing to beat Poland in their last game. Neither happened and the final ignominy occurred when Gualtieri scored for the part-timers eight seconds after the kick-off, the fastest international goal ever, and England took twenty-two minutes to equalise. Ian Wright, often summoned from the bench to save lost causes, scored four of the goals in the meaningless 7-1 victory. 'Taylor gave me my chance with England but, I have to say, he talked for England,' said Wright. 'Never stopped talking.'

There was a fascinating sequel to the press conference in Rotterdam where Taylor had lost his composure. Most people would have been upset with Shepherd's conduct that day and the relations of the two men would have ended in recriminations. But a few years later Shepherd was charged with assaulting his wife in a restaurant in Beckenham and was harshly imprisoned for four months. One of the first people to write to him in prison and offer encouragement was Graham Taylor. Shepherd said, 'That's him. He's a good bloke. I had good contacts in that team and they told me what was planned for the game, that's why I asked those questions. Afterwards, we met for dinner and we sorted things out.'

After the San Marino embarrassment, he went to the FA offices to tell Graham Kelly, the FA secretary, that he was thinking about quitting. The next day he resigned. Gordon Taylor, the chief executive of the PFA, called for the resignation of one of his mentors, Charles Hughes, but Hughes ignored him. Out of the thirty-eight matches he presided over, Graham Taylor had his star player, Gascoigne, available for only ten, excluding the one against the Irish when he chose to leave him out. He capped fifty-nine players and gave twenty-nine debuts and there were nine players – Tim Flowers, Nigel Winterburn, Gordon Cowans, Andy Gray, Steve McMahon, Stuart Ripley, Mark Hateley, Mark Walters and David White – who appeared just once under him. Even allowing for injuries and deliberate withdrawals by selfish club managers, it was an indictment of his indecision. He selected six captains, two a year.

He was on a basic annual salary of around £150,000. Twelve years later, Sven-Goran Eriksson was earning twenty-five times as much. Although he didn't have an agent, Taylor knew how to handle his financial affairs. He received around £100,000 from the FA for the final eight months of his contract and he also made a considerable sum from Channel 4 for the documentary entitled *The Impossible Job*. The programme was filmed over a period of eighteen months and it provided riveting viewing. But it didn't enhance his reputation as a decent family man. There were far too many swear words – but football people understood how it happened. The man who attracted more criticism than Taylor, though, was one of his coaches, Phil Neal, whose banal comments like 'You're right, boss' gave the impression of someone close to power behaving like an unintelligent yes man. Nine months earlier Hunter Davies had interviewed Taylor and, in an article in *The Independent*, he wrote, 'He never swears, except in private with the lads.' By this time the pressure had got to him.

One of his most astute moves was to sell his story to the *News of the World* after his resignation. The cash was probably adjacent to the amount the FA paid him each year and it was a kind of revenge against News International, the owners of the world's biggest selling Sunday newspaper. The 'Screws', so called because it puts the on both the crooked and the straight alike, and its partner *The Sun*, gave more aggravation to England football managers than the rest of the newspapers. *The Sun* came up with the headline 'Swedes 2, Turnips 1', with an illustration of Taylor's face superimposed onto that vegetable, after England lost to Sweden in the European Championships in 1992. It was fun at the time but, as McMenemy said, 'It stuck and it was no longer a joke.' After that, Taylor was known as 'Turnip' and in his series in the *News of the World* he stated, 'When the turnip stories started and then went on and on we just laughed about it instead of getting depressed about it. I must admit, though, I used to quite like turnips but now Rita refuses to serve them.'

The article was ghosted by Rebekah Wade, who later became the newspaper's editor. It started:

I admit that I have said to my wife, 'Without you and the family I would have been a suicide job by now.' I've been emotionally drained and felt betrayed. The yobs even spat at my wife. I'd wake up in the morning with my pyjamas wet. As soon as I resigned, it stopped. These last five days have been great – dry pyjamas for the first time in six months.

The foundation of Taylor's successful life was his early marriage to raven-haired Rita Cowling. They first met when he was thirteen and playing Lord Drizzle in the Scunthorpe Grammar School production of *The Tragedy of Tom Thumb*. She was three years older and doing the make-up. They have been friends and soulmates ever since. They were married at Scunthorpe Congregational church when Graham was twenty and they now have two daughters, one an Everton supporter. According to his family, the man of the house has just one annoying trait – he never clears up his nail clippings.

Taylor was born on 15 September 1944 at a farm in Worksop and two years later his parents Tom and Dorothy moved to Scunthorpe. Tom was a sports reporter working for the local newspaper and one of his tasks was to report on the affairs of Scunthorpe FC. At one time his by-line was 'The Lincolnshire Poacher' and he often brought Graham along to press the knob on his stopwatch to time the goals. Dorothy worked for the Post Office and encouraged her son and daughter Christine to take up athletics.

But Graham's second love, next to Rita, was football. He was picked for Scunthorpe Under-15s and graduated to the England Under-15s as a wing half. At seventeen he signed for Third Division Grimsby Town, making his debut on his eighteenth birthday. A new manager named Jimmy McGuigan took over and soon became his mentor, persuading him to change to left-back and encouraging him to take up coaching. Taylor achieved the FA full badge at the age of twenty-one, being one of the youngest to do so. He was self-motivated, a rarity in the ranks of professional footballers, and wanted to improve himself in every possible way to reach the top of his profession. He put himself down for a journalistic course 'but I wasn't allowed to take the exams because I wasn't employed as a junior journalist. That knocked me back at the time. I thought it was bloody stupid.'

He knew his value and after five years he asked for a benefit. 'I found players were coming into the club and getting signing-on fees whereas I'd been there for years and got nothing,' he told Johnny Rogan, the author of *The Football Managers*. So he moved to Fourth Division Lincoln and their directors were so impressed with his coaching flair and cheeky confidence that they appointed him player-manager of the team in November 1972 at the age of twenty-eight. By this time his playing career had been ended by a calcified hip problem after 189 appearances for Grimsby and 150 for Lincoln. For a man who believed in attacking methods, he scored just three goals, one every 113 games.

His salary when he took over the management of the team was £45 a week and after his first nine games the team had yet to win. Even living in a cathedral city with passive supporters, dissatisfaction was creeping in and 'Taylor out!' was soon a common chant at Sincil Bank. His P45 was looming. 'With a wife and two children under six and paying off a mortgage for the past four years, that was pressure,' he said. 'If I'd lost my job then I doubted whether I would have been able to make my mark in football again because I had no background.' With a patient chairman, the results improved and in 1975/76 he took Lincoln into the Third Divison with a record 74 points and 111 goals scored from his all-out attacking policy.

Lawrie McMenemy, ten years older, started his managerial career at Grimsby in 1971 and there began a long friendship between him and Taylor. Both men share the same distinction – they have worked in all four divisions. Taylor gradually attracted more supporters with his friendly PR approach and he toured the foundries whipping up support and organising charity runs. It was the start of becoming a community club. West Bromwich Albion's directors soon recognised his talents but he turned down their overtures, despite them being in the First Division. It was too soon. He wanted to continue his apprenticeship. Many football managers now start at the top, which is why so many are sacked.

In June the same year he was offered the job at another Fourth Division club, Watford. The main difference between their status and that of Lincoln was that Elton John was the new chairman at Vicarage Road. If the pop singer had wanted to run the club, Taylor wouldn't have accepted it. But that was not Elton's intention. Taylor said:

> I wanted the power to give me the chance to be successful. Success or failure would be down to me. Everything was ideal as long as you were willing to accept the responsibility that a chairman like Elton John gives you. His attitude was 'You're the manager, get on with it. That's what I pay you for.' Elton wanted to take us to Europe and we did it. The idea of developing a team as part of the community stemmed from Elton and myself, nobody else. We seemed to have a kind of telepathy.

They used to run up huge telephone bills. Elton John was touring around the world most of the time and often wanted to hear the commentary on the matches. And with Taylor's chats the long-distance calls certainly enhanced BT's profits. One of the first people to write and congratulate the new manager on his appointment was Bertie Mee, the former Arsenal manager who was in charge of the 1971 double-winning side. Taylor was at Wembley when the Gunners won it and the two men had a great respect for each other. Mee was still only fifty-seven and still had a lot to give. In his final two years at Arsenal he had suffered from stress and he had resigned in 1976 to be replaced by Terry Neill, a former captain of the club. Mee's letter contained a hint that he might be helpful to the thirty-two-year-old manager and Taylor followed it up. They met and soon agreed terms. Mee wasn't given a fancy title like 'director of football'. He was assistant manager and he proved to be a great asset, especially with the signing of Watford's finest player, John Barnes. Mee knew Colonel Ken Barnes of the Jamaican Army, who had managed the national side. Arsenal had toured El Salvador and a friendly game was about to kick off when police called it off. They feared a riot. The two men became friends and Mee encouraged the colonel to allow his son to play in England. The scouts of the big clubs failed to see his talent and Watford signed him from Sudbury Court in the Middlesex League. It was a considerable coup.

Elton John was a bubbly, talkative and expressive man who liked football but didn't interfere. He had a great sense of humour and he shared many jokes with Taylor in their travels around the football grounds. Taylor upset the fans early on, criticising them, and at the next home game he walked out to the middle before the kick-off holding up a sign saying 'Sorry'. After another bad result, he lectured his young players at great length and a reporter wrote in a national newspaper that he threw a cup of tea in the dressing room. Taylor rang him up. 'You've got your facts wrong,' he said. The reporter said, 'I know what happened and what I've written is true.' Taylor said, 'Yes, but it was a cup of bovril, not tea!'

One press box regular said, 'He WAS the club. He ran it from top to bottom and he had time for everyone, right down to the tea ladies. They loved him.' Taylor introduced the 'Watford Way', direct football which put pressure on the opposition from the first kick to the last. He talked about 'the second knock-down' – if the ball didn't reach someone's head first time, the second header would do it. Mee recommended Pat Rice, his ex-skipper at Highbury, and Taylor signed him. Eddie Plumley, the highly regarded secretary of Jimmy Hill's Coventry, was signed up and another new recruit was the marketing manager Caroline Gillies, one of the first women to hold a senior post at a football club. Like Taylor himself, all these people were genuinely nice people. It encouraged enthusiasm and self-esteem.

Taylor introduced a family section and a youth set-up which eventually produced enough quality players to replace the older, experienced ones who were set in their Taylor-made ways. There were plenty of critics, both inside and outside of the game. One of Taylor's chief debunkers was Terry

Venables, the man who took over from him as England manager. He criticised the long ball game and it became personal. Once they had a row in Majorca before a pre-season tournament and it ended with Taylor, at 5ft 8½ins conceding half an inch to Venables, squaring up. Later in the day they sat down at dinner to resolve their problems. Taylor claimed that his views had been misrepresented and if some people felt that his style of football was crude, well, others had the same opinion of Venables' offside game. Several hours later they parted without reaching a consensus.

The quarrel started in 1981 when Watford were chasing promotion from the Second Division. Venables' then club Queens Park Rangers were in a similar position. Just before Christmas Watford beat QPR 4-1 in the League Cup and there was an exchange of words between the young managers near the press room. Three months later, Taylor's Watford beat Rangers 4-0 in a League match to prove conclusively that his team was the better of the two at the time. Watford finished as runners-up and were promoted to the First Division while Rangers ended in fifth place. Venables reckoned that Taylor was a goody-goody type of man who was doing immense harm to the game. Privately, Taylor thought his rival was a wheeler-dealer working for a detestable chairman, Jim Gregory, who had a dodgy business background. Gregory once rang Harry Harris, the *Daily Express* football writer, formerly with the *Daily Mirror*, and threatened to have him kneecapped. Venables and Taylor were never going to be friends. They came from the opposite end of the spectrum.

Venables was influenced by the coaching beliefs of Malcolm Allison, another opponent of the long ball, and he succeeded Allison as manager of Crystal Palace a few months before Taylor joined Watford. Venables gained promotion from the Third Division in his first season and Taylor did the same from the Fourth, taking Watford up by an eleven-point margin. They represented two totally opposing schools – the classy, passing game against the more rudimentary long ball game.

Incredibly, in six years, Taylor took Watford from the Fourth to the First Division, arriving in the top flight in 1982, the same summer the club won the FA Youth Cup. They made the rapid ascent quicker than Wimbledon (1979-1987) but slower Northampton (1961-1966), the other clubs who did it. It was the highlight of Taylor's managerial career, which lasted twenty years. He must have got a few things right on the way. Elton brought out the champagne after Watford beat Sunderland 8-0 in their first season at the top. A week later Taylor was asked to take over as manager of the England Youth side and he accepted. There were shivers down the backs of a number of managers and Allen Wade, the FA director of coaching, said:

> Playing football the Watford way worries me stiff. It could kill the game. The minds of players are drilled to fulfil certain requirements, irrespective of their own inclinations. I don't want to knock Graham or Watford, quite the reverse. I admire what he has achieved with limited resources. The problem is that the Watford way shouldn't be the England way.

Within a year Taylor had resigned as England junior coach because he had too much to do. His team's progress towards the top of the First Division was astonishing and they finished second to Liverpool, beating the champions 2-1 in the last game of a momentous season. Early in the season, a young Watford team without any stars defeated Tottenham 1-0 at White Hart Lane and Jeff Powell, the *Daily Mail* football correspondent, a much-decorated winner in his field, wrote, 'It was like a pack of wild dogs smashing themselves into a brick wall.' Taylor responded saying, 'He never once took time out to come and talk to me. Oh my goodness, he is going to put the game back a generation!'

Venables was born in Bethnal Green in 1943 and went to school in Dagenham after the family moved to a house half a mile from where Sir Alf Ramsey was born. Powell was born a year earlier, also in the East End of London. The two men are still close and it was inevitable that Powell would back his friend in any future election for the next England manager. He took every opportunity to attack Taylor and his methods and a number of other writers joined in. By the time Taylor was given the senior England job, half the commentators were ranged against him.

Even Elton John and his wealth were unable to provide the elixir to keep Watford marching in step with Liverpool and the other big clubs but there was a pleasant interlude in the 1983/84 season when they qualified for the UEFA Cup. The exotically dressed chairman went on the away trips and delighted the players, press and officials with his antics on the flights. He was in raptures after they walloped the German side Kaiserslautern

3-0 at Vicarage Road after being beaten 3-1 away. A 1-1 draw at home against Levski Sofia lowered morale but in soulless Sofia Taylor's Hornets came back to win 3-1 after extra time. So many players were injured that someone at the club put an advertisement in *The Times* that read, 'Wanted: professional footballers, men (or women) aged 18-80, preference given to applicants with two arms and two legs in working order.'

With this spirit they might have gone on but the Czech players of Sparta Prague ended their adventure in freezing conditions in Prague with an aggregate of 7-2. Elton took the mike on the way back and congratulated the young players and their loyal fans. 'We're the best family club in the world,' he said. There was just one hurrah for Taylor after his side reached 1984 FA Cup final. Taylor described their 2-0 defeat at Wembley at the hands of Everton as an anticlimax and some of his players literally froze before the kick-off. Taylor said, 'As a manager you lead the team out but you're not important enough to go up those steps. When it is all over, people only want to know the winners.'

He signed a six-year contract in 1984 but he never served it. Halfway through his new contract he surprised everyone by resigning after ten happy and often glorious years and accepting an offer from Doug Ellis to manage Aston Villa, who were in chaos after being relegated from the First Division. 'I didn't want to run Villa, only the footballing side,' he said to reassure their supporters that there is only one dictator at Villa Park. Astonishingly, he brought them back up at the first attempt while Dave Bassett, his replacement at Vicarage Road, took Watford down. After just missing relegation by one point in 1988/89 he took Villa to the runners-up spot behind Liverpool the next season.

Winning top jobs is down to timing more than anything else and Taylor's performance to resurrect Villa was brilliantly timed. Inside Lancaster Gate senior officials were coming to a consensus that they would not require Bobby Robson's services after Italia '90. Oddly, that decision was made before the outcome of the World Cup and if England had won it – and Robson still swears that England were a heartbeat away – the FA would have been acutely embarrassed. They already had Graham Taylor, a decent, honorable man who wouldn't attract damning headlines, lined up. Taylor had attended many of England's internationals and was ready to take up the mantle. He was touring round Italy, watching games and doing media work. He got to know the

English journalists and, except for two or three, they liked him. His planning was as thorough and detailed as a field marshal's about to go to war.

Robson wanted a two-year extension on his contract but covered himself by speaking to Kees Ploegsma, the general manager of PSV Eindhoven, who wanted a new coach. They were old friends and if Robson wasn't required by the FA there was a safe job waiting for him. At a meeting at Lancaster Gate, Robson asked FA chairman Sir Bert Millichip if he was going to be retained. Millichip replied, 'If you have a good offer don't let us stand in your way.' PSV were willing to pay Robson twice as much as his £80,000 salary at the FA but if the FA had changed their minds he would have been keen to stay at the same money. The news leaked out on the day of the FA's annual general meeting just before the start of the World Cup. Robson was upset that he hadn't told his assistant Don Howe. 'You don't have to explain to me,' said Howe. 'In six weeks' time you could have been out of work. You've done the right thing.'

Taylor created a good impression at his inaugural press conference after his appointment. He said:

> It is my intention to be the most track-suited manager England have ever had and my name will be at the bottom of all the team selections. Lawrie McMenemy is joining me as my manager's assistant, as opposed to assistant manager, and I am confident I will be able to say about Lawrie what I said about Bertie Mee during my time at Watford. Bertie was my first appointment and my most important.
>
> I'll be bringing in different people to have a smell of international football. Some will take to it like ducks to water, others will have problems. But there is bags of talent and experience out there and I will be trying to create a structure for the future. I'll be visiting club managers at their clubs to exchange views.

Somewhat disturbingly, he spoke for a long time and some of his sentences were rather convoluted.

His opening game secured a 1-0 victory over Hungary at Wembley in September 1990 and his honeymoon period lasted one day short of his first year, when his much-changed team lost 1-0 to Germany, also at Wembley. He had kept the same side in his first two matches but that didn't happen again. His second game was in the European Championship qualifiers against Poland and England were comfortable 2-0 winners. With new men brought in, Peter Beardsley and Chris Waddle were left out and Gascoigne's omission from the 1-1 draw against the Republic of Ireland in Dublin brought smatterings of criticism.

By the end of 1991 the still consistent Gary Lineker scored the goal against Poland in Poznan which guaranteed England's place in the European Championship Finals in Sweden and Taylor's ratings were high. He was the first England manager to qualify for a championship in his first attempt and was now seeking a quality finisher as back-up or even a replacement for Lineker. But during the summer tour of Australia, New Zealand and Malaysia, Ian Wright, a possible heir apparent, claimed a comment from the bench at Kuala Lumpur persuaded Taylor to leave him out of the squad in Sweden. Wright, the winner of the European Golden Boot for scoring the most goals that season, ahead of Lineker, was standing up during the final game and Paul Parker said, 'Why don't you sit down?' Wright replied, 'F—— that, I'm not used to sitting down on benches.' He wasn't picked again for eighteen months, missing the European Championships. Lineker scored all four goals in the 4-2 win over Malaysia.

England's opening game in Sweden ended with an unmemorable 0-0 draw against the Danes and, after the second match against France finished with the same score, Taylor's side had to beat hosts Sweden to stay in the competition. 17 June 1992 signalled the first major low point of Taylor's reign with Sweden winning 2-1 in the game that ended Lineker's career. It was Lineker's twenty-first game under Taylor, in which he had scored thirteen goals, but in his six previous games he had failed to score. Jon Holmes, Lineker's agent, thought the relationship between the manager and the star striker had deteriorated.

Just past the hour mark, an agitated Taylor gestured to the UEFA official that he wanted to make a substitution, bringing on Arsenal's Alan Smith, now a football writer who writes his own material, in place of Lineker. Taylor's bold decision severed the fragile relationship with a single stroke. Lineker tore off his skipper's armband and threw it down towards Carlton Palmer, the hyped-up midfield player, as he walked off. If England had won few people would have made an issue of the substitution. At thirty, Lineker still had plenty to offer. One stab of a foot could have changed the plot completely. He would have been England's joint record scorer. Taylor later said:

> People made it out that my decision was personal. I cannot stop them think-
> ing that but I honestly swear that I never saw it that way. I had in my mind,
> rightly or wrongly, that he had got in a rut. Things were not happening for
> him, even on the training pitch. All I could see in that final game was that the
> ball was not sticking up front.

Lineker maintained a dignified pose as the storm enveloped the manager and his team. Later, he announced his retirement and went off to play in Japan in the following season. 'We were beaten by stronger and bigger ath-letes,' said Taylor. 'And they played direct football.' That was the type of football he preached himself in his early career. The tirade of abuse shocked Taylor and his family and things were never the same after that.

In the *Daily Mirror* Sir Alf Ramsey, or rather his ghost writer Nigel Clarke, proclaimed:

> England were not only beaten, they were embarrassed. And that hurt me as
> much as losing to an ordinary Swedish side. I can't believe that this would
> have happened if Terry Venables had already been in charge. He is not only
> the outstanding coach in the country, he is also a clever, shrewd and moti-
> vated tactician. Taylor, for all his talking, all his confident predictions, was not
> up to the job.

No one has investigated the probity of the UEFA and FIFA draws for the European Championships and World Cup but some of England's oppo-nents, like Poland, Turkey and Norway keep appearing. None of these countries appeal to potential England hooligans – Poland is drab (poor beer!), Turkey has a tendency of banging hooligans into primitive cells and Norway, well, it's extremely cold in the winter and there's not too much light by tea time.

After taking on Turkey and Poland in the European Championship qual-ifiers, England were drawn against, yes, Poland and Turkey, plus San Marino, Holland and Norway in the qualifiers for USA '94. Too many points were dropped against moderate opponents and it needed a rare goal from a rare appearance from Ian Wright to keep England in with a chance after drawing 1-1 against the moderate Poles in Chorzow. Four days later came the Oslo fiasco.

England's 1993 summer tour was arranged to acclimatise for the 1994 World Cup in the USA but they lost their first game to the host country by two goals to nil in Boston, a city which had embarrassed Her Majesty's red shirts on an earlier occasion. An honourable 1-1 draw with Brazil and an unlucky 2-1 defeat against the Germans failed to expunge the shame of Boston. A 3-0 win over Poland three months later acted like blowing on the embers, only to see the fire extinguished in Rotterdam. Taylor admitted his responsibility and duly fell on his sword.

Before he was appointed he had given an interview in which he said:

> The way we treat England managers in our country is disgraceful. What makes a man like Sir Alf Ramsey not talk to his fellow human beings? What makes someone like Don Revie defect? What makes a man like Ron Greenwood resign before getting to the World Cup Finals? What makes a man like Bobby Robson look like he does?
>
> It's people with petty jealousies feeding the press. People in our profession are a bit naughty and do feed these stories. They don't want us to do well. Bobby Robson had an absolutely first-class record with England yet they were making badges saying 'Robson must go'. What a way to treat human beings. They destroy us.

He was destroyed and he knew what was coming. He returned to club management and did well but never won a trophy. For all his enthusiasm and passion he didn't quite have the final parts to make himself into a great manager. He represented a near miss.

TERRY VENABLES

1993–1996

Was He English Football's Sergeant Bilko?

P 24	W 11	D 11	L 2	47%

Terry is an extraordinary man and a very controversial figure who is still revered by the majority of football lovers. He was certainly the newsiest of the England managers. Whether he lived up to his reputation, which he created himself, with his widespread range of talent and ideas, aided by so many influential friends and commentators, has to be doubted.

Andrew Neil, the television pundit and newspaper editor, said, 'He could have been the first England manager to have ended up in prison.' That fear, expressed by two senior members of the FA international committee, chairman Noel White and Ian Stott, the chairman of Oldham FC, took a prominent part in forcing Venables to resign as England coach at the end of the European Championships in 1996. 'He has far too much baggage with him,' said White, a former chairman of Liverpool, now a club director. Venables had four court actions looming as the competition kicked off and after a judge described his evidence as 'wanton' the committee members declined to back him. They refused his request to extend his contract by a further two years, which would have taken him up to the World Cup in France in 1998. He was bitterly upset. It was his last chance to end his career as a definitive hero. Born in Dagenham, like Sir Alf Ramsey, he could have emulated Ramsey's unequalled achievement of winning the World Cup.

Instead, he went back to his house in Kensington, England's most expensive Royal Borough, with a near miss on his CV after England lost to Germany on penalties in the semi-final of the 1996 European Championship Finals. His players had to play in battleship grey in the world's second-rated nations' competition because of the FA's contract with Umbro, their kit suppliers, and if they had used their traditional red shirts perhaps they might have succeeded. We now know that red is a more successful colour than any other, particularly battleship grey. Manchester United lost matches wearing battleship grey and eventually ditched the idea.

Afterwards, Venables lost a few court actions, including the £101,000 damages paid to his hated adversary Alan Sugar, but the only severe legal action imposed on him was a seven-year ban from the Department of Trade and Industry preventing him from acting as a director of a company. In 2005 the ban was lifted. Robert Maxwell, the feared tycoon who tried to take over Tottenham Hotspur when Sugar and Venables were contesting the ownership of the then stricken club, was once banned for a similar time by the DTI.

Would Sugar welcome Venables as an entrant for his popular television programme *The Apprentice*? Perhaps, but only to humiliate him again. The problem with Terence Frederick Venables is that most things about him never seem to be as they appear. Like the the word 'wanton'. The public thought it had a slightly dishonest look about it. But the dictionary says, 'Unrestrained, playful, dissolute, without motive, luxuriant, loose, lewd.' These descriptions could fit Venables – except he might be ready to sue if he was called 'lewd'.

During the 1990s he, or his advisors, filed 149 complaints to the Press Complaints Commission. At the last count none of them had been taken up. A spokesperson at their offices off Fleet Street confirmed that fact in May 2005. If he had been wronged, he could have picked up hundreds of thousands of pounds in damages for libel. He and his courtiers threatened countless writs but the writs were binned. There were two press campaigns about him. The first, a supportive one, was headed by most of the football written press including Martin Samuel, then of *The Sun* and now *The Times*, who ghosts Venables' column in the *News of the World*; Jeff Powell of the *Daily Mail*; Rob Shepherd, formerly of the *Daily Express* and the *Mail*, now freelance; Lee Clayton, when he was one of the youngest sports editors at the *Daily Star*; and a few more who backed him through and through.

The second campaign was aggressively conducted by the Gang of Four – Harry Harris, then with the *Daily Mirror* when he was the chief spokesman for Robert Maxwell, now with the *Daily Express*; Mihir Bose of the *Daily Telegraph*; Patrick Collins of *The Mail on Sunday*, the most decorated sports writer in English history; and Richard Littlejohn, who is now with the *Daily Mail* after transferring from *The Sun*. In his book *The Best Game in the World* Venables said of the Four:

They are the only journalists who have maintained a vicious and malicious attitude towards me whatever I do. Harris and Bose, both friends of Irving Scholar, have tried to discredit me with a series of so called exposés and Collins and Littlejohn, from observations of me from a distance, think of me as a kind of Cockney wide boy.

He named two others as accessories in the campaign: Alan Sugar and former Labour Sports Minister Kate Hoey, who denounced him in the House of Commons. 'Unfortunately she didn't have the courage to repeat her claims outside the House,' said Venables.

With so much publicity about his activities it was unlikely that Venables would be ignored by the FA, who wanted to appoint a high-profile celebrity manager to succeed Graham Taylor. It turned out to be a long, drawn-out referendum in the pages of the newspapers with the majority going in favour of the cheeky chappie from Dagenham. No England manager had more supporters from Her Majesty's Press than Venables. Those who tried to ruin him were totally outnumbered but it didn't mean they were wrong. The verdict on the tangled business career of Venables had to be 'not proven'.

In the mid-1980s, when Crystal Palace were supposed to be ruling over English football, the popularity of Venables was at its peak. In 1985 he won the Spanish League with Barcelona but failed to reach the very top of European football. The next season, Barcelona lost in the European Cup final to the Romanian side Steaua Bucharest, who beat them in a penalty shoot-out after a 0-0 draw in a sterile tactical battle. Some of his critics hailed it as a tactical success. His employers at Barça had other ideas – they got rid of him. However, he was one of the longest-serving coaches at the club.

As a player, he was rated one of the outstanding passing midfield players in his time and appeared in 508 League matches for Chelsea, Tottenham, QPR and Crystal Palace, scoring 50 goals between 1959 and 1975 before a weak ankle finished his playing career at the comparatively early age of thirty-one. For all his flair and brains, he was capped for England just twice. 'He had a lot of competition at the time,' said one of his acolytes. He gained his FA full badge, taking over as manager of Crystal Palace from his bombastic and popular mentor Malcolm Allison, the man who wore a fedora hat and smoked large cigars to attract publicity. Allison was another man who worked hard on his image without matching his many loud boasts.

Venables is the only footballer to have represented England at Schools, Youth, Amateur, Under-23 and senior level, a record which will never be equalled as the amateur side was later discontinued. He could have been another Winterbottom but wasn't. Perhaps there was a bit too much of Walter Mitty about him. When he was manager of Palace between 1976 and 1980, Palace were labelled the 'team of the eighties'. He took them up from the Third Division in his first season and in 1978/79 they won the Second Division title before Venables left to take charge of Queens Park Rangers, owned by the notorious Jim Gregory. But the Eagles failed to soar during that period, as everyone suspected.

Venables helped pioneer artificial pitches, putting in an Omniturf surface which he forecast would be the end of grass pitches. The ball bounced far too high, the joints of the players rebelled and the rock-hard Omniturf pitch was dug up. As a teenager, he had impressed as a crooner at dance halls and later he helped a hard-drinking and talented journalist, Gordon Williams, to write a moderately successful book entitled *They Used to Play on Grass* about the future of the game. He also contributed to the Hazell detective stories which were turned into a popular television series. His chief aim was to own a big club himself. From his money acquired in Spain and various business deals, he bought into Tottenham in 1991 and became chief executive. And with Alan Sugar ignorant of many aspects of the professional game and picking up the tab, he figured briefly as the kingpin of White Hart Lane before Sugar summarily dismissed him two years later.

He still lived like a millionaire, presiding over afternoon drinks sessions with his many friends, but few of his objectives were fulfilled. They carried a nice-looking veneer, yet lacked substance. He owned a large basement drinking club under Barkers, the Kensington store next to the offices of Associated Newspapers, the publishers of the *Daily Mail*, the *Mail on Sunday* and the *Evening Standard*. Its position was against him because most of the London drinking clubs are in St James, within walking distance of the main-line rail stations. Kensington is better known for shopping than late-night drinking. He introduced karaoke, which appealed to a different clientele and the club, 'Scribes', went into bankruptcy with Associated Newspapers as one of the major creditors. It was launched several years too soon for the age of the obscenely highly paid footballers of the Premiership.

In Spain he was called 'El Tel' but Graeme Souness and his playing contemporaries at White Hart Lane knew him as 'Bilko'. One of the favourite anecdotes of the period was about the long-standing knee injury of Roger Morgan, who was ordered in for morning, afternoon and evening sessions under the physiotherapist Cec Poynton, the humourless and demanding club trainer. After three weeks of this punishing regime, Morgan said to Poynton, 'Cec, I've got a family engagement tomorrow, can I have a day off?' Poynton said, 'No, you keep working. Getting fit to play again is more important than your family.' Morgan was very upset. The next morning he went to Venables, explained his predicament and said, 'What can I do about it?' Venables said, 'I know, send your brother Ian instead.' The Morgans, both wingers, were identical twins and the switch was duly effected and Roger went to the party. It may be an apocryphal story but it sounded good. For a while the nickname 'Bilko' stuck with him, mainly because he watched the *Sergeant Bilko* television series imported from America. Bilko, portrayed by Phil Silvers, was a likeable wheeler-dealer type who cut a few corners, a bit like Venables. Venables still has a full collection of the *Bilko* tapes and a similar collection of the *Laurel and Hardy* tapes. He loves a laugh and a joke and his laugh is Premiership class.

In his autobiography, the book which led to the £101,000 libel case, he claimed that he might have been one of Hermann Goering's victims in the wartime Blitz:

> It was nearly a short life. The house in which my Mum had been living before I was born was bombed flat to the ground the night after she left to stay with my grandparents. Had she stayed twenty-four hours longer, or the Luftwaffe arrived twenty-four hours earlier, Alan Sugar's future might well have been less complicated.

He was a war baby, born on 6 Janary 1943 in his grandparents' house at 313 Valence Avenue, Dagenham, the only child of Frederick Charles and Myrtle Eileen Venables. (Some of the quoted facts about Venables' family history are wrong, including the one in many record books that said he was born in Bethnal Green.) His father Fred was a Cockney with a wonderful sense of humour, which he passed on to his son. Fred was twenty, serving in the Royal Navy in Halifax, Nova Scotia, when his only son was born. Halifax was the place where the world's biggest man-made explosion took place in 1918 when two ships packed with armaments collided and blew up.

Myrtle was born in Clydach Vale, a mining village near Tonypandy, the birthplace of Tommy Farr, the former British heavyweight boxer who put up a highly creditable performance against World Champion Joe Louis just before the outbreak of the Second World War. After he retired, Farr used to deliver groceries to the family. At fifteen, Myrtle moved to Dagenham and three years later she married Fred after a brief teenage courtship. Six weeks after Terry's birth, she and her son were evacuated to South Wales. Later they moved backwards and forwards and at both places Terry spent a considerable amount of time kicking balls outside in the streets, fields and playing grounds. At eight he wanted to be a professional footballer. At eleven he decided that he wanted to captain Tottenham Hotspur, which he went on to do.

Myrtle wanted him to be named Duncan but Fred insisted on Terence. 'I was walking down the road and saw an advert for Terry's chocolates on the side of a bus,' he said. 'That decided it.' Fred and Terry were great pals right up to the time Fred died. Hardly a day went by without them chatting over the phone. One of a family of nine, Fred was a goalkeeper at Barking FC and he also played for the Royal Navy, despite his lack of height. He was so proud of his son that he wrote a book about him.

Ford's factory was nearby but few of the family could afford a car. After being demobbed, Fred worked as a lorry driver and then became a publican and was still running a pub in Chingford when he died. Everyone liked him and Dagenham was a place where it was easy to make friends. When anyone was in trouble, there were plenty of volunteers to help out.

The name Venables is derived from the French 'venari', the hunt, and it comes from a parish in the arrondisement of Louviers in Normandy. So Venables may well have been descended from the Huegenots, the more distinguished citizens of the French Republic before they were ordered out after the Edict of Nantes was proclaimed in 1694.

Myrtle taught dance and also worked in the restaurant at the local Odeon cinema. She insisted on immaculate table manners – 'Hold your knife and fork properly, no elbows on the table, don't talk with your mouth full, always tip the bowl away from you when you have soup and don't take a drink until you have finished your food.' She was strict whereas Fred was soft-hearted and tended to spoil Terry. Someone once said there were more footballers coming out of Dagenham in the 1940s and '50s than automobiles and he had a point. In the same town there were Jimmy Greaves, Martin Peters, the Allen dynasty, Ken Brown and many more. Younger and smaller than most of the others, Venables soon emerged as a leader of the group. He was to be called 'The General'. He won swimming events, had trials with Essex County Cricket Club and won schools cross-country races in his football boots. 'I was completely dedicated to football and would make any sacrifice to succeed, no matter how painful,' he said.

His parents bought him an expensive bicycle but the famed Chelsea scout Jimmy Thompson, who had courted him and his parents for years, told him not to use it. 'It will shorten your hamstrings,' he said. So Venables refused to ride it. He made his debut for England Schoolboys at the age of fifteen, up against Billy Bremner in the Scots side, in front of 100,000 people at Wembley. He was the star of the team and West Ham, Chelsea, Arsenal and Tottenham invited him to train with their clubs. His heart said West Ham but his head voted for Chelsea because he felt he had a better chance of making the first team at Stamford Bridge.

Thompson was probably the most celebrated scout of all time. He was a talkative, persuasive man who tried to hide round bushes to avoid fellow scouts while watching schools' games but at six feet and attired in a pinstripe suit and a bowler hat, carrying a rolled up brolly, he was an easy target to locate.

He earned fortunes and spent large sums on horses, often placing bets on behalf of rich punters. He invested a lot of time and money in the Venables signing, which was effected on amateur terms on his fifteenth birthday. In those days the clubs would offer large sums to parents but the Venables family got round that when Chelsea signed Fred Venables as a scout, earning more than his son.

Thompson built up his prodigy into 'another Duncan Edwards' and there was plenty of resentment about the arrival of this cocky upstart. On his first day, groundsman Harry Winston lined up the new recruits and said, 'Right, which one's Venables?' Terry said, 'Me' and Winston said,

'Okay, I've got a right shit job for you.' It was to sweep out the whole of a stand by himself. When he started the lapping with the professionals, the late Peter Sillett told him, 'If you show me up I'll smash you in the chest.' Playing in Chelsea's FA Youth Cup-winning side, he soon moved up to the first team, making his debut just after his seventeenth birthday. The match was against West Ham and he was on the wrong end of a 3-1 defeat. He soon learned a lesson. At half-time, having played poorly, the side's most talented player, Johnny Brooks, went to him and said, 'How am I going, Terry?' Brooks wanted reassurance from a debutant because he never had confidence in his ability. Venables had the necessary confidence. Even if he struggled, he still exuded confidence throughout his career. It helped to cover any deficiencies. A confident sportsman wins more than a diffident one.

Chelsea dropped down the league table and the pressure was on Ted Drake, their much-respected manager who had a gentle nature. One day Peter Sillett joined him on a car ride home and was surprised to see Drake sitting at the wheel failing to accelerate away from the green lights. They remained stationary for some time and a police officer tapped on the side window and said, 'Is there a problem, sir?' Drake looked startled. 'My God, Peter,' he said. 'I thought you were driving.' In his autobiography Venables told a similar story when he was manager at Crystal Palace, with him the victim.

Drake had to go and Tommy Docherty, the opposite in personality, with his cruel jokes and impetuous decisions, appointed Venables captain at the age of nineteen. Now he was living close to Bobby Moore and they were drinking partners. Soon Venables was stopped for driving 'too slow' in a 30mph limit and was banned for a year. While still banned he drove the car of his new wife Christine, whom he first met aged sixteen, and later a friend said, 'You've been driving when banned.' He denied it but the man who spotted him was a policeman and had shopped him. In Dagenham no one would rat on a mate. But now, living in Loughton, he had soon learned another lesson.

He was very close to his parents. Myrtle shaped the more responsible part of his life with Fred supplying the humour and confidence. They ran pubs and he blamed that on the breakup of their marriage. She moved back to South Wales and introduced a 'women only' bar in her pub, one of the first in the country. She died in 1990 from cancer of the lung when Terry was forty-seven. Her premature death was probably caused by her lifetime exposure to smoking. A third of the 110,000 people who died of cancer in 2004 died from lung cancer, and this form of the disease still causes more deaths among women than breast cancer, which is decreasing.

In 1964 Terry Venables was capped by England, just twice, and he said it was 'the zenith of my playing career'. But his international career lasted only six weeks. He provided a goal in the first game against Belgium on Trafalgar Day, a 2-2 draw at Wembley, and he made the equaliser against Holland in a 1-1 draw in Amsterdam. He said of Alf Ramsey, 'I held him in very high esteem but he wasn't an easy man to know. I still have the accent of the people where I grew up in Dagenham and Alf came from three streets away but you couldn't tell that from the way he spoke. He spoke posh.'

At his first England training session, he approached Ramsey and said, 'Sid, your old next-door neighbour from Dagenham, sends his regards.' Ramsey turned and walked off. 'I got the feeling that Alf's Dagenham roots were not a subject that he was keen to discuss,' said Venables. Ramsey picked him for a third game but Venables was injured and Johnny 'Budgie' Byrne of Crystal Palace took over. Venables was chosen in the original World Cup forty but failed the cut for the final selection of twenty-two.

There were more setbacks for Venables. Docherty had flair and motivational qualities and built one of the most exciting young sides in the country, but if someone upset him he would ditch them and so it proved with Venables. Maybe the Doc was jealous of his popularity. There were several rows over late-night drinking and the club's Kings Road image was worrying the directors.

The catalyst was the Blackpool incident when Docherty sent eight players home the night before a match at Bloomfield Road and claimed that Venables was the ringleader. The eight were George Graham, Barry Bridges, Eddie McCreadie, John Hollins, Joe Fascione, Bert Murray, Marvin Hinton and Venables. Four of these men went on to be managers. In a normal football club, the manager would have called the players in to sort things out. But Venables recalled, 'I heard nothing from Docherty until the following Friday night. The phone rang at home and Fred answered it. "This is Tommy Docherty," said the caller. "Tell Terry he's not playing tomorrow and he's not captain any more." Docherty put the phone down.'

Venables played his last game for Chelsea at the Nou Camp in the Fairs Cup and before the kick-off Docherty introduced Charlie Cooke as his new star. Cooke, one of the greatest dribblers in Britain, was to replace a player who was a passer. The two were total opposites. 'If Docherty had kept that side together we would have gone on to be as dominant as Leeds or Liverpool in that era,' said Venables, and he was probably right. Tottenham and West Ham bid for him and Spurs' Bill Nicholson won the race, paying out £80,000. Nicholson almost signed Bobby Moore, according to Venables in his book. What a team they might have had at White Hart Lane!

Venables was there for three unhappy years and, again, he didn't reach the heights. The crowd turned against him from the start. They thought he wasn't a John White, or even a Danny Blanchflower, but a cheeky upstart who needed to be taught a lesson. And that happened on his first day, training in the gym at the rear of the main stand. As Venables tried to take the ball past Dave Mackay he found himself being punched by Mackay in the testicles. 'The next time I got the ball, I slid the ball past him again and once more he whacked me in the balls,' he said. 'I turned and punched him in the face and unfortunately I had a ring on my middle finger and it sliced his cheek open and damaged my knuckle.' A few days later Venables invited him for a drink at a nearby pub and relations were restored. But Mackay was the master in charge on the field, not Venables.

In his brief time at Spurs Venables won just one accolade, an FA Cup winners' medal. The 1967 final was one of the drabbest finals of that period, a 2-1 win over Docherty's Chelsea side. Docherty said in a pre-match interview, 'I don't expect too much trouble from him. I don't think he is as good now as when he was at Chelsea when he was a big fish in a young pool. In training he thought he was the boss – I knew I was.' With something to prove, Venables played reasonably well but didn't dominate. Mackay did. In 1969 Nicholson cut his losses on Venables and sold him to Second Division QPR for £70,000.

'It was one of the best decisions I made,' said Venables. 'I had one of my finest spells as a player and it was the most satisfying.' There was little laughter and fun at Tottenham – everyone was under pressure to win something – whereas at Loftus Road it was the opposite. Les Allen, his former Chelsea and Tottenham teammate, used to live in Bonham Road, only a few yards from where he grew up in Dagenham, and was the titular manager. The real manager and supremo was the chairman, Jim Gregory. 'I struck up a rapport with him from the start,' said Venables. Not too many people liked the ruthless Gregory. He had a habit of inviting players or colleagues to go to his office and come up with a proposal they couldn't possibly accept. The meeting would soon end and the man would go off only for Gregory to tell his secretary to ring him back and ask him back to discuss another offer. It was a cruel way of running a business.

Gregory sacked more managers than any chairman of his time and Allen soon left. Gordon Jago, a devotee of Walter Winterbottom, was Allen's successor, known as 'High Heels' because of the odd way he walked. He was constantly ribbed by players like Rodney Marsh, Stan Bowles, Terry Mancini, Don Shanks and Frank McLintock and there were daily wind-ups, cards sessions and practical jokes. Mancini showed what he thought of Gregory by pulling down his shorts and exposing his posterior in his direction in his final game.

At twenty-seven, Venables was elected vice-chairman of the Professional Footballers' Association and represented his members in disciplinary cases. Once he won a watershed victory over Bob Lord, the Burnley chairman who was the last of the Victorian tyrants. But he had so much to do that he soon gave up the job. There were too many tasks to tackle properly and with so much socialising going on it was virtually impossible to think of him being the boss of the PFA. Not that he wanted the job. He started a clothing company in Soho as well as a music business in Tin Pan Alley, sang with the Joe Loss Band at Hammersmith and learned to type, among other things.

Though there were happy times at Loftus Road there were an inordinate number of fights among the players, with Venables often the peacemaker. Mark Lazarus knocked Tony Hazell down once after Hazell made a remark. Hazell got up and repeated the comment. So Lazarus, a very tough cookie, knocked him flat again. Fighting among players is still common because players are always being wound up, insulted or over-hyped by others. One of the most extraordinary mass brawls in English football took place at a televised *Russell Harty Show* to celebrate the twenty-fifth anniversary of the start of ITV. It started well with Venables crooning, 'What Do You Want to Make Those Eyes at Me For?' Hazell, who was constantly ribbed about his appearance, took exception to a remark made by Ian Evans, now the Sunderland assistant manager, and he punched the former Welsh international in the face. The rest of the players joined in with the wives shouting and screaming to tell them to calm down. If the news had leaked out, Venables might well have ended up defending his own players in an FA disciplinary case.

For one season Venables figured on the credits of *The Big Match* after an incident when he was booked at a game at Derby. The cameras caught him turning to the crowd and rolling his eyes and waggling his eyebrows and the amusing cameo caught the public's imagination. He was a celebrity before the word became overused and it helped to make him more popular.

Gregory had the ruthlessness of a Robespierre and to the dismay of Venables, the favoured son was the next victim to face the guillotine. Early in the 1974/75 season, Gregory called him in and told him he had done a good deal: Venables and Ian Evans in exchange for Don Rogers, the Crystal Palace winger who would soon be forced to retire because of arthritis in the knee. Gordon Jago hadn't even told Venables about the deal. Within a week Jago was packed off in a tumbril and the well-liked Dave Sexton was given the job.

Before Gregory settled on Sexton, a son of a boxer who knew how to handle himself, he rang Venables and offered Jago's job to him. Mad? Yes, football has always been mad, Machiavellian and unstable.

Malcolm Allison, a former professional gambler, big drinker and self-publicist, was the boss at rundown Selhurst Park and wanted to add some glamour – like posing with a nude Fiona Richmond in the team bath. Three months later Allison called in his new signing and friend and said, 'You're finished. You're too slow. I want you to coach the players.' At first Venables was reluctant to change tack but, with his thirty-second birthday close, he decided that Big Mal, who was always late, was right.

A talented young side was emerging but the bad publicity and bad habits of Allison caught up with him and in 1976 Ray Bloye, the eccentric Palace chairman, sacked him and appointed Venables at the age of thirty-three. Bloye spoke in riddles, a trait shared by a number of chairmen, including some of today's. The idea is to fool all the public all the time. The admired Venables coaching skills led to an astonishing offer – from Arsenal. Denis Hill-Wood, Arsenal's Old Etonian chairman and friend of Sir Stanley Rous, invited Venables to his home for tea. At fifty-six Bertie Mee was comparatively young but two barren seasons had taken its toll on him. Hill-Wood wanted a bright and enthusiastic young man to take over. The idea was hugely appealing but Venables, recovering from serious injuries to his ear and hand, sustained when he crashed into the sea para-sailing in Majorca, said he had promised Bloye he would stay at Palace despite not being on a contract. English football might have been transformed. With cash and top-class players, Venables could have been the Wenger of the 1980s and '90s. In a world where few keep their word, he kept his and Hill-Wood respected him for his sense of fair play. Four days later Venables learned that Palace were so broke that BT cut off their phone lines!

In his first year in charge, he took Palace out of the Third Division, despite having seen the directors sell his best player, Peter Taylor, to Tottenham Hotspur for £200,000 and in 1978/79 he piloted his young side into the First Division. Ron Greenwood recruited him as a coach working alongside Dave Sexton with the England Under-21s and his reputation was further enhanced. Palace, perpetually in debt (they still are), was proving more of a yo-yo club than the 'team of the decade' and their directors were so short of cash that after losing 9 out of the 10 matches of the season, the players had to have a whip round to pay for the train tickets to the town staging the eleventh. Venables insisted on the money being paid up front. The directors refused... and behind his back, they interviewed Howard Kendall as a possible next manager. The story soon came out and Jim Gregory was soon on the line, ringing Venables at dawn to offer him the job, which Tommy Docherty had just vacated, for the second time.

So Venables was back at Queens Park Rangers with Gregory paying £100,000 to Palace in compensation, one of the first instances of a transfer fee for a manager. Venables told him he should have the money because Palace defaulted on a promise to pay him that amount as a bonus from taking them into the top division. Gregory said no. He was a hard man. Together, this odd pairing took Rangers into the FA Cup final in 1982, losing to Tottenham in a replay and earning promotion to the First Division the next year on the £350,000 Omniturf artificial pitch. This time Venables got his bonus. He became the managing director and second largest shareholder.

He was getting rather too big for his boots, not for the first time in his career, when he proposed a revolutionary idea, a buy-out with him running the football side and Gregory extending the ground as sole owner, with one of his ideas being the installation of a roof. Gregory might have been nasty but he had vision. The discussions were heading for an agreement until Gregory phoned him the next morning and said, 'I don't think so. I must have had too much to drink.' Venables then asked for a thirty-three per cent pay rise on his salary of £30,000 and Gregory baulked at it.

To his surprise, a representative of Barcelona telephoned him, proposing an interview for the post of coach at the Nou Camp in place of Cesar Menotti, who led Argentina to World Cup success six years earlier. Jeff Powell, who was a friend of Menotti, had mentioned his friend Venables as a possible successor. Gregory laughed when he heard the news. And he was happy to let his manager go off for his interview.

On 22 May 1984 Venables got the job, partly because he pulled out two Monte Cristo Number Ones from his sock, one for Juan Gaspart, the director who spoke most English, and the other for himself. Gaspart wanted to offer him one but the oak box which he held was empty. In terms of one-upmanship, it was a clincher. It was said that Venables had learnt Spanish to improve his chances but that wasn't wholly true. If he had wanted to impress the Barça directors he should have picked up some Catalan instead. He had a rudimentary knowledge of both languages through his many holidays in Spain and in his introductory speech he started in Catalan, bringing roars from an audience of 50,000.

The local press opposed him and he had to win some telling battles. One was over Diego Maradona, who faced a three-month suspension for violence in a previous game and was unpopular with the directors who had to sanction his massive bills, including paying for thirty-six of his hangers-on. The directors agreed with his recommendation, selling Maradona to Napoli for £5.5 million. Asked who he thought should be his replacement, he stunned them by saying 'Steve Archibald'. They had never heard of him but Venables convinced them that Archibald, a moody but reliable Scot, was a suitable stand in for the number 10 shirt. 'Arch-goles', as Archibald was called in the press, scored twice in his first match, a friendly, and also scored in Barcelona's 3-0 win against bitter rivals Real Madrid at the Bernabeu. The Madrid fans bombarded the Barcelona coach with stones as it drove off. Back in Barcelona they were all heroes, no one more revered than 'Meester Terry'. The surge to the top kept the momentum going throughout the winter, winning the return against Real 3-2, and he was treated like a saint as he took the club to its first championship for twelve years. At New Year they laid on a dinner in honour of the Englishman and moved the clock back an hour to Greenwich Mean Time.

Life was never better for the man from Dagenham. His marriage to Christine had ended and he had a new love, the beautiful Yvette, whom he later married. A stream of Fleet Street football writers arrived to worship the King of Catalan. Another Englishman, freelance football expert Graham Taylor (no relation), fulfilled a key role as interpreter when he was needed. Venables was now about to conquer the highest peak of his life, the European Cup final in Seville on 7 May 1986, against the colourless Romanian side Steaua Bucharest. It was almost a home game and, although still on level terms after normal time, Barcelona lost on penalties. The better-known players lost their nerve. Venables said, 'I don't think I have ever been so depressed after a defeat in my life.'

The rocket was tumbling back to earth. In the second season, Barcelona came second and that wasn't enough. Arsenal still wanted him and there was an agreement that he would join them after his second season in Spain. When he heard that Don Howe, the Arsenal manager of the time, had been told by a journalist that Howe's job was being filled by someone else, Venables changed his mind. He was unsure of working with Howe as his assistant and, with his marriage ending, he feared he might be a target for unscrupulous newsmen working for the red-top newspapers in England. Against his own judgement, he signed a new one-year contract with Barça.

Before then the name 'Bilko' was back in his life. Yvette and his daughters thought it would be a good idea to have a Pyrenean mountain dog which weighed more than a heavyweight. They were living in a flat and 'Bilko's' pee not only saturated their living accommodation but the neighbours' quarters below, who took legal action against Venables. And when 'Bilko' attacked an Alsatian it was time to get rid of him and hand him over to another owner.

Archibald was also speedily deposed and the new Gary Lineker-Mark Hughes partnership failed to work. The white handkerchiefs were waving from on high – the sign of displeasure in Spain – and after losing 4 of the opening 5 matches in the 1986/87 season he resigned and moved back to London. He had no job lined up but within five days Irving Scholar, the suave, enthusiastic chairman of Tottenham, a lifelong Spurs fanatic, offered him a tempting contract. David Pleat had just been sacked over allegations about kerb crawling. Venables had some business matters to clear up and he finally started work at White Hart Lane on 23 November 1987, on half of what his salary had been at Barcelona. Some good players were on their way out, including Glenn Hoddle who had been sold to Monaco. 'I would have loved to work with him,' lamented Venables. 'He picked up his skills from watching Brazilians at a young age and it showed. It's a pity that other players didn't do the same thing.'

The love affair between chairman and feisty manager soon ended, with the meddlesome Scholar vetoing Venables' attempts to take part in business activities at the club. He liked charismatic, showy players unlike Terry Fenwick, whom Venables bought from QPR. The rows piled up and the results, both on and off the field, were poor. Scholar and his directors diversified into two women's clothing companies and a software company – all of which lost money. *The Sun* called Venables 'El Veg' as the team slid down the table but the rebellious supporters were partially placated after the signing of Paul Gascoigne for £2 million and, later, the arrival of Lineker and Nayim from Barcelona for £1.5 million.

Gascoigne startled the rest of the Spurs players by doing a George Best in training – taking on all eleven players in practice matches and often scoring goals against them. 'But he was mad, absolutely mad,' said one victim. Just before and after the 1990 World Cup in Italy, Gascoigne reached his peak before he ruined himself. He said of his manager, 'I loved him. I looked upon him almost as a father. He could handle players without getting nasty and, unusually, without swearing. I think he is the only manager I've ever known who didn't swear.'

Venables watched in horror as Tottenham went further into debt. They were the first club to become a plc in 1983 and that meant the books had to be made public. Robert Maxwell loaned the board £1.1 million to stop the club defaulting on the Lineker transfer and his crookedness heightened the crisis. Scholar had to resign as chairman of the plc as the threat of insolvency grew. Venables sought to sign rich investors to take control and the boxing promoter Frank Warren was one. He enlisted the help of two friends, Eddie Ashby and Paul Riviere, both ultimately discredited, and played a part in recruiting Alan Sugar.

The debacle arguably reached its lowest point when the team coach was towed away outside the Royal Lancaster Hotel, the habitual 'home' of Venables, and the kick-off at Chelsea was delayed. Spurs were fined £20,000 by the Football League for being late. As the shares fell, the team's fortunes rose as Gascoigne inspired an FA Cup final victory in 1991. He needed a double hernia operation but persistent injections enabled him to carry on playing. The surgery was timed so that he would recover in time for the semi-final against Arsenal, who had conceded only eighteen goals in the season.

Gascoigne was so excitable in the dressing room that his passion rubbed off on the other players and they thumped Arsenal 3-1. Venables described his thirty-five-yard free-kick as 'the finest I've ever seen'. However, his prodigy was so over-wound at Wembley that he lasted just over ten minutes after a kamikaze tackle on Nottingham Forest's Gary Charles left him with a ruptured cruciate ligament in the knee. 'He was never the same after that,' said Stuart Pearce.

Needing money desperately, Spurs had been negotiating Gascoigne's sale to Italian club Lazio. They wanted £10 million but, with a suspect knee, the clubs settled on £5.5 million in May 1992, with Gascoigne receiving £800,000 as a signing-on fee and £22,000 a week.

Scholar was living in Monaco for tax reasons and Venables and his supporters wanted him out of the club. Eddie Ashby and Paul Riviere later turned against Venables and mentioned the name of Alan Sugar as a possible saviour of the club. Sugar, born in the East End in 1947 and four years older than Venables, saw the proposed takeover of Tottenham as a way of promoting himself and making more money. His company Amstrad had supplied satellite dishes for Sky Television and the newly formed Premier League were about to sign a contract with Rupert Murdoch, a friend of Sugar's. 'I took an instant dislike to him,' said Venables later. 'And joining up with him was the worst mistake I ever made.'

Robert Maxwell owned the *Daily Mirror* and used his columns to mount a counter bid but Sugar told him, 'You can f—— off!' and the Sugar-Venables bid was accepted with each man putting in £3.25 million. Whereas Sugar was one of Britain's richest men, Venables had to borrow most of his share, using his company Edennote, which was soon exposed by the Sugar camp as being highly questionable. The lawyers were swarming around the club, taking fortunes out it, and this period was one of the worst in the history of Tottenham Hotspur FC. It was a place of hate, from the boardroom to the seats filled by angry supporters. One relief, only a brief one, was the mysterious death from drowning of Maxwell off the back of a yacht. There was now one less shark in the sea.

Sugar discovered that Ashby was still working for the club as an undisclosed bankrupt and there was open warfare between the two factions, conducted in the press. It was nasty and vindictive and White Hart Lane wasn't a welcoming place to go, as Bill Nicholson, their greatest manager, quickly realised. He kept turning up to attend matches and studiously kept out of the infighting. The purchase of Teddy Sheringham from Nottingham Forest brought matters into the open with allegations of a £50,000 'bung' being featured in a damning *Panorama* programme on BBC television. Nothing was proved and the police dropped their inquiries in 1994. But the net was closing in. Sugar, whose son Daniel worked in a senior post at the club, with his daughter Louise also employed in the set-up, took over full control in 1992 and sacked Venables the day before the 1993 FA Cup final.

Not knowing the full facts, the Spurs fans rounded on Sugar and his family and some tried to barricade them in their house in Essex. He received death threats and needed police protection. 'I feel like the man who shot Bambi,' he said. It had been a long, bloody battle with Sugar eventually winning easily on points and Venables bloodied and battered, left still on his feet but with a badly tarnished reputation. His daughter Tracey, whose salary had more than doubled to £40,000 at White Hart Lane, was sacked along with physio Dave Butler and chief scout Ted Buxton, two of the most popular men in the game.

The torrent of publicity precipitated official inquiries into the affairs of Venables, set up by the DTI, the Customs and Excise branch of the Inland Revenue and the Serious Fraud Office. No one in the game has ever faced so many inquiries and he claimed he paid out £1 million in legal fees. It may well have been more. On 17 June 1994 Tottenham were punished by the FA for financial irregularities and their punishment was to have six points docked and a fine of £1.5 million. This was for matters that had arisen during the Scholar regime.

At the time Venables still faced several pending court actions. Graham Taylor had been sacked by the FA and they were struggling for an acceptable successor. The men charged with the task, FA chairman Sir Bert

Millichip, Noel White of Liverpool, Ian Stott of Oldham and Graham Kelly, secretary of the FA from 1989 to 1998, had never played the game professionally. They wanted a former international player turned head-hunter to mark their cards so they chose Jimmy Armfield, the England and Blackpool right-back who was fifty-eight and still worked on Radio Five as a summariser and wrote columns in newspapers. So much corruption had been uncovered in the game at this time that it was essential to enlist a man with an impeccable reputation and Armfield, a Christian and church organ player, was ideal. A genuinely nice man, he took his duties seriously, interviewing every possible candidate. He said:

> As I got around the country I discovered that the majority wanted Terry Venables. He'd been involved with the England set-up since 1978, had a good record and was outgoing and was a Londoner, which is important. His critics called him an East End wide boy but that wasn't fair. Noel White didn't want him at any price, Bert was almost as strongly against him and Stott and Kelly wanted to see how it went. He had baggage, but I gave him the benefit of the doubt.

Armfield found it very amusing when Venables picked him up in his Mercedes at Euston Station reeking of garlic. 'I love it,' said Venables. That may explain why he has a big heart. After four meetings, Armfield made his mind up – it had to be Venables. The selection committee assembled in the Football League offices off Edgware Road and were shocked to see a woman about to throw herself off a parapet on top of a nearby block of flats. The emergency services arrived and talked her down, to everyone's relief. Apparently it was a regular event. She was a serial suicide threatener.

The FA panel members agreed with Armfield's recommendation, except White. Earlier, Armfield had been to see White's friend and working colleague Peter Swales, the former FA international committee chairman who was about to retire. 'I wouldn't touch [Venables] with a bargepole,' said Swales. For a while, Armfield continued his trawl. Alex Ferguson told him he backed Venables. So did Gordon Taylor, the PFA power boss.

Armfield originally offered the job on a part-time basis and Venables refused. He wanted a proper contract and the FA were reluctant to give him one of more than two years. A month later, on 25 January 1994, they settled the deal, with the salary well under £200,000. They compromised on a contract for two-and-a-half years with a clause to end it if any more damaging allegations emerged. He selected an experienced team: Don Howe and Dave Sexton as coaches and Bryan Robson and Ray Wilkins with the Under-21 squad.

When he started work at Lancaster Gate, Venables was horrified to discover there was no database on England players or on players from other countries. Not even a blackboard to work on. Soon he won respect within the building with his enthusiasm and ideas and introduced the Subbuteo board to demonstrate his tactical ideas. He ditched the boring 4-4-2 formation used by Ramsey and others and introduced the 'pyramid', later called the 'Christmas tree', which employed only one front man with the other striker playing behind him. It worked so well in the friendly games that one observer said that 'he kept producing Christmas presents every match!'

Most doubts about the appointment were removed when he emerged from the tunnel before the kick-off in his first match, a friendly against Denmark. As he walked out of the tunnel, well after the players, he was met with a roar of delight from a crowd of 72,000, almost double the attendance for the previous game. 'It was almost alarming in its intensity,' he said. A goal from David Platt meant the game ended in a slightly frustrating 1-0 win. 'Should have been more,' he said. The players soon responded to him. He didn't preach, he didn't shout and he kept instructions brief. His predecessor, Graham Taylor, had been the opposite.

In the five weeks leading up to the game he was involved in four court actions. On the day of the game, one of his former lawyers issued writs against him claiming over £312,000 in fees and two months later his company, Edennote, was wound up in the High Court. He was unruffled. His hair had already gone grey. There were euphoric moments two months later when Greece were beaten 5-0 in front of 23,569 supporters after a proposed game against Germany, arranged on the birthday of Adolf Hitler, was called off for fear of hooliganism.

His third match changed the mood. The Norwegian players, like the Swedes, are tough competitors and a dour game ended in a 0-0 draw. The Norwegians were the game's serial party poopers. The vengeful Sugar banned Venables from returning to White Hart Lane and Venables made no effort to convince the FA that the ban was unjust. Before his fourth game, against the USA, he predicted that Bryan Robson would be his successor. He was wrong. It was a poor game, won 2-0 without lustre and the Christmas tree was tossed away. Two weeks later Sugar issued a writ for libel over allegations in Venables' autobiography, a very detailed work which deserved better sales.

The 1-1 draw against Romania, also at Wembley, was a flop and it coincided with a second *Panorama* programme exposing the business dealings of the England coach. Graham Kelly pronounced, 'It presented no evidence to cast doubt on his qualifications to be the England coach, or in his capacity to do the job.' After a typical day's work – mornings either at the FA or working with the players, afternoon drinking sessions with his friends in four-star hotels and gladhanding his customers at Scribes in the evenings – he said he had no trouble sleeping.

Three days before the November fixture – a 1-1 draw against Nigeria, again at Wembley – Dennis Wise was arrested outside Scribes and charged with assaulting a taxi driver. In the days of Sir Stanley Rous an England player behaving like that would be instantly fired. Instead, Venables picked Wise for the game saying, 'He's another Alan Ball.' Glenn Hoddle, Chelsea's manager, was more moral, stripping Wise of the captaincy at Stamford Bridge as a punishment. When Wise was convicted in court, Venables finally left him out, omitting him from the squad for the first away game in February 1995, against the Republic of Ireland at the well-grassed Lansdowne Road. Up to then, England's warm-up matches for the European Championships had been comparable to the second-rate heavyweights lined up for Frank Bruno. Now, this event was away from Wembley and the knockout was delivered by English hooligans whose behaviour forced the match to be abandoned after twenty-seven minutes with the Irish leading 1-0. Venables called it 'organised crime'.

He was exempted from blame but a month later some of the critics turned on him after a dull 0-0 draw against Uruguay at Wembley. Brian Woolnough, once a supporter, wrote in his book *Venables – The England Era*, 'England aren't any better now than when Taylor was sacked.' Venables had provided assistance to him for the book and, always touchy about criticism, he wrote a curt letter to him saying he wasn't going to help any more and accusing him of being a Sugar supporter.

When Bobby Robson was in charge there were countless anecdotes about his use of language and other matters. He had a good sense of humour and could take the ribbing. But there are few anecdotes about Venables. Sir Bert Millichip tried unavailingly to broker a peace deal between him and Sugar and the closest the two men came after the talks, conducted by lawyer Charles Woodhouse, finally collapsed, was when they were pictured at the directors' box at Upton Park. Sugar was in the front row, wearing his Spurs product, the Hummel coat, staring ahead; Venables was two rows behind in a Mourinho-style overcoat and holding his nose as though he detected a nasty aroma.

Venables' first defeat in charge came in the Umbro-sponsored summer tournament, losing 3-1 to Brazil, England's heaviest home defeat since 1972. The other matches, a 2-1 win over a moderate Japan side and a 3-3 draw with Sweden, lacked distinction. 'Judge me in a year's time,' he said. He had put a lot of weight on at these soirees, and at hotels and Scribes, so he changed his diet and lost twenty-eight kilos. Someone had mentioned the risk of a heart attack when he was in the most stressful job of them all.

Two more 0-0 draws, against Colombia at Wembley and Norway in Oslo, the city which has brought most trouble to England managers and coaches, attracted dismal notices. The day Venables announced his squad for the Norwegian game he was due to appear in the High Court. Tony Berry, a former director of Tottenham, had taken exception to a paragraph from the Venables autobiography. If the case had gone the distance, up to two weeks, Venables may well have missed the Oslo trip. Two hours later the two sets of lawyers worked out a settlement and Berry got an apology and £20,000.

Yet another book about Venables was about to start and the author, Colin Malam, revealed that Terry had received an offer to coach Inter Milan. In Oslo, Venables talked publicly about his future. 'I would like it discussed and sorted out before the European Championships,' he said. There was a private meeting between Millichip and Kelly about the subject and they wanted Venables to be given an extension to his contract. Noel White and Ian Stott disagreed. The game against Egil Olsen's Norwegians – devotees of the long ball game – turned out to be dire.

Whenever England played, writs were being served – and it was no coincidence. Venables claimed there was a witch hunt against him with certain people leaking information and often stealing key papers to help ruin his name. David Webb, Venables' former teammate at Chelsea, was dragged into it and insisted that his telephone had been bugged. 'I am an honest bloke,' he said. 'Now I can't trust anyone.' David Davies, the Head of Communications at the FA, issued a strong statement refuting the suggestions that his international committee members were wavering about extending Venables' contract. The Football League investigated Webb's protestations and found no evidence.

Venables remained in a jaunty mood, as though someone had tipped him off about his job prospects. A 3-1 win over Switzerland eased the pressure but the day after the 1-1 draw against Portugal it was back on. Venables faced a claim for £20,000 from Jeffrey Fugler in the High Court and appeared in the witness box. He forgot his glasses and the Judge Mr Williams offered him a pair. 'I'll auction them,' joked the Judge. A few hours later the laughter turned into a scowl when Venables was told by the Judge, 'Your evidence was not entirely reliable, to put it at its most charitable.' The Judge decided that Fugler should receive half of what he asked for, £11,292.95, plus interest and half his costs. Venables would have to pay his costs, estimated at around £75,000. It was his first major reverse in the courts and more actions were pending.

Sunday 17 December 1995 was the turning point for Venables, the day he told the FA chiefs that he would not stay on after the European Championships. It was the weekend that UEFA were staging the draw and the day before Venables had told a slimmer Kelly – he had been on a strict diet, too – that he would quit. Kelly and Millichip tried to talk him out of it but at the meeting the next day, in a room on the eighteenth floor of the Hyatt Hotel, he announced his resignation. First he confronted Noel White, who had been quoted the previous day talking about his doubts over Venables. White is a nice man and he held his ground. The FA could have outvoted him but it was Venables who made the decision, not them. As Stott said, 'Tony Blair doesn't get 100 per cent support from his side. Who does?' Afterwards Kelly told him, 'At least you can't sue the FA – you resigned from us.' 'Don't worry,' Venables joked. 'There's still time for that.' The story broke on 10 January. The list of managers who work on after they resign is full of names who fail. Venables was the exception. He finished his work at the European Championships in June with acclamation.

But the man who should have had most of the praise was Glen Kirton, a language graduate who started working at the FA in 1971, the same way Venables was hired to work with the England Under-21 squad. They had a good relationship – on one side, the man who was in charge of the organisation of the championships, on the other, the coach. 'We wanted to ensure that we did things right and restored our reputation after all the years of problems with hooliganism,' said Kirton. 'It wasn't really about money, more about prestige.' England's share was little more than £2 million. The slogan 'Football's Coming Home' was repeated endlessly, and it was, for the first time since 1966. England were drawn in a favourable group, facing Switzerland, Scotland and Holland, with Holland judged to be the team to beat.

Another unexciting 0-0, against a cautious Croatia side, produced a storm of criticism and that was then outdone by the reaction from England's ill-advised mini-tour to the Far East a month before the start of the championships. Fresh from a 3-0 win over Hungary, the 16th victory in 18 home games under Venables, the England squad played two warm-up games halfway round the world, first an encouraging 3-0 win over China in Beijing and second a 1-0 victory over a Hong Kong XI. Gascoigne was in trouble on the flight out, scuffling with a steward and being warned by the pilot that he would be dropped off in Russia if he didn't behave. An official complaint was filed to the FA at the time so it was a risk for Venables to let the players go on a night out after the meaningless game in Hong Kong.

The 'fun' started when Gascoigne tipped a pint over Robbie Fowler's head. His book *Gazza*, ghosted by Hunter Davies (now also Wayne Rooney's ghost), details other shenanigans involving Bryan Robson, Teddy Sheringham, Steve McManaman and Dennis Wise, who hit him with 'a real upper cut'. It was Gascoigne's twenty-ninth birthday and a mix of tequila and Drambuie was poured down his throat as he sat in the now-infamous 'dentist's chair'. An enterprising photographer took pictures, which were sold to British newspapers.

Worse still, a tipsy Gascoigne started trouble in the first-class section in the top deck of the Cathay Pacific return flight on the way home. Someone slapped him in the face and he responded by damaging two mini television sets. Cathay Pacific claimed £5,000 damages and MPs called for the offenders to be thrown out of the championships. Tony Adams told the players to chip in £500 a man to more than cover the costs and Venables agreed. One dissenter was Stuart Pearce, but he paid up. It was a squalid and dishonourable way of preparing for a major competition but the FA took no action.

Perhaps they were too busy working on the Euro 96 theme song 'Three Lions' with the words, 'It's coming home, it's coming home, football's coming home.' The players sang it on the team coach and Gazza played it non-stop in his room. At the end of April, the FA had lined up Glenn Hoddle to be the next England manager – at the age of thirty-eight the second-youngest of the ten full-time managers. He was manager of Chelsea at the time – and not being particularly successful – and Matthew Harding, the club's chief backer, offered him a four-year contract worth £1.2 million. The FA's offer was slightly less but it was still almost three times the amount paid to Venables. Why was Hoddle in such demand? It is hard to answer. Maybe there was no one else suitable and he desperately wanted the post. He was looked on as a nice, easygoing guy but under the façade there was a tough character.

England's campaign started badly, with Venables upbraiding the press over the Cathay Pacific plane story, which he insisted was 'exaggerated beyond reason'. He said the players were livid and they were in the right frame of mind to give their response on the field. Most successful managers use a hostile press to rouse their players and Venables was a master at it.

When England kicked off against Switzerland they had the backing of the majority of the public, irrespective of the bad publicity, and that was a big factor in their qualified success in reaching the semi-finals. But the opening match was a let-down, with the Swiss forward Kubilay Turkyilmaz equalising after Alan Shearer's goal for the match to finish a frustrating 1-1 draw. Venables gave the squad forty-eight hours off and this led to more damning headlines. Teddy Sheringham, Sol Campbell and Jamie Redknapp were seen in a nightclub in the early hours of Sunday morning. *The Sun* encourages its readers to ring up with tip-offs about footballers' off-field activities and this was another example of it. An angry Venables responded by calling the football journalists 'traitors'.

Most of the problems with the press began to evaporate after the 2-0 win over Scotland in the second game, a match dominated by

Gascoigne, who had spent the two previous afternoons fishing in a boat with David Seaman to calm him down. Seaman told a wonderful story about the way Gascoigne tried to stop a *Daily Mirror* photographer snatching pictures of the two footballing fishermen. He chased after the photographer and as he tried to let his tyres down he nicked his mobile phone and said, 'I'll let you have it back if you hand over the film.' The man declined and drove off. 'Safe Hands' Seaman called the owner of the fishery and asked him to lock the gates to forestall the photographer, only to see him driving straight through the gates and across a main road without slowing. When Gascoigne pressed 'call' on the mobile he found himself speaking to Piers Morgan, then editor of the *Mirror*. 'You print those pictures and I'll never speak to your paper,' he said. But they still appeared. And they were highly praised except that the snapper nearly killed himself.

Shearer opened the scoring against the second-rate Scots and Seaman saved Gary McAllister's penalty with his elbow. Eleven minutes from time, Darren Anderton put Gascoigne in and Gazza flicked the ball over Colin Hendry's head to volley in the second goal – 'My greatest goal,' he said. He lay on his back on the ground, arms raised, as Shearer poured Lucozade down his throat, in a rerun of the 'dentists' chair' incident. The normally talkative Gascoigne refused to speak afterwards and went off to propose to his girlfriend Sheryl, whom he later married. He made many mistakes in his career and that was another.

Home advantage helped to lift the England players to a new peak of performance against Holland and the 4-1 hiding of the Dutch on 18 June raised hopes of a triumph in the final. 'I've never known an atmosphere like it,' said Venables, 'but let us not go too berserk.' Gascoigne praised his coach. 'He gave the most brilliant team talk ever,' he said. There were celebrations in Trafalgar Square and Venables was rapidly reaching hero status, with his financial baggage conveniently forgotten. There were calls for him to be retained and Hoddle ditched. Four days later, Spain, the team who generally promise much and produce little at major tournaments, were England's opponents in the quarter-finals and a tight game ended goal-less after extra time and went to a penalty shoot-out. England won it 4-2 with Seaman stopping the decisive penalty, taken by Miguel Angel Nadal, known as 'The Beast'.

Clichés abounded in the tabloids before the semi-final against Germany on 26 June, including headlines about 'Achtungs', 'Surrenders' and 'Heil Hitlers', which upset Venables, his players and most of the footballing public. The game turned out to be a classic battle, almost as dramatic as the 1966 World Cup final on the same pitch. Shearer headed England's early goal only for Stefan Kuntz to make it 1-1, which was how the scoreline remained after a 120 minutes. Each side converted five penalties and Gareth Southgate, as decent a man as ever pulled on an England football shirt, stepped up to place the ball on the spot. It was a poor effort, easily stopped by Andreas Kopke going to his right. After Moller scored, the tears flowed, not just from Gascoigne, and Venables delivered his final speech in charge. 'You have nothing to be ashamed of,' he said. 'You have served your country proud. We've made the rest of the world sit up and take notice. Thanks a lot.'

Back at the England hotel at Burnham Beeches, every player returned for a doleful party instead of going home. It was enlivened by Gascoigne and Robbie Fowler finding cartons of ketchup and squirting them over each other. Next morning Gascoigne found a lump of excreta in his washbag. Germany, England's old, obstructive foes, won the trophy, scoring the conclusive golden goal against the Czech Republic.

Venables faced more disappointments in various courts, eventually admitting defeat in the battle with Sugar and the DTI. He did not dispute the nineteen charges in the DTI's case and agreed to pay £500,000 of their costs. Still in demand, he took over Portsmouth from the Gregory family and found himself in another financial maelstrom before he left, after receiving a performance bonus of £300,000. The following year he was appointed coach to the Australian national side and was set to take the squad to the 1998 World Cup Finals in 1998 until Iran beat them to it, scoring a late away goal in the play-off. It was yet another cruel fall at the penultimate fence.

He was briefly appointed manager of his old club Crystal Palace by the eccentric Mark Goldberg, who, like Eddie Ashby, was declared a bankrupt. That was Venables' problem – he was surrounded by too many questionable characters. His final managerial post was at Middlesbrough, when he helped save them from relegation in tandem with Bryan Robson, whom he had always said should end up as England manager.

TERRY VENABLES

Despite his various failings, he remains a wealthy man. 'People think I'm skint,' he told Joe Lovejoy of the *Sunday Times*, 'and I'm happy to let them think that.' He bought 250 acres near Alicante after retiring from football to plan a football-oriented leisure complex and other properties. He is still smiling, still enjoying his life.

GLENN HODDLE

1996-1999

Tipped Out by 'The Thunderer'

| P 28 | W 17 | D 6 | L 5 | 60% |

Seven of England's managers have been forced out directly or indirectly by the media. The bosses of the FA have rarely stood up against the tide of criticism and Winterbottom, Ramsey, Revie, Robson, Taylor, Hoddle and Keegan were victims. Greenwood left because he was soured by what went on. He still loved the game but refused to tolerate the negativity and mean-mindedness of many observers.

England's first five managers lasted a combined forty-four years between 1946 and 1990, an average of just under nine years each. But as the media frenzy built up, with the two best-selling red-top newspapers, *The Sun* and the *Daily Mirror*, staging a tabloid championship of their own, the last five managers reigned for sixteen years, just over three years each. By this time the radio phone-in clients were weighing in with their views, adding to the clamour for personnel change. And a new generation of former players was employed to comment, in the main adversely.

Venables left voluntarily, although a strong lobby tried to get him out. Sven-Goran Eriksson proved to be the greatest survivor, impervious to the onslaught. But the one who was really bowled out by the press was Glenn Hoddle. In cricketing parlance, he almost 'walked'. When he took over, England won 9 of 10 matches, the first 6 being World Cup qualifiers. There was just one defeat, 1-0 against Italy. Unlike Venables, whose reputation was enhanced by a string of victories in friendly matches played at Wembley, Hoddle did it the hard way.

But the critics begrudged his success. Most of them thought he was arrogant and lacking in management and PR skills. They didn't warm to him. They thought he was bonkers for allowing his friend Eileen Drewery, a faith healer, to treat the players. Some, like Darren Anderton, welcomed her attentions, which included placing her hands on his head. Hoddle was open about his religious beliefs. He believes in the afterlife and reincarnation and a few words in an interview published in *The Times* in late January 1999 finally brought him down. In a country where ninety per cent of the population never go to church, a mosque or a cathedral, the majority turned against him and the FA decided to remove him.

Fifteen months earlier, Hoddle was looked on as a saviour when his team held the Italians to a brusing 0-0 draw in Rome to earn the point they needed to qualify for the World Cup Finals in France in 1998. Even when they went out, losing on penalties to Argentina, he should at least have been marked a 6 out of 10 but not a bit of it. What had happened when the Venables autobiography was published in 1994 should have served as a lesson to him. Venables and his publishers, Michael Joseph, were sued and lost considerable sums of money. The FA should have made it a requirement that no England manager should be allowed to have a book published while still in office. Instead, they ignored the danger and their executive director David Davies ghosted the manuscript of Hoddle's book, blandly entitled *My 1998 World Cup Story*, which was brought out shortly after the World Cup Finals ended.

Alf Ramsey never wrote a revealing book while he was manager. I wrote to him after the World Cup in 1966 and he replied, 'I am not considering the possibility of writing a book in the foreseeable future as my commitments during the months ahead are particularly heavy. Many thanks for your kind congratulations which are greatly appreciated.' Greenwood combined with Bryon Butler to write *Yours Sincerely* after he retired, a book without controversy. Bobby Robson has so far produced five books and none of them ended in the High Court. Graham Taylor started a book and abandoned it and Eriksson's is on the way.

Hoddle's was the most contentious because he commented about his players while he was still in charge. His revelations about the omission of Paul Gascoigne from the 1998 squad were particularly upsetting, although the facts were perfectly true. *The Sun* paid him £200,000 for the serialisation of the book and the articles were topped by lurid headlines which made things even worse. Joe Lovejoy wrote:

Hoddle signed his own death warrant as England's coach with every autographed copy of his ill-conceived World Cup Diary. A straw poll of the players, conducted in the aftermath of his dismissal, placed that book ahead of his healer-cum-guru Eileen Drewery, and the unorthodox religious beliefs they share, as the prime reason why he lost the trust of the team. Since England's failure at the World Cup, the dressing room had resembled the mess of the *Bounty*, with dissension and derision rife. The majority view was that this latter-day Bligh should have been cast adrift long before his last-straw comments about reincarnation and the disabled.

A friendly game against France approached in February 1999 but, leading up to this, Hoddle's popularity had tumbled alarmingly. A 2-1 defeat against Sweden in the 2000 European Championship qualifiers was followed by a depressing 0-0 against Bulgaria and he was booed by England's supporters. Luxembourg put up stout resistance five days later, albeit losing 3-0, and a laboured 2-0 win over the Czech Republic failed to change the mood of defeatism.

Some England managers often court the football correspondents of the more responsible newspapers. Venables and Revie did that assiduously and Hoddle started to go the same way. He had just agreed an extended contract with the FA, bringing in an extra £100,000 a year and felt it was time to do a lengthy interview for *The Times*. Unfortunately for him, Oliver Holt, the then football correspondent of *The Times* (still known as 'The Thunderer'), was in Florida for the Super Bowl. He is more of a writer than a newsman. Matt Dickinson, who undertook the task, is both and when Hoddle finally got through to him at the third attempt, the interview was conducted on the telephone with Dickinson unable to switch his tape recorder on. Instead he took notes in Teeline shorthand and the subject matters were football and religion. Asked about reincarnation, Hoddle was reported to have said:

> You and I have been physically given two hands and two legs and half-decent brains. Some people haven't been born like that for a reason. The karma is working from another lifetime. I have nothing to hide about that. It is not only people with disabilities, what you sow you have to reap. You have to look at things that have happened in your life and ask why. It comes around.

If the whole of the interview had been published on the sports pages on the Saturday hardly anyone would have taken notice of it. But when

Dickinson's copy arrived an alert member of staff saw the importance of it, suggesting that disabled people were paying for sins in previous lives. The duty news editor ordered a news item, separate from the football article, about it which included incensed reaction from organisations acting on behalf of disabled people. A spokesman for Disability Action said, 'I don't know how the FA can keep him on. How can he look in the face of all those disabled people who line the pitch at Wembley?'

It was a scoop for *The Times* and the Sunday newspapers followed it up with relish. Hoddle was aghast when he saw the original news story. After speaking to David Davies, he rushed to a television studio to explain things on the lunchtime *Football Focus* programme. He said, 'I've been misconstrued, misinterpreted and misunderstood and I am sorry for any hurt caused.' Five hours later, the FA issued a statement backing Hoddle but it lacked conviction. Keith Wiseman, the FA chairman, and secretary Graham Kelly, who were forced to resign concerning an over-generous payment to the Welsh FA, were no longer in his corner.

A clever news manipulator like Alistair Campbell might well have saved Hoddle but Campbell was working for the other side. On Monday at 11 a.m. Prime Minister Tony Blair, after speaking with Campbell, appeared on the *Richard and Judy* television show saying Hoddle's comments were very wrong and it would be very difficult for him to stay. As former BBC lobby correspondent, Davies had close links with New Labour and had worked hard over the FA's subsequent failure to stage the 2006 World Cup.

The Hoddle affair wasn't just a footballing matter. It had gone right to the top. Blair, who has studiously used the people's game to improve his chances in his re-elections, including playing head tennis with Kevin Keegan in a well-publicised photo opportunity, was like a judge pronouncing sentence. One of his Sports Ministers, Chelsea fan Tony Banks, joined in the condemnation, calling for Hoddle to go. Dennis Roach, Hoddle's long-time agent, whose activities had been investigated by the FA without any action being taken, took to the prints, saying in the *Sunday Telegraph*, 'Banks angered me most because he really ridiculed Glenn and after Glenn left, he said how unfortunate it was and what an extremely nice fellow he is. That shows the worst side of politics. I think the man is a disgrace.'

The thirteen-man FA ruling committee remained in session most of the day while Hoddle, still protesting innocence, asked for clearance to stay on.

His thirteen-year-old daughter Zara sent a text message asking for clemency, a welcome indication that he still had full backing from his separated family following his divorce. Stronger leadership by the FA could have saved him but there was none coming from Geoff Thompson, the acting chairman who was later given the job full time. Thompson shies away from the public and press. A Rous might have rescued Hoddle.

The next day the FA promised a statement by lunchtime about Hoddle's job, which was about to be handed to coaching director Howard Wilkinson on a caretaker basis. In an interview in the *Daily Mirror* Hoddle said, 'The reporter from *The Times* did not misreport me but he did misinterpret me.' At 6.55 p.m. the sacking was confirmed. The remaining eighteen months of his contract were paid up, around £500,000. He was forty-one. Ray Stirling, father of Anne, whose marriage to Hoddle ended after eighteen years, said:

> My sincere wish is that we rediscover the man I respected and loved. I feel in the last two years he has lost his way. He has fallen under the influence of a well-meant but mish-mash of pseudo-oriental spiritual beliefs. Had he stuck to football rather than theology he would have been playing on a better pitch and he knows this himself. He is a fundamentally good man. The damage is done but when you think of what a man like Saddam Hussein has done and what a wicked man he is, and then Glenn, who has been crucified, it is unbelievable.

Howard Wilkinson once said he would like to be England's coach and at fifty-three he was given his chance for a few, fleeting moments. He was more intelligent than most international managers, with a degree in physical education from Sheffield University. He had a similar coaching background to Walter Winterbottom and taught in schools before he became a manager, reaching his peak in 1991/92 when he won the First Division title as manager of Leeds United. Extremely laconic and guarded, he wasn't really equipped to handle the PR side of the national squad and after England were soundly beaten 2-0 by France he realised he had no chance of making the post permanent.

People of the calibre of Alex Ferguson and Arsène Wenger weren't interested and the field of candidates was small. No sensible manager would want the job but there was one who seemed interested – Kevin Keegan. The problem was he didn't have the top coaching awards that were needed. But most of the critics backed him, the public cheered him on and he was given the job. Amazing!

Keegan didn't have natural talent and he reached the top of his profession by his hard work and determination. Hoddle did have natural talent, as well as those qualities. 'I want to be a footballer,' he told his father Derek, a fitter, when he was five. By the time he was twelve he said he wanted to be manager of England.

Hoddle was born on 27 October 1957 at Hayes, Middlesex and grew up in Harlow, a town not renowned for football. His first present of any note was a red rubber ball and he spent hours playing, mastering it. On holiday in Bognor, he was knocking the ball up and down on both feet, trapping it and flipping it up again when a man said, 'How old is he?' His father said, 'He's five.' 'Blimey,' said the man. 'He'll end up playing for England.'

Derek played senior amateur football for Harlow, Ware and Edgware but never made the highest grade. He saw his tall, skinny son emerging as the kind of player he would have wished to be himself. He never put pressure on him. The talent came from within. Father and son were Tottenham supporters and they went to White Hart Lane when Derek wasn't playing for his clubs. They would stand outside waiting to collect autographs and Glenn's favourite was Martin Chivers. That was slightly odd because Chivers was a frustrating player, often angering his manager Bill Nicholson with his attitude.

But it was prophetic that Chivers should play a key role in Hoddle's career. When Hoddle was fourteen, Chivers was invited to give out the prizes at a prize-giving ceremony at the Harlow Sports Centre. Chivers turned to the person next to him and said, 'Who's that tall kid over there?' The man said, 'Oh, that's Derek Hoddle's boy.'

'He was a cut above the rest,' Chivers recalled. He was astonished that not a single scout had spotted him. Next day Chivers told Dick Walker, Tottenham's chief scout, about him and Walker rang Derek Hoddle to invite his son to White Hart Lane. Bill Nicholson saw the boy in action and signed him. It was a hard school and the younger players were encouraged to be aggressive in their challenges. Hoddle rode every tackle and his balance and skill marked him out as a potential Danny Blanchflower.

Nicholson was the most honest manager of his era and he never over-praised anyone. He said of Hoddle, 'In many ways he resembled Johnny Haynes in that he tended to be rather predictable, nearly always opting for the long ball.' The coaches of the day urged their players to hit the ball long because it moved the action closer to the opposing goal. It was part of the coaching courses and the argument about it is still raging. Hoddle's game, however, had much more than just long passing. He used both feet whereas most players employed one and he could use any type of pass or any trap of the ball.

Nicholson had strict standards and Hoddle observed them. He still follows that creed laid down by the former Sergeant Major Nicholson: 'Get your hands out of your pockets, get your hair cut, polish your shoes, remember who are, who you represent, and be smart.' Within a month of Hoddle's arrival, in April 1974, Nicholson resigned, saying, 'I was burnt out, I had no more to offer.' Terry Neill took over, to the fury of the Tottenham supporters. I met Neill the day he was appointed and I asked him if he had any budding stars among the juniors. 'Young Hoddle,' he said. 'He can trap a sixpence on either foot, flick it over his head and catch it on his heel. He's the most skilful young player I've ever seen.'

Hoddle's League goal record in his twelve years with Tottenham was 88 in 378 matches, almost one in four. It was marginally better than David Beckham's with Manchester United and it provokes a comparison between the two. Who was the better? Hoddle was probably ahead on pure skill but Beckham worked harder in defence. Throughout his career most managers and coaches complained about Hoddle's apparent laziness when the opposing side had the ball. Keith Burkinshaw, who succeeded Neill in 1976, was one of his greatest critics on that score. When he left, he admitted, 'I was wrong.'

When Ron Greenwood had him, he used the quarterback ploy, with hard-tackling midfielders to protect Hoddle, the man who supplied the rest of the team with his long passes. He said:

I didn't think he was properly fit. There were periods in a game when he would duck out. His shoulders would slump and he seemed short of breath. I was not talking about work rate, but total involvement and that needed mental and physical toughness. He was not as commanding as he should

have been. He is a gentle sort of chap and in those less mature days, he was
even a bit shy.

He was a lovely lad and he never gave my any problems. He lacked belief
in himself. The thing that stood out for me was what I call a toe tripper. He
had a habit of drifting along and dragging his boot toe behind him. I thought
that was a clear sign of lack of belief. It was a give away for me.

Hoddle is still reserved. One of his former Tottenham colleagues said:

He's not an exhibitionist. He talks in that serious way of speaking, with his
brow furrowed, rubbing his rather square chin. He talks as though he's posing a question, as if he is waiting for approval. He liked a pint when he was
younger but never went overboard. In a way, he was the odd man out.

He married young, as Greenwood used to preach to his players. He married Christine Anne Stirling in 1978 at the age of twenty-one and, both
Christians, they led a happy, fulfilled life for years but then divorced in
1999. Anne was a French teacher, which proved very useful when he signed
for Monaco in 1986. They have three children, Zoë, born in 1983, Zara in
1986 and Jamie in 1992. Their friends were shocked when Hoddle moved
in with his long-term friend Eileen Drewery before setting up home with
his new lady friend, Vanessa Shean. Ray Clemence said, 'It was a mystery
and I was totally saddened to hear the news.' Hoddle said, 'The marriage
ran out of steam.'

In 2000, Hoddle married Vanessa, a former British Airways hostess, who
was previously married to Jeff Shean, whose company builds hotels around
the world. The Sheans, who have three children, were friends of the Hoddle
family and lived nearby in Ascot before the affair began. They were members of the exclusive Royal County of Berks Racquets and Health Club
and Hoddle met Vanessa there playing tennis.

Hoddle's years with Tottenham were largely unfulfilled. Burkinshaw
brought two Argentinians from the 1978 World Cup-winning side, Ossie
Ardiles and Ricky Villa, to the club in a magnificent coup which began the
influx of overseas stars. But two FA Cups in 1981 and 1982, beaten finalists
in 1987, and beating Anderlecht 4-3 on penalties in the 1984 UEFA Cup
final failed to placate Tottenham's hard-headed supporters who hankered

for the Nicholson glory days. The problem was money and its misuse. Without an Abramovich, they will never compete again at this level.

However, there was plenty of entertainment on the field, much of it from Hoddle and he probably reached his peak in his time at White Hart Lane in 1978/79 when he scored 22 goals, most of them coming from outside the penalty area. He scored from twenty yards on his debut for England against Bulgaria that season, a spectacular volley, and some experts prophesied he would be an all-time great. Sadly, he failed to take his opportunities and was unable to keep a regular place. 'He needed a good run in the side,' said Burkinshaw in Brian Woolnough's *Glenn Hoddle, the Man and the Manager*. 'He was so good that he should be up there alongside the world's best players.' But he wasn't quite up there. With his very short shorts and his shirt outside them, he stood out. Perhaps it was something to do with his height. He is six feet tall, above average height for a midfield artist. Outstandingly great players like Pelé, Maradona and Best have been of medium size, with powerful thighs and they could tackle as well as they passed the ball. Hoddle was a poor tackler, as everyone agreed. With his long, elegant legs, he had the appearance of a graceful gazelle. Eight goals from his 53 international matches had to be counted as a modest return.

Ron Greenwood was reluctant to use his services when the pressure was on and Bobby Robson was suspicious of the whole Hoddle package. Greenwood left him out of the side against the Republic of Ireland after his debut and that lowered his self-belief. Over the years, Hoddle developed something of a persecution complex. Realising that he needed Hoddle's accurate, long passing in the rarefied atmosphere of Mexico City, Robson played him in every game in the 1986 World Cup Finals. An indication of Hoddle's alertness came when he was the first to shout, 'Ref! Handball, handball!' when Maradona patted in the 'Hand of God' goal. 'I always felt I missed out,' he said. 'I never really stamped myself on the tournament.' Robson said:

> I got on well with him on a one-to-one basis and enjoyed talking football with him but never felt he would stay in football once his playing career ended. He had some good ideas but I didn't think for a minute he would relish man management and the aggression you sometimes need to be a

manager. Sometimes you have to be a bit crude and rude and I couldn't see him doing that.

Hoddle and Chris Waddle were good friends and there was an anecdote which typified Robson's reign. Before the squad left for Mexico, the party went training and Robson discovered that he had left his boots behind. 'I'll have to borrow a pair,' he said. 'Anyone got a pair of nines to lend me?' he asked the players. 'I've got a pair of nines,' said Hoddle, handing over the boots. After a while Robson complained about the boots. 'They're too tight,' he said. He took one off, stuck a hand in and pulled out a rolled wad of paper. Everyone roared with laughter. They all loved him.

In their final season at Tottenham, Hoddle and Waddle were asked to record a song called 'Diamond Lights' and it went to number ten in the charts. Hoddle loves music, but he does not have a good singing voice. One of the first things Irving Scholar told him when he joined the Tottenham board was to join a foreign club because he was a Continental-style foot-baller and would thrive abroad. Hoddle never forgot it. Scholar was a lifelong Tottenham fan who made his money when he was comparatively young and had to exile himself in Monaco for some years for tax rea-sons. Personable and handsome, Scholar had an encyclopaedic knowledge of football, particularly anything to do with Tottenham, although many of their fans had opposite views about his business acumen.

In 1987 after David Pleat led them almost to a treble using the 4-5-1 formation, Hoddle had made his mind up and was ready to go to France, with his loyal soulmate Anne acting as his interpreter. His agent Dennis Roach began negotiations with Gerard Houllier, coach at Paris St Germain. Everything was settled, or so it seemed. Hoddle wanted to go out on a high note but the defeat in the FA Cup final by Coventry soured his hopes. His sensational goal against Oxford in his last appearance at White Hart Lane didn't alter that. At Bill Nicholson's funeral on 7 November 2004, attended by 8,000 people at the ground, the organisers showed highlights of the great moments of Nicholson's footballing life and most applause, break-ing into cheers, came after the showing of Hoddle's goal against Oxford. Hoddle picked up the ball close to the halfway line and ran towards goal on his own as goalkeeper Peter Hucker came off his line to narrow the angle. As the ball went on, Hoddle stepped over it, dummied him, and saw the goalkeeper dive one way only to see the ball run on as Hoddle went by the other. The ball finished up in the back of the net without Hoddle needing to touch it again. Pelé did something similar but not as striking as Hoddle's goal. It summed up his genius and the fans loved it. 'That was Glenn Hoddle at his very best,' said Scholar.

The talks with Houllier had been ongoing for three months when Mark Hateley, on the staff at Monaco, told Arsène Wenger, his manager, that Hoddle was available. According to Roach, they reached an agreement with Monaco in ten minutes and the deal went through the next day. That call from Hateley, son of former Liverpool striker Tony Hateley, changed Hoddle's life. Hoddle earned a huge tax-free salary plus bonuses and came under the influence of Wenger, the scholarly Frenchman who bore many resemblances to Walter Winterbottom. Wenger told him, 'I want you to do the things you are good at. I want to you to play in their half of the pitch and do damage. I don't want you to chase back and tackle. That would just be a waste of your talent.' Wenger also told him to change his diet and lose weight and Hoddle soon lost a stone. It gave him some extra pace.

Monaco won the French championship in Hoddle's first season. He scored 18 goals and Michel Platini said of him, 'Had he been French he would have won 150 caps.' Wenger said:

> From the start we had a good relationship. He was good at analysing situations and was ready to speak up for himself. He was very single minded. Without doubt, he was the most skilful player I have ever worked with. He had perfect body balance and I couldn't understand why he hadn't been appreciated in England.

In his third and final season, wracked by wear-and-tear injuries, Hoddle was ready to return home. Wenger said to him on many occasions, 'You must take up coaching, it suits you.' It planted the seed and the day he was paraded as England's manager in 1996 his first words were about Wenger. 'Without him I would not be here today,' he said. 'I owe him a lot. Monaco was a vital part of my life. I will never forget it and am grateful for what I learned there and what I discovered about myself.'

The man who propelled Hoddle into management was Peter Day, the former Tottenham secretary, now an agent. He was chief executive of Swindon at the time and at lunch before a Saturday game at West Bromwich Albion he told the directors that Hoddle was interested in the job that had become available with the departure of Ossie Ardiles to Newcastle. Ray Hardman, Swindon's chairman, was excited. He had obtained Hoddle's autograph on a business flight from Monaco previously and was starstruck. Hoddle had no UEFA coaching certificates, now obligatory, and he readily accepted Hardman's offer of £100,000 a year at a subsequent meeting. At thirty-three, Hoddle wanted to continue playing and often used himself in the sweeper role. It was a fascinating experiment – a near-great ball player trying to persuade ordinary players to play like him. In one game Swindon were 4-0 down and Hoddle moved himself into midfield and they won 6-4. He was soon labelled 'the miracle man'.

He introduced the Nicholson code, the players wearing blazers and ties and being harshly dealt with if they were late. He brought in a masseur and introduced a faith healer. It was optional: he didn't insist on players meeting the faith healer. He never spoke about religion to the players, only about how to play the game better. In his third season Swindon beat Leicester in the Second Division play-offs to win promotion to the Premiership in its inaugural season but by then his halo was slipping. There were rumours that he was about to go to Chelsea. Banners were held up that read 'Don't Go, Glenn!' Part of Hoddle's contract mentioned a get-out clause if another club wanted him and a day after the open-topped bus parade that celebrated promotion, Hoddle and his assistant John Gorman went to see Hardman and handed in their resignations. It was a put-up job. Ken Bates, the irascible chairman of Chelsea, was on his way to Swindon to sign the pair. 'That's a coincidence,' said Hardman. A decent man, Hardman had to accept the inevitable but there was acute resentment among the other directors, and also the bulk of the supporters.

The board voted in favour of demanding £1 million from Chelsea in compensation for Hoddle's playing contract, infuriating Hoddle. An FA transfer tribunal ruled that the fee was £75,000 and an extra £2,000 for every appearance for Chelsea. Hoddle played 31 games, bringing in £62,000. Gorman, the friendly Scot, took over briefly at Swindon and they failed to stay up. It was a sad end to a happy little story.

Hoddle's success, or failure, at Stamford Bridge depended on his relationship with the volatile, dictatorial Bates and his reign was to last three seasons, the average time for most managers. He took Chelsea to the FA Cup final in his first season, where they lost 4-0 to Manchester United. In his second season, Chelsea went out to Real Zaragoza in the semi-final of the European Cup-Winners' Cup and in his last season they lost 2-1 to Manchester United in the semi-final of the FA Cup. That was enough to keep the fans interested but Bates was quick to point out that he hadn't improved on the club's position in the top flight, failing to get into the top ten in all three seasons. By the end of his term the two men weren't talking to each other and Woolnough wrote, 'Bates found Hoddle self-centred, aloof and only interested in two things: himself and his bank balance.' The same words could have applied to Bates except that he wasn't aloof.

Hoddle's record of buying talent was questionable, with Bates asking most of the questions. Players such as Paul Furlong, bought from Watford for £2.3 million, Mark Stein from Stoke for £1.5 million, Scott Minto, £1 million from Charlton and the late David Rocastle, who cost £1.2 million from Manchester City, were hardly up-and-coming Premiership stars. Bates was always looking for big investors and one he courted assiduously was Matthew Harding, the hard-drinking chairman of the Benfield Insurance Group who answered an advertisement in the *Financial Times* appealing for Chelsea investors. Harding was a louder version of Scholar, a lifelong fan of Chelsea with immense knowledge of everything about the club, and he claimed he lent the club £5 million without charging interest to help build the North Stand. Bates soon realised he was a threat to his position. Harding was continually boasting that he would take over soon.

The press has always played a key role in football politics and those who are seeking high positions befriend as many journalists as possible to aid their cause. Bates always had favourite journalists he would leak information to but he often fell out with them. Harry Harris was one and when he displeased Bates the chairman sued for libel and won the case. Bates took delight in putting a notice on the press toilet that read 'The Harry Harris Room, sponsored by Harris'. Harding also lined up his journalistic cronies, inviting them to binge-drinking sessions in his favourite pub, close to Stamford Bridge. If you were on Harding's list, Bates would make sure that you were not welcome.

Harding's biggest recruit was Hoddle. The two men got on well and Bates became more and more annoyed by what he thought was a plot against him. When Bates was ill with pneumonia at his farm near Beaconsfield, Hoddle never sent him a card or gave him a telephone call. Harding said of Hoddle, 'He has enormous self-confidence and he's an achiever. He appears a bit arrogant but he is far from that. He is a self starter who doesn't suffer people he doesn't like or admire. He has little small talk and doesn't waste his time.' Harding often spoke of his long-term plans for Chelsea but sadly he died in October 1996 in a helicopter crash when returning from a game in Bolton.

Someone planted the idea with the FA that Hoddle would be interested in taking over from Terry Venables at the end of the European Championships and in March 1996 Jimmy Armfield had a secret meeting with the Chelsea manager. Others who were approached, Kevin Keegan, Bryan Robson, Alex Ferguson, Gerry Francis and Frank Clark, all ruled themselves out. The field was down to one – Hoddle. Graham Kelly rang and he asked for forty-eight hours to think about it. Sir Bert Millichip, the late chairman of the FA, described him as 'a gentleman, very articulate and I can see him doing the job for the next ten years'. Hoddle was paid twice as much as Venables without having the highest coaching certificates. He was thirty-eight, five years older than Winterbottom when he started at the bottom of the pile.

In his first press conference Hoddle spoke at length without making any promises but Sir Bert's description of him being 'articulate' was not entirely appropriate. Like a number of previous England managers, Hoddle was often too verbose, with his words jumbled up and interspersed with 'you knows' and boring clichés. A good communicator puts his message over in short, clear sentences, followed by a brief period of silence so his listeners can assimilate his meaning. Hoddle has never been comfortable addressing the media, especially as the army of journalists has risen from around thirty to more than 250 at international matches. Brian Woolnough, one of the longest-serving journalists to have followed the careers of England's managers, said, 'You get the impression that he would simply like to stay on the training pitch with his squad, and that he fears the media want something from him.'

His first match in charge was in Moldova, not a welcoming place, and a 3-0 victory gave him a wonderful start in the World Cup qualifying group. He set the right tone by refraining from any rash forecasts and raked up a couple of clichés, saying, 'We looked as if we had a cutting edge but there was not enough quality in the last third of the pitch.' His first game at Wembley, a month later against Poland, was unsatisfactory because the Poles played most of the football, although England won 2-1 with both goals from the new captain, Alan Shearer. 'They didn't do what I told them,' said Hoddle. He didn't show much emotion, or nerves, and Shearer was the same. As spokesmen, they talked freely without revealing their inner thoughts.

Hoddle kept the squad together for nine days at Bisham Abbey, a training centre on the river near Marlow, and the players found it rather restrictive. England footballers used to train on steak, chips and peas. Now the manager was banning red meat, substituting chicken (without skin) instead, and the Mediterranean-style diet wasn't quite what today's players were used to at their homes. They were allowed one glass of wine for their meal and beer and fizzy drinks were banned before matches. He was right about fizzy drinks. Pumping hundreds of bubbles into your stomach doesn't help digestion!

Hoddle came up with more sound ideas to reform his players, seeking to turn them into the kind of squad Wenger assembled at Arsenal. He arranged counselling for Gascoigne, saying:

> The ideal [situation] would be for him to eventually become a role model, for kids and people with similar problems to those he has suffered. I know I keep going back to this thing of forgiveness but that is what this is. The very example of Christianity is forgiveness. If Joe Public had done the same and the police were not involved then he wouldn't have got the sack or lost his capacity to earn. We are helping Paul to change and that surely has to be a good thing. I am prepared to give him a chance. To cast him outside now would be detrimental, long term for him and his family.

That was a reference to Gascoigne's physical assault on Sheryl, his former wife.

Bringing up his religion on a footballing matter may well have lost respect from some of the players who weren't believers. But if you believe in a god, you should have the courage to speak up and Hoddle did that. Two years later that was to be held against him.

Tony Adams and Paul Merson, former alcoholics and occasional trou-blemakers, were included along with Gascoigne on the trip to Tbilisi for Hoddle's third game, against Georgia in November. Their inclusion revealed forgiveness by their manager and it was an indication that English football had been too lax in the past. We were left behind the rest of the footballing world over diet, drink consumption, behaviour and fitness in the days of the Hungarians in the 1950s and are still behind now. In France they don't present a bottle of champagne to the Man of the Match, like they still do in England.

Georgia away, in the south of the former USSR, was seen as a tough match and England played so spiritedly that a 2-0 win boosted the confi-dence of the whole squad. 'It's a great way to end the year,' said Hoddle. 'I can have a good Christmas now.' But his short run of success coaxing good performances out of 'difficult' players came to an abrupt end when he chose Southampton's Matthew Le Tissier, the first player from Guernsey to be selected by England, for the home game against Italy. Hoddle saw him as a similar style of player to himself – highly skilled, a great passer, unequalled on set pieces (he converted all but one of his penalties), yet lacking pace and fitness and unable win many tackles. At the time the twenty-eight-year-old Le Tissier was at his peak, scoring a goal every 2.6 games. He was the eighth highest scorer in the Premiership that season.

Hoddle's secrecy about details of fitness of players and the composition of the starting line-up went to extremes and he was caught telling fibs in the pre-match build up. He claimed that Shearer, Gascoigne and David Seaman were fit on Monday but of these only Shearer played – and he was still unfit. Le Tissier wasn't mentioned by the commentators in their predicted sides, except for a report in *The Times* by Martin Samuel, who correctly forecasted that the Southampton player would be in. FA officials were livid and sought to find the source. Someone at Southampton's local radio station rang Le Tissier's brother Carl to check the story and was told it was true. Le Tissier lasted an hour in the game, which was dominated by the Italians, before he was taken off. 'I should have kept him on,' Hoddle said later. Gianfranco Zola, the popular Chelsea forward, scored the only goal.

Morale was hardly affected with Hoddle's men winning 2-0 against Georgia at Wembley and by the same score against Poland in Katowice.

Italy remained top but England's 4-0 win at home against Moldova closed the gap. Only one country could go through automatically and England needed a draw in Rome on 11 October.

Normally Hoddle handles pressure well but this time he started sweating profusely. The tension heightened in the previous days because he had decided to separate from his wife Anne and their three children. He spent hours on the telephone to them from his luxurious training camp at La Borghesiana. He had no one else to confide in. 'It was my secret, something I carried alone in the preparation for the biggest match of my life to date,' he recalled in his ill-fated book *My 1998 World Cup Story*.

Like many sportsmen he is superstitious and on the flight to Rome he opened the astrology page of the *Daily Express* and saw this: 'The situation at home is now moving through a more contented atmosphere. You are moving slowly but surely on to a new emotional base.' 'It was spot on,' he said later. While most managers, and players, need sleeping tablets before big matches, Hoddle slept his usual seven or eight hours, despite being woken by the barking of the guard dogs outside.

He had settled on his preferred team in the previous month and he chose men of character like David Seaman, Tony Adams and Teddy Sheringham, who had all missed the first match against Italy. Alan Shearer would also have been in but he was unfit. Ian Wright took over and hit a post in the heroic 0-0 draw that took England to the finals in France the following year. It was one of the oldest England teams of recent years.

The bigger the match, the more propaganda is pumped out on both sides. Hoddle asked some of the sports editors to ask their writers to throw in a few misleading names to confuse the Italians. And Cesare Maldini, the Italian coach, fed a few false steers about his line-up, including a mention of Attilio Lombardo, who was playing for Crystal Palace at the time. In one of the training sessions, Hoddle pulled off David Beckham ten minutes from time to provoke some headlines about injury scares.

An insurance company paid for the wives to go to Rome and Debbie Wright, wife of Ian, made a gracious speech of thanks at a lunch at a £300-a-night hotel on the Via Veneto. It was a pity that Wright wasn't a regular. Debbie would have been a great ambassador for English football. After the game the coach had to wait for three hours before it departed because hooliganism had erupted around the Olympic Stadium during the game and the hundreds of *carabiniere* were taking no chances outside in the streets. Sheryl Gascoigne went up to a well-dressed man and asked, 'What's going on? I want to get back to London. Let's get moving.' 'I am your host,' said the man. 'And we are providing a ticket for you. Please show patience. We are in the hands of the police. It will be down to them, not me.' Gascoigne should have been one of the all-time great footballers from these isles but this tormented genius was unlucky with love. Most geniuses are like that – George Best, Diego Maradona, Pelé, the list goes on.

Tony Adams would usually have been captain in the absence of Shearer but was yet to return to full fitness, so Hoddle gave the captaincy to Paul Ince. It was an inspired decision and Ince rose to new heights. When Hoddle was eventually toppled from his job, Ince was one of the few players who stood up and spoke favourably about him. 'He should never have been have forced out,' he said. 'He was doing a good job.' Two days before the kick-off in Rome, Ince was convulsed with stomach pains and Hoddle thought he was dehydrated. He helped to administer an osteopathic massage on the abdomen and it worked. He first heard about it when he was at Monaco. One of his predecessors, Don Revie, used to love performing massages on his players.

David Davies advised Hoddle to reduce the amount of time on press interviews and also ban Gascoigne from the microphones and tape recorders, both wise decisions. Too many England managers have been too loquacious, jumping into unnecessary controversies. As the coach roared through the traffic to the Olympic Stadium, Hoddle arranged for the playing of two videos, the 1966 World Cup and Euro 96, with one of the accompanying songs being 'Search for the Hero Inside Yourself'. Ince found it in himself that afternoon. In the dressing room Hoddle exuded confidence, saying, 'We will win. I've got a great feeling about it.' Outside, the atmosphere was thunderous, almost terrifying and it affected the Italians, not the English, who found it uplifting.

Several times Hoddle said prayers under his breath during the taut game, especially when Ince collided with Demetrio Albertini just before half-time. Ince's face was covered with blood and Gary Lewin, England's long-serving physio, signalled to the bench that he needed stitches. It was a long walk to the dressing room and when they arrived, accompanied by the equally long-serving Arsenal doctor John Crane, they discovered that the door was locked. Lewin had to sprint back to the dugout to retrieve the key before sprinting back. He is a very fit man.

Hoddle lost his temper for a second or two, shouting at Crane about the delay. Later he apologised. The upshot was that he persuaded the FA to have a stitchman on the bench in future, like the ones who treat boxers on their stool. Ince soon returned to the action and continued playing in the same aggressive manner. Christian Vieri's header just missed a post, about the only effort to come close to an Italian goal. The final score of 0-0 meant that England topped the group and qualified for the World Cup Finals, whereas the Italians would have to appear in a play-off.

Wright was in tears at the end and Gascoigne, one of the more flamboyant players and a big success on the night, play-acted to the English section of the crowd. Hoddle came up with another prayer of thanks. Before leaving, he went to the officials' room to congratulate the Dutch referee Van den Ende, whom he praised for his impartiality and fairness. On the flight back, Hoddle said very little. He felt no feeling of triumphalism. The aircraft landed at 4.40 a.m. in the rain at Luton airport and there were plenty of supporters waiting to cheer the players before their chauffeurs drove them home. A family friend drove Hoddle to his home and he slept most of the way. For a while, he was a hero.

The draw took place in Marseilles and England's opponents were Romania, Tunisia and Colombia, none of them feared opponents. But off-field problems about key players caused considerable worry for Hoddle. Tony Adams had a longstanding ankle injury and hadn't finally dealt with his alcoholism, Gascoigne was in a similar position and needed an hour-long talk with his manager prior to the disturbing 2-0 defeat by Chile in a friendly, when David Beckham collected a needless yellow card that ruled him out of the game against Brazil in 'Le Tournoi' – a friendly tournament in France in the summer of 1997 – when England lost 1-0. Hoddle was criticised for bringing in too many mediocre players like Chris Sutton and Andy Hinchcliffe, among others.

Hoddle had flu-like symptoms including a temperature of 102°F before the 1-1 friendly against Switzerland in Berne and cut short his interviews with the television companies. That roused resentment but being continually asked the same question is upsetting to most people, particularly highly stressed football managers right after the end of matches.

For years there were stories about Hoddle's relationship with Eileen Drewery and to pre-empt any more revelations in the run up to the World Cup Finals he came out with his version:

> To begin with, the reaction was precisely what I would expect. There were plenty of references to barmy armies, voodoo managers and mumbo jumbo. One TV man went so far as to ask me to my face if I was a crank. Others were more open-minded, sceptical maybe, but not blatantly hostile. The story certainly made the headlines and predictably, Eileen got the full media treatment. Journalists and photographers camped outside on her doorstep and followed her for days. What I hadn't bargained for was the stories continuing for so long after my announcement, or the ferocity of the criticism from some ex-professionals like Alan Mullery and Martin Peters.

Hoddle first met Eileen Drewery when he was eighteen and playing in Tottenham's first team. Her daughter Michelle went out with him for six months and after he tore a hamstring muscle she told him she could cure it. She said she intended to pray about the injury and things would soon change. Next day Hoddle realised there was no pain. Mike Varney, the then physio at White Hart Lane, had reckoned he would be out for six weeks. Two days later, Hoddle resumed training.

Another incident in 1984 convinced him that there was more to life than football: God came into his life. He had an inflamed patella of the knee which didn't heal up. Even the ministrations of Mrs Drewery failed to work but she explained, 'I have a gift handed down from God and I am a channel for it.' When he realised he had discovered God, the injury cleared. His faith grew stronger and on a footballing trip to Israel just before the 1986 World Cup he experienced a watershed in his life. 'Everything started falling into place,' he said. 'I would talk to Eileen for hours and she explained how healing works and I would go off searching for my own answers. It comes from love.' She touched people on the head and they felt better afterwards but Robbie Fowler, a sceptic, made a tart comment and rushed out of the hotel room.

One of Mrs Drewery's successes was Hoddle's father Derek, relieving his arthritis of the back. Aferwards he began playing golf regularly. There were other examples of miracle cures.

When Hoddle became England's manager he spoke to the players about her powers and suggested that if anyone wanted to see her – there was no compulsion – they could meet her and more than a third took up the offer, including Darren Anderton, David Seaman, Gareth Southgate, Paul Merson, Les Ferdinand, Ian Wright and Sol Campbell. For a time Anderton met her every week and she saw him as a changed man, with a much more positive approach to life. Unfortunately, Anderton never really made the top grade. He had too many injuries. Hoddle has remained loyal to many of his players and Anderton was a good example. When he signed Anderton for Wolves in August 2005, he said, 'His label of forever being injured was cruel. He is one of the best athletes I have ever worked with.'

In the lead-up to the World Cup, Gascoigne featured in a number of newspaper stories about his excessive drinking – he had been pictured in clubs drinking with Chris Evans and Rod Stewart – and Hoddle asked him if he was available to meet Eileen Drewery. A chauffeured car paid for by the FA picked him up and took him to her home and after a chat and putting her hand on his troubled brow, she said he had demons coming out of his head. According to Gascoigne's latest book *Gazza*, she opened the door to let them out but told him not to smoke or drink beer, otherwise they would be back. Next day Gascoigne was back smoking and drinking – both habits which Mrs Drewery followed herself.

Hoddle encouraged the players to pay her for her services, around £20 an hour. But as the campaign against her continued the FA advised him to back off and she withdrew. She wrote a book about her experiences, serialised in *The Sun*. That didn't benefit her or Hoddle, though they remained good friends. There was an odd moment in England's 1-0 win over Morocco, watched by 80,000 frenzied locals in Casablanca in the King Hassan Tournament, part of England's warm-up. Michael Owen was knocked out in a collision and, as the medical staff treated him, Hoddle came over, put a hand on his back and offered a silent prayer for his speedy recovery. When Owen came to, he said, 'I don't want to come off, I won't come off.' And he didn't, going on to score the goal. Two days earlier, Hoddle had a dream about Gascoigne. He dreamt that he was sitting across a desk from Gascoigne, who was crying.

Most football clubs now have sports psychologists and some of them are boring. But if someone can improve the confidence of the players, whether it is an Eileen Drewery or the current England football psychologist or whoever, that must be beneficial. The biggest part of succeeding in professional football, next to ability, is confidence. Whether Mrs Drewery was able to cure the injuries of players is debatable but if someone believes in it, then that is halfway to achieving it. David Seaman was a believer. He had a lingering shoulder injury which failed to heal and after seeing her he reported 'a big improvement'. He defended her, saying, 'The truth was that Hoddle never put any pressure on players to see her. She was just there as a resource if we chose to use her.'

Before leaving for La Manga, the training camp Hoddle had chosen for the squad in Spain, he held a gathering of the sports editors and asked them to refrain from writing damaging stories about the players. 'If you do, it will harm our chances of winning,' he said. Gascoigne soon altered things, inspiring the most embarrassing stories by his lack of self-discipline. The FA arranged a golf day at Stoke Poges in early May and Hoddle was almost poleaxed by Rob Shepherd, Graham Taylor's old adversary of Rotterdam. Shepherd's wayward drive crashed into Hoddle's buggy, just missing him. To minimise the dangers presented by overly keen red-top pressmen, Hoddle refused to let the press stay at the same complex in Spain or fly with the official party.

The England party flew from Murcia, the nearest airport to La Manga, to Casablanca for the two King Hassan Tournament matches and the second game was a 0-0 draw against Belgium, with the Belgians winning 4-3 on penalties. At half-time Hoddle almost exploded, forsaking his usual, calm approach. 'You aren't doing yourselves any favours,' he said. This time the stadium was almost empty. Gascoigne had been late for the coach and came off early in the second half with a 'dead leg'. By then Hoddle had virtually made up his mind that he was to be among the six he left out of his final World Cup squad. He believed he wasn't fit mentally or physically.

The next day, after a round of four-ball with Terry Mancini against Darren Anderton and Gary Neville, Hoddle finalised his plans. He was asking every player to come to see him individually, with five minutes allocated per player, the next afternoon. That night the players were given permission to have some drinks in the hotel bar and when Hoddle rejoined them later in the evening he realised that Gascoigne, singing lustily on the karaoke, was very drunk. David Seaman had to put him to bed.

Ian Walker, Phil Neville, Dion Dublin, Nicky Butt and Andy Hinchcliffe were all duly ushered into the Royal Suite the next day to receive the bad news from the manager and, at 5.30 p.m., twenty minutes behind schedule, in came Gascoigne.

There were two versions of what happened next. Hoddle's version, from his World Cup book, is as follows:

> There was a bang on the door. He was more drunk than I thought he would be. I sat him down and he said, 'I don't believe this.' I said, 'Well, you're not fit enough. It's nothing to do with anything else.' And he began to cry. He got up and said, 'Gaffer, my career is finished.' He came closer and shook my hand. 'I'm going to wish you all the best,' he said.
>
> I wanted to explain the situation, how he could help himself but he turned – and then suddenly flew into a total rage and kicked the chair. It was a full-blooded volley from a bare foot. He could have broken it, he kicked it so hard. Thank goodness I had moved those wine glasses. He was a different person now. He had snapped. Then he came back with a barrage of abuse. He turned and then stopped, like a man possessed. By this time, I had my arm ready. I thought he was going to hit me. There was a lamp to my left and he punched it. The glass shattered all over the room. As Glenn Roeder and John Gorman heard it they steamed straight in and ushered him out.

Gascoigne's version from his autobiography was:

> He was treating us like school kids. I wasn't drunk. Not at all. I burst into the room and went ballistic. 'What the f——ing hell are you doing? You know what it means to me, you f——ing bastard.' 'Let me explain,' Hoddle said. 'I don't want any explanations. You know what you're doing to me?' I walked over to the wardrobe and kicked in the door. Then I overturned his table, smashing a pottery vase, sending it crashing to the floor. In the process, I managed to cut my leg so now there was blood all over the place. I didn't attempt to hit him, though I would have liked to. I suppose, deep down, I still respected him, as a player, if not as a manager. I was in a complete fury. It wasn't long before he led me to believe that I was in the twenty-two, telling the world that we hadn't seen the best of Gazza yet.

'Gazza, just calm down.' 'Just shut up, you bastard.' 'The thing is, Gazza, your head isn't right.' 'I got you to France, I saved your skin, your job, and now look what you're are doing to me.' I was about to start smashing all his windows when David Seaman and Paul Ince burst in and managed to restrain me. Then they called for the doctor who gave me a valium to quieten me down. I was taken to my room.'

A few hours later he flew home with the five other dropped players. He cancelled the holidays of his family in France and was welcomed, temporarily, by Sheryl, his wife. He didn't watch the World Cup on television, not a single kick. A few days later he was embroiled with an intrusive photographer and hit him, damaging his car and his camera. He could have ended up in court but the police were lenient – sensibly. In his book, he recalled:

What really pissed me off was when, almost immediately after the tournament was over, Hoddle published his World Cup diary. He should not have written about it while he was still the England manager. He was just cashing in on his position, making money out of my misery. I thought it was disgusting. I was not the only one who thought that.

Few of the ninety-two councillors at the FA would have agreed with Gascoigne about many things, but they did that time. It was a clear breach of etiquette, abetted by ghost writer David Davies, one of whose earlier jobs was to tidy up the columns 'written' by the players and keep out contentious matters. Now Hoddle was coming out with material which had embarrassed the whole England set-up. He should have been censured but the contents of the book were held up against him later when his next major mistake, the reference to disabled people, erupted on the front pages.

Seaman summed up the view of most of the players that Hoddle was badly at fault. In his book *Safe Hands* he wrote:

It was something he did not need to do and left him open to the charge of doing anything for a little extra money. I simply couldn't fathom out why Gazza had been dropped and Hoddle certainly never explained his decision to us. It was a massive shock to everyone but we had to get on with it.

Tuesday 9 June was England's D-Day, with hundreds of British Airways staff spilling onto the runway to wave goodbye. It was like Euro 96; the whole nation was backing Hoddle and his boys. The aircraft landed at Nantes en route to allow the players to play a practice game at Caen, a town renowned for its bitter fighting in the Second World War fifty-four years previously. It proved to be a bad idea. The locals kicked out at Hoddle's stars and the rain poured down. At La Baule, the beach, which was described as 'one of the best in the world', was just as wet and windy.

England's base for the early stage of the World Cup was the Hotel Du Golf International near La Labule in Brittany, where for much of the time they were there it rained. Perhaps that might have been a bad omen.

Except for being provided with a bumpy training pitch – soon rejected, with a much better one found nearby – Hoddle was happy with the preparations. A key man was Dr Jan Rougier, a friend of Arsène Wenger who advised on diet: when the players should eat, how they eat (he recommended excessive chewing), their vitamin and mineral supplements and the controversial addition creatine. Robbie Fowler, who had taken part in the early stages before being ignored, said, 'You had to have creatine. I was very suspicious of that stuff. There were injections and then there was Snowy White's 'Bird of Paradise', the song Hoddle always played to soothe the players.'

Before England's opening game in Marseilles, against moderate opposition in Tunisia, Hoddle called his players to the centre of the training pitch and announced his XI. He told them not to tell anyone, even their agents or relatives. Hoddle had given David Beckham his debut against Moldova the previous year and he had been an ever-present in the World Cup qualifiers but now he decided to leave him out. 'There was a vagueness about him,' Hoddle said. 'I'm sure he was missing Victoria, who was away a greal deal.' On the morning of the match Hoddle was rung by someone saying, 'The Prime Minister wants to talk to you.' Hoddle thought it was a hoaxer. He was wrong. Tony Blair told him what everyone knew, that the nation was behind the team, and he apologised for not being able to watch the game on television. He was attending a summit meeting – 'But I'll make sure the tea break starts at the right time,' he said. A few months later the premier came out with the fatal words on the *Richard and Judy* programme which sealed Hoddle's fate.

Before the kick-off at the Stade Velodrome, Hoddle went to the middle and prayed, not for victory, he said, but asking for an energy to help overcome any negativity. The players arranged a book for their bets on every game at the hotel and one of the people with the worst records of forecasting results was Hoddle. He tipped a 1-0 win this time. He was a goal out – it was 2-0 with Alan Shearer, from a stunning header, and Paul Scholes scoring the goals. A short time earlier, Shearer was so upset about allegations that he had deliberately tried to kick Neil Lennon in the head in a domestic match, and the FA charging him with the offence, that he was thinking of quitting. Fortunately for Hoddle and his camp, Shearer was absolved.

Back at the hotel Hoddle banned alcohol for the two days before matches. 'Alcohol is the last thing the body needs when it is dehydrated, when there is lactic acid building up in the muscles,' he wrote. But for the Wenger connection, English international footballers might still be boozing away. Some of them still do!

Instead of celebrating throughout the next day, Hoddle took time out to raise the subject of a story on the front page of the *Sunday People* about David Seaman's private life. It was a serious breach of his agreement with the sports editors and in a live televised interview, he came out with some strong words. Neil Wallis, the editor, refused to back down. Seaman very sensibly didn't mention this controversy in his book *Safe Hands* but he admitted he was nervous before the two opening matches.

The truce with the sports editors had ended and the press opened fire with all barrels, particularly the *Daily Mirror*. It criticised Sir Brian Hayes, the FA security advisor for having a few days off and published pictures of Paul Scholes' house, while another newspaper published a made-up interview, supposedly with Scholes's wife. Armed French equivalents of the SAS followed the team everywhere.

England *v.* the Press is a long-running saga in World Cups, with the team manager forced to spend almost as much time on that as on the training pitch. Alex Ferguson, never short of a few critical comments when he thinks it affects his players, attacked Hoddle for letting David Beckham be interviewed about his omission. Hoddle declined to respond despite tremendous pressure from the journalists. He was learning fast.

On the way to the match against Romania in Toulouse Hoddle had a feeling England would lose. He was right: they lost 2-1 to a late goal scored by his former Chelsea teammate Dan Petrescu, who shot through the legs of Seaman. But the real culprit was Graeme Le Saux, who let Petrescu through. Hoddle was angry with him but later he was also angry with Kevin Keegan after watching the match again on television and hearing Keegan in his role as summariser saying, 'Well, that's fan power for you' when Hoddle brought on substitutes David Beckham and Michael Owen twenty-five minutes from time. 'Absolute rubbish,' he told his staff. Owen scored the goal, reigniting the press campaign calling for him to start the matches.

On the way back the players, and also the staff, were totally depressed, especially as their loved ones had only seen them for a few minutes before they flew back to their base. Peter Taylor, the most upbeat in the group, started whistling 'Always Look on the Bright Side of Life'. The mood slowly improved. In the days that followed, Alan Shearer and Gareth Southgate, both leaders, thought up a good way of poking fun at the press. It was a competition among the players to come up with song titles in their answers in interviews. Shearer, a Phil Collins fan, took an early lead with 'Against all Odds' and 'Something in the Air Tonight'.

Some of the players had fears that they were on their way out. Seaman wrote, 'We were all taking extra vitamins to lift ourselves and make us a little bit more lively.' Hoddle relaxed listening to Celine Dion and when he woke up in the team hotel near Lens, ready for the game against Colombia, he told John Gorman, his always-cheerful deputy, 'I've got no nerves and I'm totally confident.' In his diary, he wrote, 'The players picked up on my mood. I remember the anxiety of Bobby Robson and Ron Greenwood unnerving the squad when I was a player.'

The English newspapers were kept away from the party – although the staff at Château Tilques distributed plenty of them before they were promptly confiscated. Hoddle read the articles, mostly on the theme of what would happen to him if England lost – he would soon be sacked. As usual, he prayed on the coach going to the ground. There was little to worry about. The Colombians were overawed and went down quietly to goals from Anderton and a Beckham free-kick, one of his best. Back at La Baule, the champagne was poured and Vanessa, soon to be Hoddle's new wife, kept everyone in hysterics with jokes. Hoddle was still in a job. The FA had already told him they wanted him to stay at least until 2000, what-ever the outcome in France. The Prince of Wales was at the game, along with Prince Harry, and afterwards his private secretary rang Hoddle to thank him for inviting them.

The next posting was at St Etienne to take on Argentina in the second round and Graeme Le Saux asked David Davies if he could be excused from attending press conferences because his wife is from Argentina. Permission was soon granted. Even now, England have a 3-2 lead over Argentina in World Cup matches and this contest was seen as revenge for the 'Hand of God' defeat in Mexico City in 1986. Hoddle was fifteen yards behind when Diego Maradona palmed the ball into the empty net but said later, 'I didn't blame him. It was the officials who really angered me.' It was England's third match in eleven days and several players had injuries. Beckham had a lactic acid build-up in his thigh and was forced to postpone a session or two practising his famed free-kicks.

Hoddle had bad memories of St Etienne's Geoffroy Guilchard Stadium. Playing there with Monaco he had contracted an infection of the cartilage which stopped him playing for almost two years. His throat, after too much shouting in the Colombia game, was very sore and the BBC's Ray Stubbs eased his distress by giving him half-a-dozen Fishermen's Friends. In the hour before kick-off at 9 p.m., Hoddle went round to each player with instructions and advice. Whether he overdid it only he will know after England went out on penalties. (During the Ashes series in 2005, England coach Duncan Fletcher made just one point to Matthew Hoggard, the Yorkshire bowler who, batting-wise, is looked on as a blocker, in the final hours of the Edgbaston Test which England just won. He said, 'It will be easy to hit the seamers so get ready if you are given one to hit.' Brett Lee bowled a full toss and Hoggard, up on his toes, whacked it for four. That was good management.)

After only six minutes, Argentina were awarded a penalty when Diego Simeone conned the Danish referee Kim Milton Nielsen. Seaman explained:

> I was coming to the ball and maybe I should have stood up a bit longer but once I committed myself, Simeone knew what he was doing. He tapped the ball to the side of me, ran into me and went over. No complaints, it was a penalty but he definitely played for it.

The incessant showing of videos makes it easier these days for goalkeepers. Seaman knew that Batistuta would shoot to the goalkeeper's right and he did. He got a decent hand to the ball but it was too powerful a shot. Seaman was cautioned for bringing Simeone down.

Four minutes later, Owen was awarded a penalty in almost the same circumstances and Hoddle praised his 'professionalism'. Shearer blasted it past Carlos Roa. Hoddle was incandescent when the referee failed to caution the moustachioed keeper. He kept raging at the fourth official, a Norwegian who said, 'What can I do, Glenn?' Owen added a brilliant second in the sixteenth minute. Sitting high in the 30,600 crowd, the wives of the England players stepped up to the barriers and removed the blue and white Argentinian flags and replaced them with Union Jacks and the flag of St George. The Argentinians retaliated, taking down the Union Jacks and putting up theirs. And so it went on until officials intervened… leaving the English flags on station.

On the field the oscillating battle grew in intensity. Javier Zanetti made it 2-2 right on the break after Le Saux was at fault at the free-kick. In the fiftieth minute Beckham went down under a rugged challenge from Simeone and, as he lay on the ground, he flicked his boot at the Argentinian. A flick of a horse's tail would have done more damage, but the tall Nielsen brandished the red card. Beckham said in his book *My Side*, ghosted by Tom Watt, 'I don't know how I did it but Simeone tugged my hair first and then went down like he was shot.' It was another example of Beckham's poor discipline, like the previous year when an unnecessary booking had stopped him playing against Brazil at Le Tournoi.

To Hoddle's surprise, Argentinian coach Daniel Passarella failed to change his formation against England's ten. It was as though he was content with 2-2 and penalties at the end. England felt that they had won it near the end when Sol Campbell rose to head in but again Nielsen penalised England. Seaman was one of the few who looked at the replay later and admitted the referee was right. Shearer had fouled the keeper. Hoddle was further incensed by the referee's failure to see Chamot's arm reach up to the ball as he challenged Shearer in extra time. He believed England were robbed by three decisions. The third decision wasn't as clear as the 'Hand of God' but it should have counted against Argentina nevertheless.

Does Hoddle have extra-sensory perception? As the chosen players assembled for the shoot-out he recalled later, 'I could tell immediately from their reaction that they weren't up for it. The defenders looked particularly unhappy.' He listed his five penalty takers: Shearer, Ince, Merson, Owen and Batty. Shearer, Merson and Owen took penalties for their clubs. Only Batty, brought on near the end, had never taken a penalty, and he was very confident of putting his away. The referee dealt one final blow to England's cause, deciding that the penalties would be staged at the end where the Argentinian supporters were on their feet.

Shearer slammed in his kick. As Seaman waited on his line, missiles were thrown. The officials took no action. Crespo missed! The heroic Ince missed! Veron... scored. Merson scored. Gallardo scored, Owen scored, Ayala scored. Now it was the last man, Batty. He shot appallingly, too close and at a convenient height and the ball bounced off Roa's chest to the roars from the Argentinians. There is nothing worse than losing a shoot-out. Sick, sick, sick! Hoddle sat on his haunches, tears in his eyes as he looked up to his children and former wife sitting mournfully in the stand. In the dressing room, the angry players sat around without a word. Hoddle praised them. 'You did everything you could. The decisions went against you and I'm not going to blame anybody. Put your chin up and walk out with pride.'

Beckham finally spoke up, saying to Shearer, 'Sorry Al!' By this time his relationship with Hoddle was irrecoverably severed. 'He was my hero when I was a boy,' said Beckham. 'But I don't know what went wrong. When he left me out for the Tunisia game he told me, "You aren't focused" which was rubbish. I think I found out the reason later, all of the party went off to play golf except me – I went out with Victoria for the day.'

As the England coach drove off, another coach filled with Argentinians waving their shirts and mocking Hoddle's players, drove alongside. It was their team coach. Rattin, Ramsey, Malvinas, Maradona – the hate had lingered on. Back at La Baule Prime Minister Blair rang to commiserate. The squad were going to take a BA charter flight back to Heathrow but BA offered the use of a Concorde. Hoddle took up the offer. On the short flight, Hoddle and Beckham stood in the narrow aisle for a while and Hoddle warned him about further excesses. 'It's the end of the line as far as learning lessons are concerned,' he said.

They were similar players, similar personalities, decent, family men. Greenwood and Robson hadn't succeeded in fitting Hoddle into their team plans and it seemed that Hoddle had the same problem with Beckham. Both were great passers at distance but both needed more to complete the whole package. They were gallant losers on too many great occasions. The fates, and a referee, were against them. The press savaged Beckham for some time afterwards – one tabloid newspaper pictured him with a noose around his neck – and Hoddle thought he should have some counselling, perhaps from Eileen Drewery. Hoddle's biggest mistake, he said afterwards, was 'in not getting Eileen out to join us from the start'.

He revealed that Real Madrid had offered him a coaching job. If that had happened, he and Beckham would have been working together again in another country and who knows what would happened? Hoddle stayed in charge of England for four more matches, a damning 2-1 defeat by Sweden in a European Championship qualifier at Stockholm, a dismal 0-0 draw against Bulgaria in another qualifier at Wembley, a limp 3-0 European Championship success in Luxembourg and a 2-0 victory over the Czech Republic in a friendly at Wembley.

Between these matches Hoddle's position was becoming increasingly less secure. Graham Kelly, the FA secretary who was on his way out himself, tried to mediate between him and his agent Dennis Roach with the members of the international committee who, except for one, refused to give Hoddle a two-year extension to his contract. Roach was pressing for more money and Kelly revealed in his book *Sweet FA* that 'there was a six-figure sum between the two sides'. Kelly warned Hoddle several times that the members wanted no more books, no more truck with Mrs Drewery and that the Under-21 squad had to be under the control of Howard Wilkinson, the FA's technical director. A stubborn man, Hoddle agreed about no more books but offered the members a chance to meet Mrs Drewery. And he wouldn't budge on the Under-21 issue – he wanted to be in charge of them. Kelly said, 'I was beginning to feel that I might need the services of Mrs Drewery the way things were going.'

Just before Christmas Kelly quit over money paid to the Welsh FA. Chairman Keith Wiseman departed in January and Hoddle followed a few days later. Kelly said:

Without doubt the FA hung Glenn out to dry after his interview in *The Times*. I still believe, however upsetting his comments will have been to disabled people – and I sympathise very much with the hurt they will have felt – he did not need to lose his job for personally-held opinions.

Roy Hodgson was keen on the job but Noel White did not want him. As for Venables, Kelly said, 'Jack the Ripper had a better chance than him.'

Robbie Fowler, not always the best advertisement for English football, wrote in his autobiography:

> One or two of the senior players made it clear to the FA that the manager had lost the players and there was little chance of qualifying for Euro 2000. That set the alarm bells going and when they found an excuse to ditch him – for saying those things about disabled people – they moved faster than David Beckham does to join in the celebration when an England striker scores a goal. He couldn't relate to us. He talked to us like we were kids.

That is a cruel analysis. Some people on the staff at Tottenham, and many of the club's supporters, contributed to Hoddle's fall at White Hart Lane at the end of his spell as manager there between 2001 and 2003. But his fifth club managerial job, when he took over from David Jones at Wolverhampton Wanderers in the 2004/05 season, proved to be more rewarding.

Overambitious, perhaps he was too early for the England job. The FA botched his case and was still botching six years later when the *News of the World*, the scourge of the FA, revealed that they were still paying Hoddle's mobile phone bill until it was cancelled.

KEVIN KEEGAN

1999–2000

The Man Who Walked Away

P 18   W 7   D 7   L 4   38%

Early in his brief nineteen-month reign as England manager, Kevin Keegan was at the FA offices when he met Ted Buxton, the former scout who worked with Terry Venables. 'How's it going?' asked Buxton. 'I don't need all this,' said Keegan. 'If Terry wants it back, he can have it.' He wasn't joking.

A sensitive man who resented criticism, Keegan was an odd man out among England managers – he walked out before he was sacked. And not just with England but with his club management jobs too. It was seen as dereliction of duty but a minority had other views. They thought he acted quite reasonably to protect his wife Jean and their two daughters Laura and Sarah. If someone doesn't like his job any more, and the hassle goes with it, why should he have to carry on?

When Keegan resigned from his England post – after the 1-0 defeat by Germany on 7 October 2000 – a number of the 1966 World Cup winning heroes were present to pay homage at the last game ever played at Wembley. Jack Charlton was one and he said of Keegan, 'He's left us high and dry.' At the time the public conception of Keegan was that he walked away from trouble instead of confronting it. Charlton, of course, was a stout-hearted warrior who would never quit. But the truth is that, like Keegan, Charlton resigned from top managerial jobs in similar circumstances.

Charlton's last job in club management was at Newcastle and just before the start of the 1985/86 season he was booed by a 5,000 crowd in a friendly against Sheffield United. His response was to resign. He said to his assistant Willie McFaul, 'I don't fancy this one bit. I don't need it.' Charlton had quit as manager of Middlesbrough in 1977 and six years later had resigned from Sheffield Wednesday. Both Charlton and Keegan claim that they never applied for a footballing post nor were they ever sacked.

Charlton's departure from his job as manager of the Republic of Ireland in 1994 wasn't tantamount to being fired, but close to it. After a shameful 0-0 draw in Liechtenstein, Ireland lost 2-0 against Holland at Anfield in a European Championship play-off and Charlton was talking about resigning. He lingered for a month before the Irish FA told him that he would have to go. Obstinate up to the end, he finally bowed out.

Throughout his career, Joseph Kevin Keegan OBE was a paradoxical character. Only 5ft 8ins tall, he nonetheless seemed to tower over his colleagues in English football, setting an example to everyone, not just in England but in Germany where he played for Hamburg. Not a single player from the Home Nations could boast of being European Footballer of the Year as he was in 1978 and 1979 and Bundesliga Footballer of the Year in 1978. He had a big heart and knew what he wanted from life – to become the best footballer around. He wasn't blessed with natural talent but he worked prodigiously to turn himself into a great player. His sturdy frame made him stand out like a pocket Hercules. His long, permed hair, almost like one of the three musketeers, personified his cavalier approach. His passion for the game, backed up by an idyllically happy marriage, eventually carried him to the top.

When he retired as a player in 1984 at the age of thirty-three he had no thoughts of becoming a manager. Instead, he migrated to the south of Spain to play golf and enjoy life. He named his luxurious residence, looking over the seventh green of the Rio Real club, a few kilometres from Marbella, 'Seventh Heaven'. He avoided mixing with the villains of Marbella and Puerto Banus and one of his golfing friends was Don Revie, who was wasting away from motor neurone disease. He wrote in his autobiography, 'I watched him die. He was a smashing man, even nicer away from football and it was hard to watch someone who had been so fit and healthy fade away like he did.'

Keegan divorced himself from football but after seven years of apparent bliss, bringing his golf handicap down to five and making up valuable time with his family after being away so much with football, the attractions of sun and holes in one began to fade. A friend, Derek Pavis, a former chairman of Notts County said, 'Pure and simple, he wanted to become England's manager. To do that, he had to take a manager's job first and the one closest to his heart was Newcastle.'

In 1990 the Keegans moved back to their farmhouse in Hampshire, near Broadlands, the former home of Lord Mountbatten, and Kevin was often quoted in the press, on the radio and on television. The clamour for him to save Newcastle mounted and, two years later, without any senior coaching qualifications, he succeeded Ossie Ardiles at St James's Park. He kept the club in the Second Division and in his second season, following the formation of the Premiership and the renaming of the divisions, Newcastle won the Division One title by eight points to join the Premiership. There were many who felt he had the qualities to become England manager, including himself.

Graham Taylor was foundering and Sir John Hall, the Newcastle chairman, even suggested that Keegan could manage England on a part-time basis and still remain the manager of Newcastle. He told some of the FA councillors 'He could do it, you know.' Six years later, when he was manager of Fulham, Keegan was approached by the same people. He was the people's choice for England, said FA chairman Geoff Thompson, and he was signed up for four games at £50,000 a game.

The FA had had Keegan on their shortlist after Terry Venables resigned in 1996 but he had signed a ten-year contract at Newcastle and ruled himself out. One of the few English managers ever to have a ten-year contract was Bobby Robson when he was at Ipswich. Robson started coaching when he was a player at Fulham and by the time his playing days ended he had the FA full badge and was ready to go into management. Keegan hadn't coached anyone at that stage of his career. He never studied the game except through his own observations as a player and a television viewer. So why did the FA finally recruit a man without qualifications? Someone should have pointed that out to them.

It is now obligatory for a manager to have a UEFA licence before they can manage a Premiership club. It should also apply to England managers but for some reason the FA were reluctant to discuss, certain outstanding footballers, including Hoddle and Keegan, were exempt on the grounds of their footballing prowess. Sir Clive Woodward was on his way to qualifying for his UEFA licence when he joined Rupert Lowe's Southampton and he admitted in an interview with Matt Dickinson in *The Times* on 25 September 2005, 'The irony is that I never took a single rugby qualification and won the World Cup.'

As Woodward knows full well, technology has taken over. No longer is it possible for a successful manager to say to his players, 'Go out and enjoy it.' Analysts record every move of the players on their laptops and up to a dozen 'experts' prepare the way for the manager to make his final plans. Keegan was severely handicapped without the necessary training and that was why he failed. He once said, 'You don't need an FA coaching certificate to be manager of England. The best qualification I had is that I played at the top level from the age of twenty-one until I retired at thirty-three.' He was wrong. If you want to teach anyone, you have to learn to teach.

A Catholic sister played a big part in Keegan's development as a goalkeeper at his first school. Sister Mary Oliver was the headmistress of St Francis Xavier School at Balby Bridge, near Doncaster, and she doubled up as games teacher. 'She encouraged me in my football dreams,' said Keegan. 'The trouble was that I was Jack the Lad, the class idiot.' His father Joe, a miner who worked in pits in the North East before moving to Armthorpe, soon put him right. He fought as a Chindit sergeant in Burma in the Second World War and lived for seventy-one years despite severe bronchitis, silicosis and eventually cancer without receiving the full pension he should have deserved.

Although the Keegans – Doris and Joe, sons Kevin and Mike and daughter Mary – lived in poor circumstances in a terraced house in Doncaster, their famous son was born in Armthorpe in a house rented by Aunt Nellie, on St Valentine's Day, 1951. They were Catholics, but not devout. Joe liked a flutter and a drink and sometimes brought out the strap when the offspring misbehaved. Too small to put newspapers in a letter box, his older son switched to cleaning cars to provide some pocket money. He was far too small to remain a goalkeeper – he was 5ft nothing at fourteen and was told to play outside right instead.

Kevin Scott, one of his colleagues who played alongside him in the Mayor's Under-14 Cup, said, 'He was known as Shorty and in those days size seemed to be more important than your skills. But he's done brilliant in his career. I introduced him to chips and peas, I remember.' Another, John Sheridan, said, 'He just played for football. He was so small, the ball used to come up to his knees. I never thought he would play for England, and certainly not manage England.'

He loved running, particularly the mile and cross-country, and he also loved watching the races at Doncaster Racecourse, where he developed a love of horses. He first met Jean Woodhouse, later to be his wife, there when she was sixteen and he was nineteen. She was a bright, vivacious young lady who gained A Levels in Economics and German, which proved useful when they lived in Hamburg. She soon started to watch his games and never lost her enthusiasm for watching him in action. When he joined Liverpool, she wore red knickers at Anfield… to bring him luck.

His academic record was more modest, two O Level passes in art and history, before he left school to work as a cheeky tea boy and messenger at the Pegler's Brass Works for £6 a week. Pegler's senior football team turned him down. So did Jimmy Hill's Coventry and his hometown club Doncaster Rovers. He always had to prove himself and that continued throughout his life in football. At sixteen he made the breakthrough and was signed by Scunthorpe, a club which lacked every finery. In just under three seasons he played 120 matches. Eventually he overcame his fears about being too small and too frail after watching Derek Hempstead, a right-back 'who had the best physique I ever saw'; Hempstead showed how to run up and down the terraces carrying dumb bells. 'If you lift dumb bells in the gym, you get musclebound,' Keegan explained. 'But on the run, you don't.' So that was the explanation why he was so fit.

Several clubs watched him and Arsenal wanted to invite him on a close-season tour to assess him but the rules forbade it. Preston and Millwall made bids and Bob Paisley saw him at Tranmere without making a move. The 1970/71 season was nearing the end and Scunthorpe and Tranmere had staged cup ties on their grounds without a result and they tossed for the right to pick the venue for the third tie. Tranmere won and decided to play it at Goodison Park. 'That was my guardian angel bringing me more luck,' said Keegan. Because, unknown to him at the time, Bill Shankly was in the crowd. The week before the FA Cup final – in which Arsenal beat Liverpool 2-1 to win the double – the twenty-year-old Keegan was summoned to Anfield.

He always had a streak of independence in him and when the £33,000 deal was about to be concluded Shankly said, 'We're going to pay you £45 a week.' Keegan looked disappointed. 'What's wrong, son?' said the legendary manager. 'I was expecting more because I'm on £35,' he said. Ron Ashman, his club manager, looked shocked. 'What about £50?' said Shankly. Keegan smiled his acceptance. Shankly then promised him £100 every time he played in the first team as an incentive and, despite turning up late for his debut against Nottingham Forest, he was never dropped. In his five years with Liverpool he earned the same money as the big-name internationals.

Coincidences followed him everywhere. At Scunthorpe, when he moved into his digs at 37A Lilley Road he found that he had the room which Ray Clemence had previously occupied. The two men made their England debuts on the same day, and were dropped on the same day.

Keegan celebrated the goal scored on his televised England debut by ditching his battered Cortina and buying a Datsun 240Z costing £2,468. He revered Shankly, who, like his father, was the son of a coal miner. 'He told me I was going to play for England and I never doubted it,' he said. 'He had a great depth of understanding of his players and their excesses.'

That quality was severely tested in the 1974 Charity Shield match against Leeds at Wembley when Billy Bremner launched himself into a dangerous tackle which Keegan managed to jump over. He had already been incensed by Johnny Giles catching him with a worse tackle earlier and swung a punch. Bremner retaliated and the middleweight midfielders continued to punch at each other. When it was all over Keegan joked, 'It was down to my fighting spirit, or my Irish ancestry.'

Keegan had played cricket with the referee Bob Matthewson a week before, but Matthewson had no alternative but to show two red cards. As Keegan turned to go down the tunnel, he tore his shirt off and threw it to the ground. Behind him, Bremner did the same. Both bare-chested contestants were pictured in every newspaper in the land. Again, Keegan's guardian angel came up with a palliative after the players were banned for eleven matches and fined £500 apiece. The five weeks off enabled him to marry his childhood sweetheart in secrecy at St Peter in Chains Roman Catholic church in Doncaster on 23 September 1974. Only the two families were present. This Garboesque feature reappeared on numerous occasions after that, emphasising that he wouldn't be used by the media at the expense of his private life.

He learned a lot from Shankly and used it when he became a manager. He admired his passion for the game, his honesty, his humour, his compassion and his obvious love for his family. The two men shared the same qualities and they admired each other immensely, so much so that Keegan wanted Anfield renamed as the Shankly Stadium. Shankly said of him:

> He is like a whippet, like a weasel after rats, always biting and snapping at your legs. He reminds me of Denis Law when he was sixteen. He has everything: fantastic ability, two good feet, good in the air, is energetic and courageous and has the will to win. He's perfect in size, like a full fledged middleweight, the greatest fighter of them all.

Shankly, who had a playing career of 16 matches for Carlisle followed by 297 games for Preston between 1933 and 1949, winning the FA Cup in 1938 and gaining 5 caps for Scotland, managed Liverpool from 1959 until he suddenly retired at the age of sixty-one in 1974. The James Cagney-like Shankly wasn't a coach. His successor, Bob Paisley was the qualified coach and he was different in many ways, less passionate, less humorous and more serious-minded.

Keegan told a very funny story about Shankly's funeral in 1981, which brought the city of Liverpool to a standstill. Keegan was too small to be a pallbearer but was still invited to the modest Shankly home to view the coffin in the front room. The undertaker came in and explained that the handles of the coffin were made of plastic and that they shouldn't use them because they could break.

'Bill hated anything that was fake,' said Keegan, 'and here he was going to his final resting place with plastic handles. Big Ron Yeats waited for the undertaker to leave and, imitating his manager's gravelly voice, said, "Jesus Christ, a plastic job!" The pent up emotion poured out and were we streaming with tears of laughter.'

Under Paisley, Keegan quickly attained superstar status. The medals and the honours poured in and he was talked into taking part in the televised series called *Superstars*. Injured in a fall in a cycling race, he should have quit but his will to win kept him going and he eventually won the $2,000 prize. The next day he finished up on a drip in Northampton General Hospital. Harry Swales, his agent, brought in extra income as he moved towards millionaire status. Another of his mistakes was to have his hair permed like an Elton John wig. His nickname at the time was 'Andy McDaft' and he said, 'My flares were so wide that I couldn't see my shoes. And then there was that haircut!'

He made his international debut in 1972 under Alf Ramsey:

> …and in the year I was with him, I suppose he spoke no more than two or three dozen words to me. He was so posh, like a teacher from Eton rather

than a footballer from Dagenham. But I admired him for bettering himself. Wealth without education can be a dangerous thing: you only have to look at some of the lottery winners to see that.

Keegan was on the bench when England were put out by Poland, not long before Ramsey was sacked. Close to the end someone shouted, 'Kevin, get changed.' Keegan got up and Ray Clemence, eager to get his mate on, started pulling down his shorts, exposing his buttocks. Then there was another order: 'Not you, Kevin Hector.' The Derby forward was almost too late. He was on the field for just over a minute and almost scored. If Keegan had been out there, well, England's and Ramsey's destiny could have been much different.

Keegan welcomed Joe Mercer as caretaker manager in 1974. 'He was a delight,' he said. 'He wanted to give us a taste of how football was really meant to be, how enjoyable it could be.' Uncle Joe was loved by everyone. He always had a smile and was still smiling when he took the squad to Leipzig, Sofia and Belgrade for the close-season tour despite being racked by back pain. He often forgot players' names and when Duncan McKenzie turned up for the departure to Leipzig he thought he was an autograph hunter.

This casual approach rebounded against Mercer when the squad arrived at Belgrade Airport. There were no supporters on the flight and, with the England players dressed in assorted clothing rather than their England blazers, an over-authoritative policeman must have mistaken Keegan for a hooligan. Liverpool colleague Alec Lindsay was sitting on the baggage carousel, close to Keegan, as it started up, and suddenly the policeman lashed out at Keegan and started beating him up. More policemen ushered the shaken Keegan into a room and the beating started up again. An English journalist alerted Ted Croker, the FA secretary, who went into the room. Keegan's passport was on a table and Croker held it up to the man in charge to prove his identity. Keegan was released and the England players held a meeting and voted to go home. Mercer talked them out of it, saying, 'Our answer will be on the pitch. We'll stuff them!' Not quite. Keegan scored the equaliser in a 2-2 draw.

Mercer's seven-match assignment was followed by the arrival of Revie, who soon realised that most of the international players weren't used to his odd practices at Leeds. Keegan didn't mind carpet bowls but he hated the dossiers. Before the game in Belfast, the first visit there by an England side in four years, Revie suggested to him that he ought to have a few days off. Keegan had received a death threat but he insisted on turning out. 'I kept to the middle of the pitch and never stopped,' he said. Before the next match, against Wales at Wembley, Revie read out the names, omitting Keegan. Keegan was stunned. He expected an explanation but none came so at 6 p.m. he drove to his home in North Wales and took his phone off the hook. 'It was one of the worst mistakes I ever made,' he said. Revie rang later and explained he was resting him ahead of the match in Scotland three days later. It was another example of Keegan's pride being dented and him reacting impulsively. A few months later, in March 1976, Revie appointed him captain in place of the injured Gerry Francis, one of five captains Revie chose in his twenty-nine matches.

Keegan won a second championship medal the following season, and followed it up by scoring the winning goal in the UEFA Cup final, beating Bruges 4-3 on aggregate. He was now talking about moving abroad. John Smith, the laconic Liverpool chairman, did a deal with him – one more season from Keegan in exchange for releasing him for a set fee of £500,000. It was like doing a Tony Blair, naming his own departure date and his own terms. And it worked. Inspired by Keegan, Liverpool almost won the treble. They won the League title, lost 2-1 to Manchester in the FA Cup final and won the European Cup for the first time, beating Borussia Moenchengladbach 3-1 in Rome. Bertie Vogts, his marker in the Olympic Stadium, kept hold of his shirt so much during the game that Keegan said, 'You can have it after the game, not now!' Vogts joined in the Liverpool celebrations afterwards and the two men have been firm friends ever since. They finished up victims of witch hunts when they eventually lost their managerial jobs with England and Scotland respectively.

It needed guts to uproot to another country and start afresh in the best league in the world at that time, the Bundesliga, and Keegan made it work after a few false starts. There was no rush of bidders and only Hamburg came up with the £500,000 fee. Part of the agreement was that he should have a house in the outskirts so that the Keegans' pair of Old English sheepdogs Heidi and Oliver should have regular exercise. Instead, he was housed on the nineteenth floor of a city centre hotel, a worse scenario than the

Venables episode when Terry had to get rid of his outsize dog in Barcelona. Eventually Keegan bought a bungalow in a nearby village and soon spoke fluent German.

The arrival of Gunther Netzer as boss changed things for the better. The home fans soon relished Keegan's honesty on the field and at the end of his first season, he was voted European Footballer of the Year and West German Man of the Year. Interviewed by Ian Wooldridge, he said, 'Technically, I am probably the worst player to win the award. But kids don't need to be born footballers. If they work and work, they can get to the top.' Uwe Seeler, the great German striker who is still president of Hamburg, said of him, 'For me, Keegan is a little Volkswagen, running forever. He fights the ninety minutes with full speed and full heart. I never saw a player who was so professional.'

After escaping from being kicked by Johnny Giles and his Leeds colleagues, Keegan found that German football was much more robust than English football. Man markers left some nasty bruises on his anatomy. And after being smashed to the ground three times by Erhard Preuss, a Lubeck player, Keegan retaliated with a punch that Shankly would have loved. Preuss was knocked out and Keegan was sent off. He was fined and banned for three matches and part of the punishment was to return to Lubeck to apologise to the elders at the town hall, carrying a bouquet of flowers.

A hard-drinking Yugoslav, Branko Zebec, trained the players so hard that most of them were sick almost every day. It must have worked because in his second season Keegan helped Hamburg to win the championship and he was voted European Footballer of the Year for the second successive time, the first man to do it. By now he was a multi-millionaire and, like many rich people, he wanted more and more. Washington Diplomats offered him £250,000 for four months in the summer playing in the USA and he accepted, despite the risk of injury playing on artificial pitches. Luckily for him, Netzer discovered a rule that would bar him playing in the European Cup until the later stages so the deal collapsed. Johan Cruyff took the job instead.

Keegan's phenomenal record in Germany tailed off in his final season as Moenchengladbach finished runners-up to Bayern Munich in the Bundesliga and lost 1-0 to Nottingham Forest in the European Cup final. He had fallen out with Forest boss Brian Clough who said, 'Any

Englishman that plays football in another country to make money makes me vomit.' They appeared on television panels together in England and there was always frostiness between them. Keegan's final act was to make a record, 'Head Over Heels in Love', for which he was paid £20,000. He had many lucrative sponsorships and was just as enthusiastic about his promotional work as his football.

His next aim was to play in Italy after the drab port of Hamburg but Jean told him if he went he would be on his own. He bowed to her judgement. Late in 1980 Lawrie McMenemy, who had been appearing on television panels with him, rang supposedly to ask about a light fitting which he said was made in Hamburg. But he really wanted to find out whether Southampton had a chance of buying him. The fee, laid down by Keegan himself, was £500,000. The persuasive McMenemy kept quiet about the negotiations and on 11 February 1981 Keegan flew into Southampton Airport and was driven to the Potters Heron Hotel near Romsey. The club had arranged a press conference and most of the journalists thought it was about plans to build a new ground.

Twenty-odd media men were sitting, rather bored, when McMenemy appeared from behind a curtain and said, 'Gentlemen, this is our new signing, Kevin Keegan.' It was the shock of the season. A homely club with limited resources had nabbed the twice European Footballer of the Year. When Keegan kicked off at the start of the next season Southampton FC and the whole of Hampshire were transformed. The training on Fridays took place in the gym and players like Keegan, Alan Ball, Mick Channon (who now trains Keegan's racehorses), Charlie George and a fiery Steve Williams kicked, shoved and cursed for an hour or more like a footballing version of *Rollerball*. It was reminiscent of what happened at Tottenham Hotspur when Dave Mackay sorted out Terry Venables in what they called 'The College' at White Hart Lane.

Keegan had his first major injury when the Saints finished sixth, their highest position up to that point, and his fame brought him more problems when McMenemy talked him into taking part in an expensively sponsored friendly match in Casablanca. His hamstring strain was so sore that he decided to remain in his hotel room. McMenemy rang and said, 'There are 70,000 here and they won't start until you play. It could be a riot.' So he had to go, and limped around, further damaging his leg.

In his second season he was soon disillusioned when he realised that Southampton would never compete with the richer clubs. He fell out with McMenemy and in his book he claims that the manager had called him a cheat. The two wives, Jean and Anne, remained friends and, over a period time, the menfolk made it up but when he left, to join Second Division Newcastle in another secret deal, for a set fee of £100,000, there was still a lot of bitterness remaining. The light fitting, made in Hamburg, is still working in McMenemy's home in Braishfield, Hampshire.

Keegan's arrival at Newcastle outstripped his welcome at Southampton by some distance. Hysteria took over. He was greeted as the people's hero, a grandson of a North East mining hero who saved dozens of lives in a local mining disaster, who would save Newcastle from relegation from the Second Division – which he did. Keegan told the local reporters, 'The passion in the North East is similar to Liverpool.' The difference was that Newcastle hadn't won trophies for decades whereas Liverpool monopolised them. Newcastle were almost broke and Keegan negotiated his own terms, once again showing his business acumen and independence. He asked Stan Seymour, the Newcastle chairman, to pay him fifteen per cent of the increase in gate receipts, which couldn't cost him anything. Seymour thought it was a good idea, and the attendance bonus also applied to away matches. As the talks were about to conclude a light bulb above his head came on. He saw it as an omen.

Swept along by the Toon hysteria, attendances at St James's Park rose to an average of 24,000, 7,000 more than in 1981/82. He was embarrassed by the new wealth rolling into his bank account – but he earned it with his sweat, as well as through his name. The ground was sold out for his debut match and he scored in a famous victory over Queens Park Rangers. Bobby Robson had just taken over as England manager and was sitting in the stand. Keegan himself admitted that he hadn't had an outstanding game. Without speaking to him, Robson made his mind up not to pick him for England. Keegan was furious and his resentment and anger lasted a long, long time. 'He dropped me like a hot stone,' he said. In the same year the Queen presented him with the OBE.

Keegan was frustrated by the poor standard of most of his teammates and after they lost 4-1 against Fulham he seized the inoffensive Kenny Wharton by the throat when he said he had enjoyed the game. Arthur Cox, the manager, had to break them up. In the second season, with Peter

Beardsley and Chris Waddle emerging into influential players, Newcastle won promotion, but an incident in the 4-0 defeat at Liverpool in the third round of the FA Cup made Keegan suddenly decide to retire. He knocked the ball past Mark Lawrenson, expecting to go on to shoot, but Lawrenson caught him up and took the ball off him. It was time to go and, with a theatrical flourish, he announced the news on St Valentine's Day, 1984, his thirty-third birthday. His racing friend Mick Channon, who had been on loan at Newcastle, said, 'The trouble with Kev is that he dreaded going downhill as a player. He wanted to go at the top and he certainly did. Once he has decided to do something, he is very single-minded and goes ahead with it.'

He played his last competitive game against Brighton, the FA Cup finalists of the previous season, and scored. The club hired a helicopter to land on the pitch to whisk him away to a party at the Gosforth Park Hotel, the hotel he stayed at for much of his time at Newcastle. As the chopper lifted away he dropped his number 7 shirt on the centre circle. More than 1 million people watched Newcastle's home matches that season and it made him a very rich man. In the pay league, he was ten years ahead of his time.

He had plenty of time to enjoy his wealth when he quit the country to make a new life in Spain. But the longer he stayed away, the more he missed his real desired vocation, leading a major English club and, ultimately, the national side to success. Towards the end of his seven years abroad the family agreed to return to their other home in Hampshire. Almost the same stature as Napoleon Bonaparte, his self-imposed exile was longer than the Emperor's in Elba but the sequel, for him personally, was bloodier. In April 1991 Jean and their daughters had flown home earlier and he was setting off on his last drive back to England in his Range Rover. Except for a short break in a roadside rest, he drove the 1,600-mile journey without sleep. Back on English soil, he was driving along the M25 on a bright spring evening when he nodded off and was wakened by hooting from a driver behind. Less than fifty miles remained of his journey but he took the sensible course and took the next exit, signposted Reigate, and parked up in a quiet lane. He was soon asleep, his head resting on a pillow against the driver's window.

Suddenly and brutally he was woken by the sound of a lump of concrete smashing through the window. A young man began beating him around his head with a baseball bat and when he tried to get out of the vehicle, he shoved the bat into his mouth, causing serious facial injuries. There were four men and Keegan asked one of them, 'What do you want?' 'Money,' said the first man. Keegan pulled out his credit cards and cash, mainly pesetas and francs, and handed them over. It turned out that they were drug takers and drug runners, from Newhaven. One was eighteen and he was the one who wielded the offensive weapon. After the men ran off, Keegan discovered that his tyres had been slashed and he stood by the side of the nearby road trying to wave to a friendly driver. It took some time to find one. Keegan had had a lucky escape. He needed only eight stitches and his bones and teeth were unharmed.

One of the criminals turned Queen's Evidence and the other three were sentenced to a lenient sentence of four years apiece. The Recorder who heard the case, Edward Southwell, said, 'It was a disgraceful use of criminal violence against a defenceless individual.' Because the incident happened in a lovers' lane, malicious, totally untrue rumours were aired in the press. One implied that Keegan was homosexual. His injuries healed quickly and he was soon settled in a contented routine, rising at six o'clock to muck out at the family's stables, involving himself in PR and promotional activities, speaking at dinners and appearing on Sky as an analyst.

Early in 1992 his friend Andrew Wilson from Scottish and Newcastle Breweries asked whether he was interested in becoming the manager of his old club. Second from bottom with debts of around £7 million and a struggling young side, Newcastle were in a dire position. Ossie Ardiles, the manager, was on the way out and the directors offered Keegan £60,000 from February to the end of the season, plus a bonus of £60,000 if he kept the club in the Second Division. He was keen and Jean's comment of 'You'll take it' clinched it.

His first move at Newcastle was to order the fumigation and painting of the dressing rooms and gym to cheer up the players and staff. It was good thinking. Within a month he decided to resign, insisting that the club's chief backer and chairman, Sir John Hall, hadn't kept his promises to him. Sir John soon calmed him down and agreement was soon reached about the amount of money available for players. Newcastle stayed up with a winning goal against Leicester in the last minute of the last game of the 1991/92 season.

Toon power swept Keegan's side to the Premiership the following season, finishing as champions, eight points ahead of second-placed West Ham, with 92 goals and an average attendance of almost 30,000, a thirty-seven per cent increase on the previous season. Keegan was an outstanding motivator, rousing his players to new heights. Over his career he read countless books about motivation, positive thinking and management skills, including the works of American football coach Vince Lombardi. He underscored points and used them in his team talks and lectures.

The early home games saw thousands of fans locked out and the police insisted on all-ticket matches in future. Keegan was on a three-year contract paying £125,000 a year and Sir John Hall, who had a new stand named after him, turned it into a ten-year one. Keegan was the first manager to talk about crooked agents who offered bungs. 'I didn't realise it was so rife,' he said. 'It stank.' Sadly, it still goes on despite FIFA's regulation that no agent can operate until he puts up a £100,000 bond.

He preached all-out attack to his players and was happy to concede goals as long as his side scored one more than the opposition. Newcastle finished sixth in the 1994/95 season and in the next two seasons it was a two-team battle with Manchester United for the title, with Newcastle finishing second on both occasions. Few complained about his tactics or his managerial qualities at that time, yet after he was with England he was branded as an abysmal tactician. He is better known for his public row with Alex Ferguson in the 1995/96 season than for his prowess as a manager. At the time Newcastle held a twelve-point lead and the frenzy mounted.

Ferguson wanted to destabilise Newcastle, and asked Howard Wilkinson, in his final year as manager at Leeds, to 'have a pop' at his players in an attempt to win the fixture against Keegan's side. According to Ferguson's book, Wilkinson agreed. In an interview after United's match against Leeds, Ferguson said that Wilkinson's team tried harder against Manchester United with ten men after their goalkeeper was sent off than they had done against most teams that season, and that he hoped they would show the same will to win in their remaining matches. A more rational man might have ignored Ferguson's psychological ploy but Keegan exploded in a television interview, earning critical stories in the newspapers. 'I would love it if we beat them [Manchester United],' he said. 'Love it!' What it showed was that Keegan was rattled, whereas Ferguson was in control. A more pointed observation made by Keegan concerned the way Sky seemed to schedule their televised matches to suit Manchester and not Newcastle, who were often told to play on Mondays and Wednesdays. For a while, he refused to be interviewed by Sky.

In the 1996/97 season the frantic pace was being switched to fast forward with the tension frothing along, especially with the manager. His mobile phone was ringing all day and there was little peace for him. The directors made him another offer, £1 million a year for two years plus £100,000 to win the Premiership. He already had an agreement to pick up £1 million if and when the club floated on the Stock Exchange. He was quick at mental arithmetic and knew how to handle these negotiations. The record signing of Alan Shearer from Blackburn for £15 million only increased the pressure. Everyone involved with the club was expecting instant success. There were daily press conferences and later he admitted that one was of his biggest mistakes. He was overexposed and when he realised his error he insisted on having a full-time press officer working on the football side. He was one of the more honest managers but with some matters, like buying and selling players, managers sometimes tell lies and he was no exception. When he sold Andy Cole, upsetting the fans, he came out onto the steps outside of the main stand to explain why he did it. Not many managers would have done that.

The Newcastle empire grew too fast and Keegan sometimes spoke of resigning control of the team after his five years in charge. He wanted to resign after the single-goal defeat at Blackburn on Boxing Day 1996. He was upset about the lack of effort from some of his players and he wasn't enjoying his work. The flotation had gone through and there was more pressure on the directors. The bank had loaned the club £6 million to complete the Shearer purchase – the £15 million was paid up front – and they wanted their money back by Christmas. Keegan felt he was isolated. Sir John Hall wasn't available to talk to him and someone on the board leaked a story to the *Sunday Mirror* saying that he was ready to resign.

On 7 January the directors presented Keegan with a new two-year contract and he refused to go beyond the end of the season. He had to go. It was a dreadful end to a comparatively happy but extremely fraught story. His salary was paid up to that day and the only gesture they made was to let him have his car and mobile phone until the money was finally received.

Most managers in these circumstances – Bobby Robson included – do not receive their settlement money for some time. Keegan was living in the luxurious Wynyard estate, 300 yards from Hall's mansion. It was the twelfth house move since the Keegans were married in 1974. The former chairman and his former manager didn't exchange words over the crisis until a few weeks later when Keegan rang Hall in his home in Spain, who said rather sheepishly, 'We'll have dinner when I get back.' They never did.

The club wanted to make the news public immediately but Keegan, still partly in charge of events, insisted on an 11 p.m. announcement. It left time for him to take his family to Heathrow for a planned flight to Florida, enabling them to escape before the press arrived outside his barred gate. His plan to fly off was thwarted because there were no seats for four sitting together. Undaunted, he jumped into his vehicle and drove through the Channel Tunnel to take a flight from Paris. The holiday in Florida was one of the best of their lives.

One of his ventures when he was out of work was Soccer Circus, a travelling footballing tuitional for children all over the country. A few months after he quit Newcastle, Mohamed Al Fayed, the man the Government have hitherto denied a British passport despite him helping bring in billions of pounds in tax from his ownership of Harrods, asked to see him about the concept. 'I was immediately impressed by him,' said Keegan. At a second meeting, one of Al Fayed's staff asked if him if he was interested in managing Fulham Football Club, owned by the hard-swearing Egyptian multi-millionaire. He said no but, told that he could combine Soccer Circus with overseeing Fulham, he changed his mind. Mark Griffiths, Al Fayed's lawyer, flew in a helicopter to Wynyard, where Keegan was still living, and they agreed a deal worth around £500,000 a year plus a five per cent stake in Fulham Leisure Ltd, the parent company. Micky Adams, the manager who had just brought Fulham into Division Two, was on his way out and Ray Wilkins was appointed team manager with Keegan the chief operations officer. Al Fayed's aim was to take Fulham into the Premiership in five years and he succeeded in 2000/01, not under Keegan but the French coach Jean Tigana, who watched matches chewing toothpicks instead of the traditional chewing gum of the English managers. By this time Fulham were able to afford an £11 million player and found themselves in High Court actions over how the money was paid.

Keegan spent four frantic days each week in London and organised a host of changes in his brief reign, mainly successful ones. He lived in a flat in Knightsbridge, within walking distance of Harrod's. When he arrived on 25 September 1997, Fulham were seventh from bottom in Division Two. At the end of the season they finished sixth. Alan Smith, the club's director of youth, said:

> No one could fault him for effort. He was a real bustler. He arrived at 8 a.m. and got stuck into his work and was often still there at eight o'clock at night. He was always putting an arm round you, praising you and that was the first time I've been treated like that in a football club. He made me feel ten feet tall. It was quite refreshing.
>
> Ray Wilkins told me, 'Don't try to outdo him and put him in your shadow. He can be careful with his money and is a bit wary of Southerners.' I found him a warm and supportive man and he raised a small club to new heights. As for his coaching, he was the most enthusiastic coach I've encountered. He charged around as though he was still playing, at 110mph. He'd rush in for a quick shower afterwards and be back in his office working away ten minutes later. Others would take half an hour.

Keegan still wasn't qualified as a coach but that was not seen as a handicap. Smith said:

> He was different to Bobby Robson. Bobby was the last of the great English coaches who spent a tremendous amount of time taking coaching courses around the country. No one put as much back into the game as him. He wasn't on huge money at the FA and you couldn't see Eriksson doing any coaching like the way Bobby did.

Wilkins fell out with Keegan the following season when Fulham finished champions. 'I think Mohamed Al Fayed wanted extroverts,' explained Smith. 'He liked being in the company of celebrities. Once he had Michael Jackson at the club as a guest and I'm sure Michael Jackson didn't know much about football.' Keegan took over as manager but was still known as the chief operations officer. Glenn Hoddle was fending off the critics in another part of London and when David Davies called him 'Mr Hoddle' in a press conference everyone knew the FA were headhunting again for a new England manager. Hoddle soon departed and Howard Wilkinson's one match as caretaker failed to impress either his bosses or the media assessors.

The same FA top brass – they usually hold on to their jobs much longer than England managers – were scouring the world for candidates and several, including Doug Ellis and Robert Chase, backed Keegan. Graham Kelly, the secretary of the FA, said:

> We were very impressed with Kevin when he took temporary charge of the Under-21s in 1994 when Dave Sexton was not available. He also worked for us at the annual all-Party Parliamentary dinner where his speech was warmly received by members of both Houses of Parliament.
>
> Tactically, at the highest level, Keegan still has to prove himself, but his enthusiasm is one of his greatest assets. In the pressure cooker world of the England job, that emotional aspect to his make up may prove to be his Achilles heel. Time will tell.

Kelly was absolutely right. Some of the London-based players turned up late for the flight from Heathrow to Vienna for the UEFA Under-21 Championship qualifier against Austria, and the next morning Keegan told them that any repeat would prematurely end their careers – it was reminiscent of Alf Ramsey, who once left the passports of some of his errant World Cup players on their pillows as a warning.

Early in 1999 Keegan firmly denied that he wanted the England job. 'I am happy at Fulham,' he said. By February, the FA's five-man international committee had approached Arsène Wenger but the Arsenal manager said, 'I believe the national coach should be British, not a Frenchman.' Now they sounded the clarion call for Keegan to succeed Hoddle and he changed his mind with rare speed and alacrity. However, he was reluctant to commit himself to a full-time post. He didn't want let Fulham down so he suggested a four-match appointment at £50,000 a match. After a two-hour meeting – most football meetings last two hours because the delegates want to catch their trains home before the rush hour – the FA accepted his terms. 'He's the best man for the job and I'm delighted to see a way of him managing his country,' said Geoff Thompson. Arsène Wenger was sceptical:

It could be done in the short term but in the longer term it is not possible. Maybe they can do it in Russia or the Ukraine where you have one team which is effectively the national team. Maybe if all the national players played at Fulham that would be all right. Maybe Mr Fayed can buy the whole England team and have them play for Fulham.

The late Emlyn Hughes said, 'He's always been a cracking lad, very genuine. Knowing Kevin, he won't stand for people telling him what to do. He can handle the media, no problem.' Terry Venables and Bobby Robson were enthusiastic about the new man but Robson warned, 'He will have to be careful about his temperament. The job will be one of great pressure and there will be inevitable flashpoints when he will have to control his emotions.'

In his first press conference a smiling Keegan promised that the national anthem would be sung at the highest possible volume, boosted by amplifiers, at the England *v.* Poland European Championship qualifier at Wembley, to rouse national fervour. It was, with some of the England players actually singing the words. But his other promise, that he would return to Fulham after his fourth match in charge, was never kept. In front of a passionate crowd of 73,836, Paul Scholes scored a hat-trick, his first and last in international football, in a 3-1 success. Chants of 'Keegan, Keegan' rang out. The footballing public loved it.

Within days the whirlwind romance between Keegan and England became a full-blown affair, as Henry Winter wrote so expressively. In an effort to win esteem throughout the land, and particularly in the Home Office, Mohamed Al Fayed said:

I am considering releasing Kevin. Kevin is my gift to the nation. If the nation wants Kevin, the ordinary person wants Kevin, the FA want Kevin, then I will give him to England. The nation comes first – the glory of the country That is a sacrifice we will make at Fulham.

Keegan responded, saying:

Mr Fayed has been very good to me. I still have to finish what I have at Fulham, not because I've got a contract or the money or because I've got five per cent of the club but because I like the man and he trusted me with something at a time when I lost a bit of faith in people in football.

There might be a solution somewhere but I am not going to look for that yet. Who knows in the future? I want to hand over to somebody else, whether it's Bobby Robson, Bryan Robson or whoever the FA decide is the right guy. Whoever it is, I would like to come and work with the forwards.

A month later, Keegan tried five new players in the 1-1 draw against Hungary in a friendly. Keegan said, 'It's time to stop playing games. I want the job.' Alf Ramsey died on 28 April to remind the footballing public that we did have a great World Cup-winning manager once. The FA talked terms with Keegan and on 13 April the deal was announced, a £3 million contract over three years. Paul Bracewell, one of Keegan's proteges, was appointed Fulham's new manager while Ray Wilkins confirmed that he was suing Al Fayed for unfair dismissal.

Scandinavia has been a deathbed for English football and Keegan's second European Championship qualifier, against Sweden in Group 5 on 5 June must have put him in danger of cardiac arrest. Sweden had just won in Poland to lead the group and a 0-0 draw at Wembley was acutely depressing. The headlines screamed, 'The honeymoon is over after the first kiss!' Four days later the downward spiral continued – Bulgaria 1, England 1 in a drab match left England with the task of beating Luxembourg and Poland in the final matches to make the play-offs. The part-timers of Luxembourg were despatched 6-0, with Alan Shearer scoring a hat-trick, but the visit to Poland yielded another dismal 0-0 draw when David Batty was sent off. Later it was revealed that Batty had had a heart condition for the past year and needed tablets.

The pressure was intensified on Keegan but few critics admitted that they had got it wrong. England's fate lay with the Swedes and when they beat Poland 2-0 in Stockholm, a relieved Keegan said, 'A thousands thanks to the Swedes!' England faced a two-leg play-off against their old foes Scotland. The first was a physical game at Hampden Park which England easily won 2-0 with Scholes scoring both goals. His tally of 9 goals in 19 games was impressive but he was booked for overreacting in celebrating his second goal. Ten players were cautioned, five from each side. Four days later, it was the turn of the Scots, who won the second leg through a goal from Don Hutchison, but it was England who qualified.

In the Euro 2000 draw Keegan expressed astonishment that Germany were in England's group in Holland and Belgium and less astonishment to discover that two familiar opponents, Portugal and Romania were included. Four friendlies were arranged and none of them gave England's supporters any encouragement. The 0-0 against Argentina on the day Sir Stanley Matthews died at the age of eighty-five and the 1-1 against Brazil, both at Wembley, were played at half pace. A limp 2-0 win over Ukraine followed and a flaccid 2-1 victory in dusty Malta completed the unsatisfactory build-up. Keegan said in Valletta, 'If we play like that in Euro 2000 we'll be out on our necks.' He couldn't be accused of telling fibs.

The departure of the squad to the Low Countries was accompanied by the muted sounding of the drums. The support troops, football's version of the Barmy Army, had little confidence in the general in charge. Some of them had little respect for David Beckham as well. Things went well for a time in the opening match against Portugal in the mind-deadening town of Eindhoven, in the south of Holland. Scholes and Steve McManaman scored from crosses from Beckham but, as Keegan said, 'The players got carried away with the euphoric atmosphere and went looking for the third goal. You'll probably say that's typical Kevin Keegan. I am not against that. But I felt we should have steadied ourselves.' Some observers saw it as a worrying sign that he kept talking about himself as 'Kevin Keegan' and not 'me' or 'I'. Inspired by Luis Figo and Rui Costa, Portugal came back, outnumbering England in midfield, and at 2-2 Keegan replaced the injured Michael Owen with the less mobile Emile Heskey. At the end, as the Portuguese celebrated their 3-2 victory, Beckham was suddenly, and cruelly, abused by half-a-dozen louts as he came off.

Victoria and her father were sitting in the crowd and before and after the match they were abused and jostled. Beckham had kept looking at them while the game was on, worrying about them. This time he was victim. He said in his book *My Side*:

They had a go about me, then Victoria and then, the most horrible thing, they shouted this stuff about Brooklyn. They were wearing the England replica shirts with the St George's cross. It still makes me feel sick to my stomach thinking about what they were saying. I was so angry but I bit my lip. I just stuck up my middle finger towards them and headed straight to the changing room.

Keegan came off a yard or two behind and he said, 'I heard it and I was ashamed. I just couldn't believe it. This was his best performance for England and what happened afterwards was totally unacceptable.'

The pictures of Beckham's rude gesture featured in many of the newspapers and some writers said he might face an inquiry by UEFA, the organisers. Within hours UEFA ruled it out. Losing their first game was a disaster and Keegan followed up with an own goal when he decided not to conduct the usual press conference the next morning, instead giving the task to Les Reed, a well respected and friendly forty-seven-year-old coach who worked for nine years under FA director of football Charles Hughes. 'It turned out to be a turkey shoot,' said the *Mail's* Martin Lipton. Reed was sacked by the FA later and sued them for unfair dismissal, a case which dragged on for years, leaving him in limbo.

The squad and its vast retinue moved on to Charleroi in Belgium and the odds of England beating Germany were rising by the day. But the Beckham factor proved a big asset: all the players were right behind him and he wanted to put on a show. In the fifty-third minute of what Beckham called 'an absolutely terrible game of football', he was about to line up a free-kick two yards inside Germany's half when the combative Gary Neville told his Manchester United colleague, 'Take a quick one!' Beckham, wanting a more deliberate approach, said, 'Gary, go away.' Like Johnny Wilkinson, he curled his kick just right for Alan Shearer to head in the only goal. Uproarious celebrations broke out in England's half of the stadium and out in the middle as the players hugged each other, only for Gary Neville to say, 'We haven't done anything yet. We haven't even qualified yet.' Keegan showed his usual enthusiasm. 'Fantastic,' he said. 'We waited a long time for this. I was only a kid the last time we beat them, I was just twelve.'

Three days later they were back at the same ground to face an ordinary Romanian side, expecting the nation to rejoice again. But it was like winding back the tape on the Portugal match – England, employing the 4-4-2 formation that had proved ineffective against the Portuguese, were 2-1 up, only to lose 3-2 and go out of the competition. 'The minutes in the dressing room afterwards was like a blur,' said Beckham. 'We felt crushed, like the fans, to be going back home.' Phil Neville conceded a rash penalty in the eighty-ninth minute, bringing down Coventry striker Viorel Moldovan, and that was it. A damning statistic was that England mustered only eight goal attempts to Romania's twenty-four.

Keegan's honesty shone through as he told the media throng, 'This is no hard luck story. We weren't good enough. I can't say the penalty cost us our place in the quarter-final. We just didn't get back to our peak. We squandered possession too easily and I take the responsibility.' In the inquest that followed, FA chairman Geoff Thompson raised the subject of 'giving Kevin some help'. Howard Wilkinson was still in a position of power at the FA, as the technical director and also manager of the Under-21 set-up, but Keegan wouldn't have wanted him as a helper. Some journalists recommended Don Howe and that idea was ignored too. Keegan already had plenty of assistance from his staff: Arthur Cox, an experienced manager, Derek Fazackley, an experienced coach and Peter Beardsley, a novice coach. Thompson's suggestion, well supported by most people, had merit but it could be seen as a vote of no confidence in Keegan.

Privately, Keegan was saying, 'It's not worth the hassle' but he carried on. As one international tournament ends, another starts and ten weeks later Keegan was back at the tiller picking a side to take on France in Paris in a friendly before England's first qualifying game for the 2002 World Cup. Michael Owen came on in the seventy-ninth minute and scored in the eighty-sixth to score the equaliser in a creditable 1-1 draw. He was one of four substitutes.

Eleven days before the World Cup qualifier, against Germany at Wembley on 7 October 2000, Keegan's mother Doris died at the age of seventy-six. He was very close to her and took it very badly. A friend said, 'That, and the constant pressure, has got to him.'

The match had particular significance: it was the last game to be played at Wembley before the Empire Stadium, opened in 1923, was demolished. The players were edgy, the old ground was almost full and history was bearing down on skipper Tony Adams and his men. Beckham thought the match was 'awful, as frustrating as I've ever played in.' Dietmar Hamann scored the only goal from a free-kick which squirmed under David Seaman and the Germans spent the rest of the seventy-six minutes holding on. The rain was pouring down and the mood changed to anger as England flailed away in vain. When the referee brought it to an end boos rang out. Beckham, substituted near the end, walked down the touchline to the dressing rooms for the last time, a few yards ahead of Keegan. The insults were hurtful and the England manager was deeply offended. The people's choice was now the people's Aunt Sally.

Back in the dressing room the players were having their drinks and none of them had started changing. *Private Eye* coined the phrase 'ashen-faced Ron Knee' many years ago as a joke. Now that expression fitted Keegan perfectly. He stood in the middle of the room and began saying, 'Lads, I have to be honest with you and honest with myself. I've gone as far as I can with this. I'm calling it a day. You've got good times ahead of you. You're very good players.' Arthur Cox, his number two, a man of few words, said, 'No, Kevin. Don't do this.' Players joined in with heartfelt pleas. Beckham said, 'We want you to stay.' Keegan refused to budge. He passed on a message to Adam Crozier, the diminutive and breezy secretary of the FA, asking him to come down. Normally the England manager goes to the press interview room up some stairs on the right, to conduct interviews in a packed room. The reporters were becoming fidgety, then agitated. 'He will be there soon,' said an official. 'He's had to sort something out.'

Crozier arrived, looking bemused. The two men went out of the dressing room into a toilet area to speak without being heard by the players. Five days later England faced another game, in Finland. 'Stay on for that one and we can talk again,' said Crozier. Geoff Thompson and David Davies joined the talks and neither of them could talk him round. Afterwards Crozier said:

> I tried everything but he wouldn't alter his mind. The timing wasn't ideal. It was a huge disappointment because the whole of the nation wanted it to succeed with Kevin. I thought Kevin felt things were not going right for him. He said he couldn't get as much out of the players as he would have liked. As soon as the game was over the reaction of the crowd pushed him further down the line.
>
> He was an inspirational coach at Newcastle and Fulham and gave it everything he had. I think the whole country wanted it to work. Everyone was willing it to work. Kevin is a very proud man. With the benefit of hindsight, it might have been better had he gone after Euro 2000 to give his successor time to settle before the World Cup qualifiers but at that stage he felt he still had more to offer.

Keegan gave one television interview before departing. He looked surprisingly calm. He said:

> I just feel I have given my best shot. I didn't want to outstay my welcome. The fans made me realise that not only did they put me in the job, but, by what they were saying when we were coming off, they wanted me out of it. I was just not up there for the job. I feel I am a little bit short at this level. Absolutely no one is to blame but myself. I did it to the best of my ability. The timing isn't great but I hoped a much better man would lead England to future triumphs.

His honesty was praiseworthy but many people thought he should have stuck it out a bit longer. If the mob can change leaders as easily as this, democracy would never survive.

Alan Shearer, who had just retired, said, 'I was amazed. He must be very hurt. The players have to take responsibility and I am among that group, because we haven't done as well and they should.' Lawrie McMenemy, back as a friend, said, 'He will be hard to replace.' Sacked Tory Minister David Mellor, said, 'He should never have been given the job. He did it badly and he walked away in the most shameful manner possible.'

Keegan went back to his family, his horses and his other, more pleasant activities, and three months later he was back in the news, in the High Court. The *News of the World* had carried a story about him supposedly acting as a bookie on betting nights among the players during the Euro 2000 campaign. They alleged his actions caused bitter rifts between the players who gambled thousands of pounds on videoed horse races. The article claimed, 'Our in-depth investigation into the England soccer gambling scandal blows away the squeaky-clean responsible image Kevin Keegan liked to present as team boss.' Keegan has spent many hours playing card games in his life but to suggest he was the organiser of a gambling syndicate, embarrassing some of his players with immense debts, was ludicrous. Rebekah Wade, editor of the newspaper, had to apologise for the stress caused to Keegan and News Group Newspapers, the company which has caused much strife to England's managers over the years, paid him £150,000 damages and paid his costs, around £30,000. In view of the seriousness of the allegations against a man with an impeccable reputation, the payment was on the low side. Keegan, with his hair almost grey after his experiences since returning from Spain, was interviewed outside the High Court in The Strand and said, 'These allegations have hung over me but I want to thank Adam Crozier for standing by me during this difficult time.'

After the Germany disaster, Howard Wilkinson resumed for a second, brief stint as caretaker manager and if the team had won in Helsinki he may have had a slim chance of succeeding Keegan. But the match finished 0-0 and he had no chance. Peter Taylor, the Under-21 manager, was appointed caretaker for the next game, a friendly against Italy in Turin. His first task was to ring David Beckham at 8 a.m. and say, 'I want you to be our captain.' Beckham had only been captain once before, in a Manchester United youth team game in Northern Ireland. Beckham was overjoyed and he thought it was the greatest thing that had happened in his career up to then. In another bold move, the forty-seven-year-old Taylor brought in some younger players. The side played with flair and, though a strong Italian side won 1-0, it left a good impression with the FA officials who accompanied the team.

Watching the game from the stands was Sven-Goran Eriksson, currently in charge of Lazio, and he came into the dressing room to speak to the players. The FA's five-man committee had earmarked Taylor as a number two behind a big-name England coach, yet to be appointed. These days he is still on the fringe. When he was manager of Southend, his birthplace, between 1993 and 1995 he was reckoned to be suffering from stress. But in recent years he has gained an enviable reputation as a coach. A popular figure, he could well reappear in the senior England set-up again. The FA now had Eriksson in their sights. He spoke English fluently and his record around Europe was impressive.

Keegan's love for the game was unabated and seven months after he walked away from Wembley for the last time he was offered a job as manager of Manchester City and he jumped at it. His five-year contract, worth £6 million, failed to last the distance. He quit at the end of the 2004/05 season after taking City back up to the Premiership in his first, exciting season when 108 goals were scored at a rate of 2.8 a game, then enduring three seasons of struggling against mounting debt, coaching a side that could muster only 1.3 goals a game.

The previous manager Joe Royle had brought City up from Division Two in the 1998/99 season via the play-offs and in his second season had taken them up to the Premiership. Not a bad record, one would think, but financial problems engulfed the yo-yo club of the North West the following season and they were relegated. Royle was dismissed and he won damages for unfair dismissal, only to be forced to repay most of the cash back to the club on appeal. In the days after his departure, he spent an agonising period defending allegations that he took his players out on drinking binges. There were several outings to pubs but to call them binges was a huge exaggeration.

When Bobby Robson's contract with the FA lapsed in 1990, Royle was on the shortlist of four to be interviewed and, according to Bill Fox, the former president of the Football League, he would have got it. However, as Royle wrote in his autobiography:

> I didn't turn up. I have a healthy regard for the preservation of my and my family's privacy and freedom from ridicule and abuse. For, as men like Don Revie, Bobby Robson, Graham Taylor, Kevin Keegan and Sven-Goran Eriksson have discovered, the media put the national team boss in a goldfish bowl – and then throw in the piranhas.

Royle's twenty years in management taught him that coaching certificates don't make you a good manager. As Lawrie McMenemy said, 'All managers can coach, but very few coaches can manage.' Personality means as much as knowledge of tactics. The ideal CV should contain many aspects, including personality, ability to lead and impart confidence to players and teach them how to become better team players. Keegan still had the passion and motivational skills and, when he left, supposedly by 'mutual consent' at the end of the 2004/05 season, some of his players complained that his training methods were inadequate and that he failed to appreciate the value of modern tactics. David James, not the man best qualified to criticise, spoke out against Keegan, saying:

> There was a lack of specifics about goal setting. The gaffer didn't seem as happy-go-lucky as I remember from working with him at England. We looked on him as a fun guy but the job seemed to have become a strain for him. Some players were unhappy with aspects of training and I was one of them.

Stuart Pearce took over and he had the coaching qualifications. With his passion and discipline, he is now another fringe candidate for the England job. Keegan has had plenty of comebacks but his assistant at Newcastle, Terry McDermott, said, 'I think this is the end for him in management. He's moved back to Hampshire and I don't think he will be back in football.' We shall see.

SVEN-GORAN ERIKSSON

2001-2005

*The Swede Who Finally
Fell Off the Tightrope*

P 58	W 33	D 15	L 10	57%

Up to 2006 World Cup qualification

Known as 'Svennis' to his relatives and close friends, Sven-Goran Eriksson was criticised from the moment the FA appointed him as the first foreigner to become England's head coach, a title which the FA preferred to 'manager'. And the criticism kept up throughout his stay, reaching a crescendo in the high summer of 2004 when 'Fariagate' erupted and eventually his five-year reign ended eighteen months later when he was toppled from his tightrope by the 'fake sheikh', the *News of the World*'s investigations editor Mazher Mahmood, in Dubai, ironically the place where Don Revie fell on his sword. Eriksson's indiscreet comments about the crookedness of certain Premiership managers, and about some of his players – all based on fact and well known in the game – finally brought him down. The FA had reprieved him over the way he courted Manchester United and Chelsea while he was under contract. They excused him over the Ulrika Jonsson embarrassment and also his affair with an FA secretary but upsetting the Premiership chairmen, the real rulers of English football, was a trip too far.

The FA have a rule to govern these matters. They have often charged players and managers with 'bringing the game into disrepute'. Now the rule, Rule E, has been extended, yet no one mentioned that Eriksson might have been a contender. There are two explanations why he got away with so much. First, money and second, lawyers. When his annual salary was doubled to more than £5 million in March 2004 by three senior members of the FA, with the others insisting that their objections to it be minuted, Eriksson couldn't be sacked without full compensation of £10 million. His lawyers would ensure that. The first articles concerning the Dubai sting, about his thoughts of taking over Aston Villa and signing David Beckham, brought dismay to his employers in Soho Square and he just managed to hang on. The following Sunday's revelations were much more damaging. On the Monday he was summoned to a meeting at the FA which lasted seven hours and late into the evening when it was confirmed that Eriksson was leaving his job after the 2006 World Cup Finals. He qualified for a £5 million settlement, half of what he should have been entitled to under his contract. The good thing was that it pushed the authorities into meaningful investigations of corruption in English football. One agent, an honest one, reckons that £100 million has been siphoned off to managers and agents since the Premiership started in 1992.

Eriksson left behind no legacy for for his successor. He hardly brought a single innovation to improve the England set-up. However, he had the best relations with his players of any England manager, if only because he handed a lot of power to David Beckham. Tactically he was poor. And he won the lottery every year, sponsored by the FA, without really earning his money.

The FA have used the same formula to pick their managers, and it is about timing. The media lobbies for the candidate who has had a winning run and it becomes an unstoppable campaign leading right up to the fourth floor of 25 Soho Square. English football's longest serving manager is Dario Gradi of Crewe Alexandra. He has produced more good young players than the Premiership managers who have been allowed to spend millions of pounds on ready-made players, mainly from abroad, with much of the money deriving from Rupert Murdoch's Sky organisation, part of the same business empire which brought down so many England managers through its best-selling red-top newspapers. A younger version of Gradi could have been headhunted by a smaller, more efficient and independent ruling body to take over from the unwieldy FA but this is unlikely to happen for some time, if ever. Vested interests still rule.

An FA councillor once said of Eriksson, 'He's a bit of a womaniser' and on 18 July 2004 Eriksson was exposed as the lover of Faria Alam, a thirty-eight-year-old personal assistant of Bangladeshi origin who worked with David Davies, the FA executive director, at an annual salary of £35,000. As Mark Palios, the FA chief executive, had also had an affair with Ms Alam, members of the FA were very angry. Most of them thought it was a sacking case. Colin Gibson, the FA director of communications, issued a statement denying the allegations concerning Eriksson while Ms Alam issued her own statement refuting the story. Within a week both statements were proved to be false.

It brought back memories of the Profumo affair in 1963 when John Profumo, the Tory Minister of War, had an affair with a Christine Keeler – while Eugene Ivanov, a Soviet naval attaché and spy, had sexual soirees with Miss Keeler at the same time. Profumo, an honourable man who did charitable work in the East End for much of his life, resigned because he had lied in the House of Commons. His departure led to the fall of Harold Macmillan's Government but, forty-odd years on, Eriksson wasn't going to resign. 'Why should I?' he asked. 'It is a private matter.' But in America, except perhaps at the White House where Bill Clinton's dalliances with Monica Lewinsky caused acute embarrassment, they don't countenance this sort of thing. It's bad business practice.

In the late 1980s another young lady from the Subcontinent, Miss Pamella Bordes, a former Miss India, started a scandal in the House of Commons involving a minor Minister, among others, but standards had fallen by then and no one resigned. When Eriksson was compromised, the average football supporter must have wondered about all the fuss. A fifty-six-year-old divorcee with the reputation of Warren Beatty having something on the side... good luck to him.

The furore built up with most of the media calling for him to be fired. Many of the pundits didn't like his lack of emotion and his refusal to say anything interesting. They questioned his tactical expertise and his knowledge of domestic football. Was David James really one of the best goalkeepers in the country?

Although many people were initially disappointed about a foreigner being appointed England manager, the resentment against him cooled for a while when he won 5 out of 6 World Cup qualifiers, including the watershed 5-1 win over Germany. And he was given a cautious reprieve when England went out of the World Cup in Japan against Brazil.

Back home the newspapers splashed his ill-fated romance with Swedish television presenter Ulrika Jonsson on the front pages, exposing him to ridicule. Some FA members thought it showed a lack of judgement. He was on a tightrope when he started in his job: now he was on the highest wire. In the Euro 2004 qualification England had wild swings in form and the David

Beckham factor came into it. Beckham was clearly unfit in Japan but insisted on going. Was he bigger than the team? Was he telling Sven what to do?

England were one of the favourites in Portugal but losing to the host country on penalties was looked upon as Eriksson's fault. The inquests were still going on while rumours about his love life resurfaced and his lawyers wrote to the newspaper editors denying that he was having an affair with a woman who was employed by the FA. The alleged affair was not with Ms Alam but another woman. Hundreds of hoax emails, written by a disgruntled former employee under the name of P.G. Enis, were sent to newspapers alleging relationships between employees.

After his summer break, Eriksson denied more rumours until the *News of the World* dropped on 3 million-plus doormats in July. One headline was 'We Flew out to Sweden for Sex – Secret Romps at his Hideaway as Nancy Stayed Home Alone'. The newspaper claimed the affair had started the previous September and 'a close friend of Faria' said, 'The sex was fantastic. She said Sven had a great body.' She also revealed that Faria was 'seeing' Palios in February 2003. 'That obviously meant she couldn't get together with Sven but in February she split with Mark, leaving the door open for Sven,' said the 'friend'. Ms Alam called Palios 'PP' for 'Pretty Poll' and Eriksson 'Sugar'.

Inside the FA there were desperate attempts by senior staff to save some credibility and retain Palios, who has four daughters. Geoff Thompson, the chairman, accepted Palios's explanation that he never took Ms Alam out for dinner at the FA's cost and there was no impropriety. 'Nothing more than a fumble,' said the fifty-two-year-old Palios. They concocted a strategy to impale Eriksson and force him out. The lawyers were in from the start and the FA were seeking damage limitation. Palios, an accountant, was on £350,000 at the FA and before the FA bosses had made their minds up he offered his resignation. He might have stayed on but for a long, taped telephone conversation between Gibson and an executive of the *News of the World*. Gibson offered a deal: 'I give you chapter and verse on her [Alam] and Sven and get her to do an interview to say she lied to everybody this week. The pay-off is that we leave MP [Palios] out.' The executive replied, 'That looks a good deal.'

At the next *News of the World* conference, the executives realised the best story was shopping Eriksson, not protecting Palios so in their next edition they printed the tape of Gibson's telephone conversation. Any credibility left in the FA was finally stripped away. Their ninety-two council members, mainly reputable people from the Shires, were furious. One said, 'We've been made idiots by all this.' Palios confirmed he was resigning and Gibson, left low and dry in a reservoir in a summer's long drought, also offered his resignation. Both men did ultimately quit, Palios going back into business and Gibson becoming the communications director of the England and Wales Cricket Board.

While the panic was at its most virulent, the FA executive director David Davies rang Eriksson on 17 July and asked him the truth of the Alam romance story. Eriksson dismissed it as 'nonsense'. Davies later issued a statement saying Eriksson denied the story, which wasn't strictly true. Eriksson had stuck to his line that he doesn't comment about his private life and the statement had to be withdrawn. It proved to be very embarrassing to the FA and the board arranged a meeting on 5 August to resolve matters. Two days before, Eriksson went to see their lawyers and insisted he had done nothing to infringe the conditions laid down in his contract with the FA. The board meeting was switched to a smaller hotel than the usual ones and it was like a John Cleese farce, with scores of television, radio and press men charging around it. After six hours of discussions, mostly over legal matters, they decided that Eriksson's position was unchanged.

Those who wanted him to be charged, or sacked, were undermined by the interview Davies gave outside the FA offices the previous Monday on his return from holiday when he gave the England head coach his full backing. By prejudging the case, he weakened the argument for disciplinary action. But Thompson, who had gone off to Lithuania, should have been criticised for not returning to Soho Square, not Davies who later announced he was to go after the 2006 World Cup. Graham Kelly, who was secretary for the FA for many years, said, 'Thompson must accept full responsibility for the shambles and resign. Eriksson is a figure of fun and should be removed.' Asked if he ever thought of resigning, Eriksson said, 'Sometimes, of course. But I don't feel I should throw in the towel because of my private life.' The other reason why Eriksson wasn't sacked was his immense annual salary, £4.5 million net.

Ms Alam was supposed to have earned £300,000 for her story – it was probably much lower – and eleven months later she claimed £30,000 damages in front of an employment tribunal for constructive dismissal, breach of contract and sex discrimination. In one document, a lawyer wrote about Eriksson, 'He had a roving eye, like a seagull who would wrap his wings around people.' That was a reference to the way Eriksson hugged female members of the FA staff at Christmas parties. The case was dismissed. Ms Alam left to work in New York while Sven stayed in his job, unsuccessfully trying to avoid the paparazzi.

He made an early start to his career as a woman fancier, and his first serious relationship began on his eighteenth birthday. He went to a local dance in his home town Torsby, a winter resort with a population of 5,000, and met Nina Thornholm, a beauty pageant contestant, and they soon lived together in a flat. Sweden was much more liberal in these matters than England. He took a job as a clerk in the social security office and was passionately keen on football, ski jumping and young ladies.

Sven-Goran Eriksson was born on 5 February 1948, the first child of Sven Senior, then a bus conductor, and Ulla, who worked in a newsagent's and a hospital. To come from that background to become one of football's most decorated international coaches showed that he possessed remarkable qualites – determination, willpower, the competitive urge, limitless charm and a willingness to improve himself. He read Ernest Hemingway and was looked on as a dedicated, well-behaved pupil. 'He always wanted to analyse things and make notes,' said Sven Senior - with a reasonable scholastic record. A hard-working midfielder, his football was described as second-rate but he was first-class in acquiring knowledge of coaching. He was an avid watcher of televised English football and adopted many of their methods. For a time he wanted to be a sports journalist, rather ironically, and after twelve monotonous months in the Swedish Army, he met his wife Ann-Christin in 1970 while studying sports science in Orebro. They married seven years later and Johan, their son, arrived after a further twenty months. A daughter, Lina, arrived sixteen years later when he was working for Roma.

Known as 'Anki', Ann-Christin said, 'His determination to achieve what he wanted in life was the first thing that appealed to me. He never gives in. He knows what he wants and goes for it.' A left-wing socialist in his student days, Eriksson qualified as a PE instructor as his hopes of being a good footballer faded. His life changed when he met Tord Grip playing for Karlskoga in the 1970s, where Grip was the player-coach. Grip, who gained three international caps, was ten years older and a far superior footballer. After five years in charge, Grip joined the Swedish Premier League club Orebro before returning to Degenfors, a club that produced more than twenty internationals, including the legendary Gunnar Nordahl. He advised Eriksson to stop playing and concentrate on his coaching, and appointed him as his assistant.

When Grip was given a job with the Swedish FA, Eriksson was promoted. A veteran Scots coach named Dave Mosson, who was in charge of one of Eriksson's early coaching courses, described him as, 'not of the dynamic sort. Swedes keep their cool and they are very polite and reserved.' Eriksson, who fitted that description perfectly, made a study of the coaching methods of two Englishmen who were very successful in Sweden, Roy Hodgson and Bob Houghton, and also asked Bobby Robson and Bob Paisley if they could let him watch their training methods in England. Robson and Paisley both agreed and he was staggered when Robson invited him to sit on the bench at a League game with him. 'He is a special man,' he said.

Eriksson's Anglicised coaching methods were so successful in his three years that in 1979 IFK Gothenburg, Sweden's top club, appointed him as coach. He was thirty-one, a penguin-like figure with a ready smile. 'He was a complete nobody and he made a terrible start,' said the former Liverpool defender Glenn Hysen. 'After losing his first three games and he asked the players whether they wanted him and they said yes. He went on to win the UEFA Cup, the first time a Swedish club had won a European trophy.' Their opponents in 1982 were Hamburg, who had lost Kevin Keegan to Southampton the season before. They were so cocky that they had already printed flags that read 'Hamburg SV – Winners of the Europe Cup '82'. Eriksson still has one at his home. 'I was the happiest man alive after we won,' he said.

His achievement was quickly acknowledged around Europe and the Portuguese club Benfica signed him to replace the Hungarian Lajos Baroti, who had done the double two years previously. The Eagles won their first sixteen matches, beating the similar records of Tottenham and Chelsea. Eriksson lost his temper once against Real Betis in a UEFA Cup tie, storming in at half-time and berating his players about their habit of settling for draws in away games instead of going for the win. He showed courage by

SVEN-GORAN ERIKSSON

leaving out Portugal's most popular player Joao Alves, who played in black gloves, and bringing in twenty-three-year-old Swede Glenn Stromberg.

In his first season, Eriksson's team won the domestic double and lost to Anderlecht in the final of the UEFA Cup. In his second season, Benfica won the title but were knocked out by Liverpool on an aggregate of 5-1 in the quarter-finals of the European Cup. He agreed another two-year contract – clubs there don't normally go in for contracts of more than two years because of the volatility of Portuguese football – only to change his mind and accept an offer to join Roma.

While he was settling up his affairs, Irving Scholar, chairman of Tottenham Hotspur, approached an agent in Cascais to make contact with Eriksson. Scholar had dispensed with Keith Burkinshaw and wanted someone from abroad after being let down by the then Aberdeen manager Alex Ferguson. Scholar got through to Eriksson and was disappointed to learn that Eriksson had given his word to Roma. Eriksson soon learned that coaching in Italy was a much tougher assignment than coaching in Portugal. The rules forbade a foreign coach and he was appointed director of football but still acted as coach. Finishing seventh was a poor record but he blamed the injuries of the Brazilian superstar Falcao, who only appeared in four matches. Falcao lived with his mother in a luxurious villa and was chauffeured in a top-of-the-range BMW to his dates with actress Ursula Andress. There was no record of Sven dating the James Bond siren!

In his second season Eriksson found himself a target for the Italian football writers and Roma were wallowing in the middle of the table until he signed the Polish player Zbigniew Boniek – soon they were challenging Juventus for the title. With the title within his grasp, Eriksson saw his players go down to the bottom side Lecce and finish runners-up. Winning the Italian Cup in the same season was no consolation. In 1987 Roma were again in trouble until an audience with Pope John Paul II helped change their fortunes and for a while they were almost neck-and-neck with leaders Napoli. Once again, they lost to a bottom club and finished up losing their last seven matches. Supporters jeered Eriksson and called for his resignation. He duly submitted his letter of resignation, saying, 'Football in Italy is not just played on the field. A coach like me could never have imagined that the real championship, the most difficult one, is played outside the stadium.' He meant the machinations behind the scenes.

At the start of the 1987/88 season, Eriksson joined Fiorentina, a club in perpetual crisis, as coach and his first signing was his good friend Glenn Hysen. Florence was a good place for Eriksson but running a successful medium-sized football team up against the giants at Turin and Milan was a daunting task, especially after the club president Piercesaro Baretti was killed when his Cessna aircraft crashed into a hill near Turin. Eriksson's side ended the season in eighth position, well below their supporters' expectations.

Next time out, Eriksson tried to improve his squad, which relied on the skill of the Brazilian playmaker Dunga, by bidding for Barcelona's Gary Lineker. But Lineker preferred Tottenham. Two months before the end of his second season, Eriksson announced that he was thinking about going back to a more gentle work environment, Lisbon's Benfica. Fiorentina's directors acquiesced at first, only to change their minds. Then the press became hostile and the directors realised it was pointless to retain him when the fans were fractious. So off he went to Portugal again, accepting a lower salary. Italian football experts reckoned that this was the time when Eriksson's career started to wane. One said, 'Tactically he was unable to come out with a formula to come up with the right answers.'

There are eighteen clubs in the Portuguese League but fifteen are only there to join in the hurrahs when Benfica (with thirty-one titles since 1935), Porto (eighteen) and Sporting Lisbon (eighteen) pick up their annual trophies and medals. Two clubs outside the Big Three have won the first prize – Belenenses and Boavista, with one success apiece. Eriksson's record on his second posting in Lisbon was not as good as he and the fans expected. In the 1989/90 season Benfica reached the semi-finals of the European Cup and their President Joao Santos was reprimanded by UEFA for asking why players from Marseilles, their opponents, weren't dope tested. They qualified for the final against AC Milan in Vienna and it was one of the worst finals ever, with the only goal, scored by Milan, inflicting Benfica's fifth successive defeat in European Cup finals. Porto won the league, leaving Eriksson's side runners-up.

The following season Benfica lost matches they should have won and confidence in the manager was fading fast. He was approached by Fiorentina, by the US Soccer Federation with a view to coach their national side in the 1994 World Cup and by Internazionale, who made a big offer which Eriksson nonetheless thought was inadequate. Benfica recovered to be crowned champions, their twenty-ninth championship, and Eriksson was content to stay on for a further year.

The key players in Portuguese football were traditionally signed from Brazil and many of them had marriages arranged to qualify for Portuguese passports. But the arrival of the Israeli agent Pini Zahavi, the man who has played a huge part in English football in the last ten years, including handling the Rio Ferdinand transfer to Manchester United and several of United's other big deals, changed the national background of the club. (Later Zahavi, based in London, tried to persuade Eriksson to become manager of Chelsea when he was manager of England, only to fail.) Zahavi took players from the former Soviet Union to Benfica, including Sergei Yuran, an errant striker who finished up being thrown out of several English clubs, defender Sergei Kulkov and Alexander Mostovoi, who married a Portuguese girl to avoid the immigration laws. In the new Champions League, Benfica showed an English audience how to play the game at the very highest level at Highbury in November in 1991, outplaying Arsenal in a titanic battle. But Benfica were unable to maintain that standard and were knocked out of the competition, and also out of the Portuguese Cup. They needed to beat Porto at the Stadium of Light to take the title but went down 3-2. With great haste, new President Jorge de Brito sounded the last post for Eriksson, bringing in Tomislav Ivic from Marseille to be the new coach.

It was reported that Eriksson had signed an agreement to replace Vujadin Boskov as coach at Sampdoria in January and it proved to be true. Off he went to a new city, Genoa, to work in Serie A once more.

Though Italian football rouses great passion and fury, in many ways its coaches have a better life than managers in the Premiership. The richer clubs do not own their grounds and this releases funds for them to purchase worldwide stars who don't need so much coaching. The deals are usually handled by the club president and his advisers. After two or three years, the coach moves to another club and Eriksson followed that pattern. Paulo Mantovani, the Sampdoria president, was terminally ill and had bought half a side in an attempt to catch the big clubs. One surprising choice was the undemonstrative Des Walker, the Nottingham Forest and England centre half. Sampdoria players enjoyed Eriksson's relaxed approach but Mantovani and his son Enrico, who suceeded him when he died the following year, wanted more sail on the ship after a middling seventh position. New stars were brought in and Ruud Gullit was bought from Milan for a derisory £500,000 and David Platt from Juventus for £5.2 million on the same day. Gullit was thirty-one and had creaking knees but he had something to prove after being discarded. Along with Roberto Mancini these different personalities scored the bulk of the 64 goals, making Sampdoria the highest scorers in Serie A. A creditable third place in the league was followed by winning the cup. Gullit said:

> I was really charmed by Sven. He's a real gentleman and would talk to you, one on one, in a very civilised way. He gave us licence to think for ourselves and we paid him back by working hard for the team. He is very knowledge-able about tactics but he believes more in the individual. He knows that it is individuals who determine whether you win games or not.

Gullit moved back to Milan but, soon realising that he had made a mistake, he rejoined Eriksson.

Domestically, Eriksson's private life changed when his marriage to Ann-Christin ended and in 1993 he took up with vivacious divorcee Graziella Mancinelli, and they set up home after a chance meeting as neighbours and parents whose children went to the same school. He took her to the World Cup Finals in the USA for a working holiday. Sampdoria finished eighth in the 1994/95 season after putting out Bobby Robson's Porto in the UEFA Cup before going out to Arsenal on penalties. Platt was sold to Arsenal for £4.7 million and the squad was changed again.

A defeat in the cup against Genoa provoked demonstrations and Eriksson's wanderlust reappeared. Reports in England and Italy indicated that his next job was to be at Blackburn Rovers, whose manager Ray Harford had quit in October. Roy Hodgson, in charge of Inter, also came under pressure in Milan and accepted an offer from Jack Walker, the Rovers multi-millionaire chairman, only to then change his mind. Eriksson moved back into the reckoning and, after some shilly-shallying, agreed to join Rovers. But in a bewildering switch Lazio swept in with a bid for Eriksson's services and offered compensation to Rovers to release him from his letter of intent. Walker was livid. 'When a man gives his word, he should stick to it,' he said.

As the merry-go-round gathered pace, Hodgson changed his mind yet again and eventually signed up with Rovers while Eriksson committed himself to

Lazio. He told football writer Joe Lovejoy, 'I signed with Blackburn and I didn't feel right about breaking it, but they were aware of certain family problems and it was very difficult. It is the one black mark on my CV. I still feel sorry about it and it won't happen again.'

Eriksson's players at Sampdoria were genuinely sad to see him go. Juan Sebastian Veron, the Argentinian midfielder, is quoted in Lovejoy's brilliantly researched book *Sven* as saying, 'He was almost a father figure when I first came to Europe when I had to live on my own, doing my ironing and cleaning. Sven was a big help, particularly protecting me from the press.' Two new, exciting developments helped ease him into his new job with Lazio. In 1997 Tord Grip became his assistant after working at Malmo, Serie B club Campobasso, the Norwegian national side, Young Boys at Berne in Switzerland, Sweden as number two behind national coach Tommy Svensson, and Odense in Denmark where he was sports director.

Also, in 1998, Eriksson had a new lover, the exotic Nancy Dell'Olio, who was born in New York and brought up in Bari. Trained as a lawyer in New York, she took a degree in a university in Rome before marrying Giancarlo Mazza, a major shareholder in Lazio. The marriage was over when Sven first met Nancy at a Lazio party. Nancy's immaculate coiffure and appearance helped to keep her name in the celebrity columns. She smartened up during their on–off–on, tempestuous relationship and when they arrived at functions they would look the best-attired pair around.

Though Italian, Nancy doesn't like pasta or bread, preferring lean meat or fish. She is glucose-intolerant, drinks a lot of water, takes a lot of minerals and vitamins and has dispensed with the use of her personal trainer. 'I think everything comes from inside,' she said. 'If you eat healthily, your skin and hair will look good. I keep fit to make love, to be in love.' Caroline Davies wrote of her in the *Daily Telegraph*, 'The adjective "vulnerable" is not one usually associated with the Italian former lawyer of indeterminate age, who for six tempestuous years has been Mrs Eriksson-in-waiting. Volcanic, triumphant, dogged, are the ones commonly employed.'

When she was twenty-one she was nearly killed when a car driver ploughed into her near her home. She said:

> I was in a terrible state, with one side of my face destroyed and I went into a coma. Awakening from that, I can only describe as like being born again. It

made me question everything and taught me so much about myself. I knew the experience would not break me. It made me so strong. I would say to anyone who is facing adversity, you can conquer it. I was always a spiritual person but my accident made me even more so.

With her Italian temperament and Sven's calmness, the relationship has lasted much longer than some people predicted.

To keep Nancy in the elegant state she craved, Eriksson needed a big salary with tempting bonuses as Cragnotti spent more and more billions of lira in a bid to win the major trophies he had missed out on. He was down-hearted when Lazio failed to win the title and capturing the Italian Cup was hardly recompense. There was added pressure on Eriksson in the 1998 UEFA Cup final. His opponents were Inter, who finished 13 points ahead of seventh-placed Lazio in the championship, and the Rome side won the game with ease, 3-0. Lazio had just floated on the Milan bourse, the first club to do so in Italy.

In the 1998/99 season Lazio were well ahead of the field in the championship by April and a journalist wrote, 'Nancy's caresses have melted the heart of the icy magician of football.' But losing to Roma in the Eternal City derby caused a breakage and Milan snatched the title on the last day from Eriksson's grasp. He calmed his president and Lazio's supporters by taking the team to the European Cup-Winners' Cup final and winning it 2-1 against doughty opponents in Real Mallorca. It was an overdue first success in Europe and Eriksson was back as a hero.

Without being a Roman Abramovich, Cragnotti sought to lavish more and more money on a collection of superstars including Juan Sebastian Veron, who cost £19.8 million and the Argentinians Nestor Sensini and Diego Simeone, David Beckham's 'friend'. The money came from a new television deal and for the major football clubs it was like printing their own money, over-inflating the transfer market – a situation which soon spread to the Premiership. Eriksson did what Jose Mourinho and other top managers now do, ensuring there was enough quality backup to rest key players. Early in October, champions Milan drew 4-4 with Lazio in the Olympic Stadium and Eriksson called it one of the finest matches of recent times. Unbeaten in sixteen matches, they lined up against their chief rivals Roma and went down 4-0, provoking a mini riot at Formello, the Lazio training camp which has guards to keep out intruders. Angry supporters climbed in and abused the superstars before being removed.

In March, Lazio lagged behind Juventus by nine points and Cragnotti was giving his coach a stern warning: win the title or go! But Lazio closed the gap and there was another riot, not unusual in Italian football, when referee Massimo de Santis disallowed a goal in the final split-second in the Juventus *v*. Parma match when Juve were leading 1-0. Television showed that the ball went in before the last blast of the whistle, denying Parma a draw. Juventus and Lazio would have been level on points had the game ended 1-1. Furious Lazio fans turned up outside the Rome police headquarters, protesting about this 'cheating scandal' and had to be dispersed by tear gas and baton charges.

On the final day of the season some of them turned up for Lazio's home game against Reggina carrying a black coffin bearing the slogan 'Football is Dead'. If Perugia managed to draw against Juventus and Lazio won, there would have been a play-off. Eriksson remained strong, telling his players it would end in their favour. At half-time Lazio were 2-0 up and at Perugia the score was goal-less. Suddenly the skies opened at both grounds, a hundred and twenty miles apart, flooding the pitches and driving the players and officials off the field. Pierluigi Collina, the eminent FIFA referee with the haunting look, tried to bounce the ball at Perugia and found it stuck in the mud. The game at the cavernous Olympic Stadium resumed and Lazio duly won 3-0. Eriksson remained calm, waiting for the resumption at Perugia. When the players re-emerged, Juventus lost 1-0 and Lazio were champions. Eriksson's players also won the Italian Cup, beating Milan, and, though they put out Chelsea in the Champions League, they lost to Valencia in the quarter-final. Winning two trophies finally satisfied Cragnotti and the timing was ideal for Eriksson, who had already had talks with the FA. Adam Crozier, the Scottish-born Sacchi and Sacchi marketing executive in his thirties, who startled the FA councillors by turning up for his first press conference without a tie, was determined to get him as England's first foreign manager at almost any cost.

Cragnotti took his spending up to £225 million, with £56 million on two more Argentinians, Claudio Lopez and Hernan Crespo, in Eriksson's last season at Lazio. They made a poor start and were sixth, with Cragnotti showing concern, when the deal with the FA was sealed. The news was announced to the fans before the laboured 2-1 victory over Brescia and they were promised that Eriksson would stay to see the season out. There was warm applause around the ground. Crozier had set up a sub-committee to find a successor to Kevin Keegan after the Finland game and used Sir Alex Ferguson as his main adviser. Arsène Wenger was approached and David Dein, the Arsenal vice-chairman and power broker behind the scenes at Soho Square, soon squashed that idea, claiming the Frenchman was not available, for obvious reasons. Wenger was fast becoming Arsenal's finest manager, outdoing Herbert Chapman.

Athole Still, Eriksson's friend and agent, got the saga moving, ringing him and saying, 'Would you be interested in the England job?' Eriksson was surprised. 'Are you having a joke?' he said. 'Have you ever heard of a foreigner being manager of England?' Still flew to Rome later in the week and told him that the FA wanted to offer a five-year contract with an astonishingly high salary. Eriksson's mood changed. It seemed a good deal. Nancy loved London, as did he, and England had a young and emerging squad. On Sunday 29 October 2000 the FA hired a private aircraft to take Crozier and Dein to Rome for a meeting with Cragnotti, his son Massimo, Dino Zoff, the former Italy goalkeeper and coach and Eriksson. Cragnotti, a tough negotiator who was skilled in publicising himself and his family, said, 'We have a very close bond but I am reluctant to stand between my friend and what he wants.' He asked him, 'Do you want to talk to them?' Eriksson replied, 'Yes, this is the sort of job I have dreamed about. It is something I have always wanted to try.'

The financial side was settled within a day and the whole operation went through inside two days. Eriksson was on £1.75 million a year, tax free, at Lazio and Crozier bettered that, offering £2.5 million a year plus bonuses, nineteen times the sum paid to Terry Venables when he took England to the semi-finals of Euro 96. The two parties compromised over the time when Eriksson could leave Lazio – from February he was to be part-time manager of the national side while still working with Lazio until the club's championship and Champions League campaigns were resolved. He anticipated he would encounter criticism and he was right. He had read a book about England managers named *The Second Most Important Job in the Country* and said, 'It showed that all of them were declared idiots at some time, even Sir Alf Ramsey, so I knew what to expect.'

He made another good point: an Englishman has managed the Sweden team so why shouldn't a Swede take England? Yorkshireman George Raynor, a 5ft 6in winger born in 1907 at Hoyland, near Wombwell, home of the Cricket Lovers' Association, became coach of the Sweden side which won a gold medal in the 1948 Olympics and lost 5-2 to Brazil and Pelé in the 1958 World Cup held in Sweden. Raynor went to Barnsley Grammar School, played for Sheffield United reserves, Mansfield Town, Rotherham United, Bury and Aldershot before retiring at the start of the Second World War. He took up coaching and organised a successful football tournament in Baghdad during his military service, which impressed Sir Stanley Rous. The all-powerful FA secretary promptly recommended him to apply for the post of Swedish coach and, to his astonishment, he got it. He had two spells with Sweden, 1946-1954 and 1957-1960, and also had brief periods with Juventus, Lazio and Coventry. By age fifty-three his career was fading and he became manager of Skegness Town while being stores manager at Butlin's. He was remembered as an amusing and lively companion.

The opposition Raynor encountered when he first went to Sweden was mild compared to what happened when Eriksson was appointed by England. John Barnwell, the long-serving and respected chief executive of the Football League Managers' Association, described the appointment as 'an insult' and Gordon Taylor, the equally long-serving chief executive of the Professional Footballers' Association, said the FA had 'betrayed their heritage'. *The Sun* said it was 'a terrible, pathetic, self-inflicted indictment of the game'. Jeff Powell in the *Daily Mail* wrote the funniest critique:

> England's humiliation knows no end. In their trendy eagerness to appoint a designer manager did they pause for so long as a moment to consider the depth of this insult to our national pride? We sell our birthright down the fjord to a nation of 7 million skiers and hammer throwers, who spend half their year living in total darkness.

Eriksson was flown by private plane to St Albans on 2 November 2000 to meet the assembled press before flying back to Rome to take training at the Lazio training ground. It meant an 8 a.m. start at the press conference and Eriksson was cheery and smiling as he looked up into the dozens of cameras at the Sopwell House Hotel often used by England and by many of the leading clubs. Sopwell House was owned earlier in the last century by Lord Louis Battenberg, a leading Admiral in the First World War, who was born in Germany. He encountered a lot of xenophobia in his time and he was father of Lord Mountbatten, who played a prominent part in winning the Second World War in both Europe and the Far East. Someone from the FA gave Eriksson a poppy to put in his lapel in an effort to placate any xenophobia at this time. Sweden took no military part in the Second World War and they have no dead soldiers to salute on Armistice Day.

A questioner tested his knowledge of English players. Who was the Leicester City goalkeeper, he asked (Ian Walker, who had a handful of England caps). And who was the Sunderland left-back? (Michael Gray, also capped). Eriksson couldn't think of either. For more than half-an-hour, he ducked and dived against persistent questioning and Rob Shepherd of the *Daily Express*, said afterwards, 'Christ, to think it's going to be like that for the next five years!' There were a number of fault lines in Eriksson's promotion – five years was too long, the wages were obscene and treating him like a billionaire and lavishing money on his travel and other expenses gave the wrong impression that the FA have limitless funds. Allowing him to stay on at Lazio was another fault. Lazio started tumbling down the league and on 9 January 2001, Eriksson announced he was quitting to join the FA full-time. It cost him £1.3 million to break his contract. That night Lazio took on China in a friendly in their centenary and as he took his seat the fans clapped and cheered him, reducing him to tears.

His first match in charge of England, a friendly that needed seven substitutes, was a happy romp with a 3-0 victory over a not-too-committed Spain. Beckham had been worried about the captaincy. Was he going to be retained? 'Absolutely,' said Sven. He told him, 'I think you will make a great England captain. The other players look up to you.' The next match, a qualifier for the World Cup against Finland, started badly at Anfield with the Finns taking the lead. However, Michael Owen equalised and Beckham scored a deflected winner. It was the captain's first goal from open play.

The best players worry about their form and Beckham is no exception. One of Eriksson's best qualities, often underrated by the critics, was that he was excellent at praising people and giving them confidence. 'He deserved credit for creating a better team spirit than I can remember with England before,' said the captain. Beckham used as an example the 4-0 defeat of

Mexico in Eriksson's fourth match, a friendly match. 'A Mexican player came through the back of me and I just limped off and got on with it,' he said. 'A minute later Stevie Gerrard had gone flying into the Mexican, legally, and left him reeling on the floor. Looking after your mate – it's an attitude I knew very well from playing for Manchester United.' England's players, particularly from United, are used to hearing the F-word in almost every sentence. To their surprise, Eriksson hardly used it. Rio Ferdinand said, 'He was so calm, so cool. He didn't rant or come in swearing his head off. I've played under a lot of managers who shout to put their points over forcibly but Sven is the opposite.'

Often Eriksson would come in at half-time and sit down for a few minutes before making his points in simple explanations. Talking to the press, he never opened up as Taylor, Hoddle and Robson had. This caused resentment among some correspondents and that was a reason why they turned on him when the results went against his side. He refused to cultivate friends among the media, treating them all the same way, with politeness and numbing blandness.

Four days after the Finland game the Foreign Office finally gave the all-clear to allow the England squad to fly to Tirana, the capital of the desperately poor, war-racked Balkan state of Albania. England were slow to start and all their goals came in the final eighteen minutes of an unmemorable 3-1 win. Tirana is a place to get out of as quickly as possible and Eriksson took Nancy on a short, recuperative holiday in Barbados, the Caribbean isle upon which hot sun never stops shining except for a few brief showers. They wanted privacy but the English red-tops use freelance photographers who are stationed in Barbados. Any celebrity is soon targeted and pictures of Nancy loosening her bra strap caused a predictable reaction. She wanted to sue but was talked out of it. Eriksson wasn't used to being constantly harassed.

He made a sound decision to give his players a weekend in La Manga, the Spanish golfing complex which has attracted bad headlines on other occasions, when English footballers have gone wild. His players concentrated on their golf, with Eriksson failing to join in. 'I don't play golf,' he explained. In Athens, preparing for a crucial qualifier against a strong, committed Greece, he took his players out training in the middle of the afternoon with the temperature touching 100°F. It showed he was willing to defy traditions. The Greeks held his side to a single Paul Scholes goal until three minutes from time, when Beckham scored from one his trade-mark free-kicks. Five wins from five matches. It was the best record of any England manager. 'Very professional,' he said of his players. 'It was no difference from Italian football.' Praise indeed.

After the scruffy game in Athens Eriksson was in amazingly high spirits before the showdown against Germany at the Olympic Stadium in Munich on 1 September 2001, a day that has gone down in English footballing history, second in terms of glory only to 30 July 1966. He was ebullient even though he had lost his unbeaten record, with England losing 2-0 in a friendly at White Hart Lane on 15 August to an experienced Dutch side. He was criticised for using twenty-two players but the Dutch used nineteen as well. In other words, it was a practice match in front of 35,238 short-changed supporters. Echoing Alf Ramsey's belief that England would beat the Germans, he said, 'We are at the same level and it will come down to attitude – and our attitude is exactly right. I felt lucky on the day – all of my twenty-five selected players were available. Beating Germany is something very few players have achieved and we are going to do it.'

There was a rude interruption when he was forced to take legal action against the publishers of the celebrity rag *Hello*, who included a five-page feature showing his Georgian house at Regents Park, which he had bought for £2.5 million. The overexposure, without permission, led to a series of break-ins, ruffling his usual calm.

On the night the weather helped, warm and comforting, and another advantage to England was that the ground, which normally held 70,000, contained only 63,000 and most of the noise came from the English fans. Carsten Jancker scored in the sixth minute but then, when Sebastian Deisler should have scored from close range, England's players sensed their luck was about to change. In the thirteenth minute the Germans failed to clear a Beckham free-kick and Michael Owen sidefooted the equaliser. Steven Gerrard drove past Oliver Kahn right on the break and in the dressing room he did most of the talking. Eriksson said little. 'Just keep doing what you were doing for the last twenty-five minutes,' he said. The players were excited, anxious to get back out there.

Three minutes into the second half, Emile 'Bruno' Heskey laid the ball towards Owen, whose volley went in off Kahn's body. Owen's hat-trick came in the sixty-sixth minute and Heskey slotted in England's fifth sixteen minutes from time, around the time when most of the locals started leaving in disgust. Five-one! Unheard of. The first question to Owen was, 'Did it happen?' He said, 'Maybe at the end of my career I'll look back and think that!' The players were delirious, so were the fans. But Eriksson kept calm, going round his staff, shaking hands with a quiet smile.

Sportsmanship reigned with the German players congratulating the victors. Liverpool's Dietmar Hamann, who scored the goal at Wembley the previous year, said, 'England beat us with a bit of the Liverpool style. They played long balls which made it difficult for our defenders to deal with the pace of Owen and Heskey.' All five goals came from Liverpool players and it was Germany's second defeat in sixty-one matches at home. The fans drank all night in the beer halls of Munich, and the journalists too, but the players had to exercise restraint. They were still three points behind Germany with a game in hand and they had to beat Albania four days later at St James's Park, one of English football's most feared stadiums.

Not having the use of Wembley turned out to be a big advantage to England because most of their matches were watched by real fans, not prawn ciabatta munchers and champagne sippers. But a passionate 52,046 crowd saw some of the gloss stripped away as England struggled to improve on Owen's forty-fourth-minute goal against a dogged Albanian side. Their second goal in a hard-won 2-0 victory came from substitute Robbie Fowler two minutes from time. Fowler later slated Eriksson in his book. 'He's not a particularly good manager,' he said. 'He's a half-decent coach who got himself a massive reputation. He hardly says anything. But if the stories about his private life are anything to go by, he's obviously a bit of a rascal, so he can't be all bad!'

The pressure was almost off. A home win against the Greeks on 6 October at another footballing hotbed, Old Trafford, would clinch the top position and send England to the World Cup Finals in the Far East. But vital performers like Michael Owen, David Seaman and Sol Campbell were injured, Frank Lampard was dropped after an embarrassing drunken incident at a hotel in Heathrow and *The Sun* reported that Steven Gerrard, who actually played, was caught drinking at 2 a.m. before the team assembled. The drink culture was still flourishing and a red-faced Eriksson refused any questions about boozing.

The portents were disturbing, more so after the Greeks, never short of commitment, dominated the first half and led 1-0 on a deadened, relaid pitch. The admirable and much-liked Cornishman Nigel Martyn has rarely let anyone down and made match-saving stops to prevent England being condemned to a play-off. Fowler was hauled off and, within a minute of coming on, substitute Teddy Sheringham, aged thirty-five, back-headed a Beckham free-kick into the net. What a relief to the 66,009 audience. But the relief lasted just ninety seconds as Themis Nikolaidis beat Martyn to put Greece ahead again. Coaches say the most vulnerable time is the period just after one side scores – the other team often scores within a minute or two. Concentration goes and perhaps the answer is to cancel all celebrations and order the players back to the centre circle with only brief handshakes.

Beckham assumed a greater role, dictating the play and inspiring his men. His anger was showing – at the sloppy way England were performing, the nasty little digs from the volatile Greeks and his dreadful free-kicks. He'd taken seven and not one was on target. The news from Gelsenkirchen was shattering: Germany 0, Finland 0 at full-time. If the England score stayed as it was, Germany would be the qualifying country and England would be forced into the play-offs.

Dutch referee Dick Jol checked his watch as the ninety-minute mark arrived and fortunately a minimum of four minutes were added. Eighty-five seconds from the end the canny Sheringham went down under a mild challenge from Kostas Konstantinidis and Beckham started to line up the ball for what should be the last free-kick. The range was twenty-eight yards, just right for him, close to the D of the penalty area. Sheringham, however, butted in and said, 'I'll have this.' 'No,' said Beckham. 'It's too far for you.' He curled an inswinger into the top right-hand corner over the startled Nikopolidis and the fans erupted. There must have been roars when Mafeking was relieved in the Boer War more than a century ago but they didn't equal the deafening noise at Old Trafford. Oliver Kahn, the controversial German goalkeeper and captain, was watching on television and burst into tears. It was the first time the Germans had failed to qualify automatically for a major competition. Soon afterwards they beat Ukraine in the home and away legs of their play-off to go through.

The first thing Beckham did was to go outside the dressing room to ring his wife Victoria who was at a working engagement in Italy. As she answered the phone he tried to talk. 'The words didn't come out,' he said. 'But she understood the grunts and gasps coming down the line.' Half an hour later, Beckham walked past the press box to a reception room and the last twenty or so English journalists rose to clap. 'That hasn't happened, ever,' he said. When he got back to training at the United training ground at Carrington, Sir Alex Ferguson said to him, 'I hope you're going to work that bloody hard now you're back!'

After being voted the UK Coach of the Year, Eriksson journeyed to Busan, South Korea, for the draw for the World Cup Finals and afterwards used the coaches' most overused word, 'disappointing', to express his feelings about his opponents, Argentina, Nigeria and Sweden in Group F, the 'group of death' according to the English journalists. Tord Grip was put in hospital with pains down an arm, suggesting a mild heart attack, but it proved to be a scare. It made Eriksson think of his health. In Italy coaches have to undergo thorough checks every six months, otherwise they can't sit on the bench. He thought the FA should follow that lead.

Eriksson was only a few months into his five-year contract when intermediaries approached him about succeeding Alex Ferguson at Old Trafford. Ferguson said, 'I think they'd done a deal all right. I'm sure it was Eriksson and I think they'd shaken hands.' Eriksson issued a statement through the FA denying any direct, or indirect approaches. Ferguson changed his mind about retiring and accepted a three-year contract for more money. On 10 April Beckham was trying to fulfil Ferguson's credo of 'work bloody hard' when he was felled by a two-footed tackle from Argentinian Aldo Duscher in United's Champions' League victory over Deportivo La Coruña. The blow broke his second metatarsal, a tiny bone in the foot, but the medical verdict was that he ought to be fine for the World Cup.

England played six friendlies before serious action began and only one, against Paraguay, which they won 4-0, was worthwhile in terms of raising confidence. They lost 2-1 to Italy at Elland Road, using all twenty-two players, drew 1-1 against Sweden at Old Trafford, 1-1 against Holland in Amsterdam, 1-1 against South Korea in Seoquipo and 2-2 against Cameroon in Kobe. It was a woeful record.

There where mutterings from the fourth estate – Sven was spending too much time promoting Playstations, egg and bacon breakfasts from Sainsbury's, classical CDs and other distracting sales pitches. They were none too happy with the mediocre results on the field either. But the FA felt they were swimming along fairly smoothly towards another World Cup Finals. That was until Hurricane Ulrika struck.

Early in December 2001 the personable, thirty-four-year-old Swedish-born television presenter and former weather girl Ulrika Jonsson met Eriksson, who is nineteen years older, at a Christmas party hosted by the reviled Richard Desmond, chairman of Northern and Shell who own the *Daily Express*. It took place at the Roundhouse in Camden and, according to the then *Express* editor Chris Williams, formerly of the *Daily Mail*, 'There was instant chemistry between them.' The Swedish immigrants were introduced by another unpopular figure, Alistair Campbell, who was spin doctoring for Prime Minister Tony Blair and New Labour at the time. It would have been a great scoop for the *Express*. Instead, they were scooped by the *Daily Mirror* five months later. Piers Morgan, the bombastic then editor of the *Mirror*, was given a tip that the *News of the World* were working on the story. He rang Ulrika's agent, Melanie Cantor, and concluded a deal, a nice payment in exchange for a 'friendly' exposure piece under the headline 'Svensational!' The other newspapers dived in and by the next day Eriksson and his employers were held up to ridicule.

A Dario Fo-style farce was enacted at the Chelsea *v.* Manchester United game with Eriksson sitting in the directors' box and Ulrika, brought along by the television presenter Angus Deayton, who had been exposed in the *News of the World* on another occasion, was positioned in a different stand, sitting next to the balding Dutch coach Dick Advocaat. And, in the radio section, Stan Collymore was acting as a summariser for BBC Radio Five. Collymore, a former lover of Ulrika, had been involved in a number of sordid episodes. He has made a lot of money from his confessions published in the red-tops. The photographers spent more time picturing the celebs than the players on the field and there were raucous shouts and chants from all quarters. Sir Stanley Rous and Walter Winterbottom, not to mention Alf Ramsey, would have been shocked by the goings-on but Adam Crozier soon assured Joe Lovejoy, on behalf of the Sunday newspapers, that Eriksson's position with the FA wouldn't be affected.

The floods of newsprint failed to abate with the nation's biggest selling Sunday newspaper, the *News of the World*, filling five pages with titillating details of the England manager and the Swedish beauty's romps at various meetings. Apparently, the lovers spoke in Swedish on their mobiles to avoid prying listeners and when afternoon sex was served, 'Pint-sized Eriksson left his built-up shoes outside the bedroom to warn the nanny that they were at it.' Back at Regents Park, one could expect an incandescent Nancy waiting at the door with a raised baton but to everyone's amazement the pair emerged later and were chauffeured to their favourite restaurant 'San Lorenzo', which was Princess Diana's favourite too. Quizzed later, Nancy said, 'That's a really stupid question. We are together, more than ever.'

The following week Eriksson faced a huge throng of media people at Burton's off Oxford Street to launch the World Cup suit. The *Mirror* was founded for women and it was no surprise when a lady reporter fired the first question: 'Who is your first choice for selection – Nancy or Ulrika?' He looked her in the eye. 'That is private,' he said. When the man from *The Sun* asked, 'Do you still love Nancy?' he replied, 'Private is private. I am sure you will find out, you are parked outside my house.' Eriksson's calm behaviour won over the hardened critics and many of them joined in a round of applause as he departed. After six days, the saga was wound up. Ulrika issued a statement saying, 'I am no longer a part of this relationship.' Eriksson took Nancy to the Arsenal *v*. West Ham game and she was applauded by a capacity crowd. Ulrika's book came out and after England qualified for the World Cup, she was hired by the *News of the World* to write a column. Her latest marriage ended with her saying, 'Husbands are only good for putting out the rubbish.' She was joking of course. In another interview three years later, she said, 'I admire Sven his staying power. I thought he'd quit the country. He behaved badly but I was really fond of him. He is kind-hearted and sweet.' They both come over as sweet people, if not disciplined and totally responsible people.

Ulrika was soon forgotten and, before leaving for the Far East, the FA paid for a five-night holiday for the squad members, their partners and families and the accompanying staff at the Jumeirah Beach Club in Dubai. The party numbered 123 and they were housed in thirty-five villas with the Beckhams given first choice. The England captain was still lacking fitness following his metatarsal injury and some managers would have left him behind. But Eriksson needed his leadership as well as his ability on the field. It was a gamble but it didn't work. He wanted the injured Steven Gerrard to travel on the same basis but Gerard Houllier, the Liverpool manager, vetoed the idea. The FA even paid the laundry bill of the players; that drew critical comments and when a news reporter discovered that a bar bill totalling £20,000 had been left unpaid, the hostile headlines started appearing.

Their travel experts chose well. The players loved the privacy of the huge, luxurious complex and when they arrived in Jeju Island, famed for its honeymoons, for the first week in South Korea they felt the hotel was very relaxing. The opening friendly against South Korea was a shambolic 1-1 draw with Danny Murphy performing so badly that he apologised to his teammates. In the next training session he cracked the same bone in the foot that had put Beckham's involvement in the World Cup Finals in doubt – and indeed had ruled Gary Neville out of the competition. More players went down with minor injuries and luck was going against the harassed head coach as he took his men to another island, Awaji, for the second stage of their preparations in Japan. The second friendly match was equally bad, with England fortunate to draw 2-2 against a stronger Cameroon side. The humidity, around forty or fifty per cent, and a temperature high in the eighties affected the players and they complained of not being able to play at a high tempo for the whole of ninety minutes.

England's first game of the tournament, against a tough but unadventurous Swedish side at Saitama on 2 June, started indifferently and deteriorated. Beckham was clearly unfit despite Eriksson claiming he was ninety-five per cent ready, and was replaced by another injured player, Kieron Dyer, in the sixty-third minute. Sol Campbell headed in a Beckham corner and it ended 1-1. Mentally, the players had not been ready. FIFA insisted that the teams should be in their dressing rooms an hour and a half before the kick-off and the players hated the interminable delay. Eriksson soon ran out of things to say and the popular FA doctor John Crane tried to lighten the mood with his anecdotes.

There were only five days before the next match, against Argentina in Sapporo, and Eriksson earned his salary with his calming words and refusal to panic. And when Beckham suggested that the strict diet should be abandoned for a day, replaced by McDonald's fast food fare, he readily agreed. 'We stuffed ourselves,' said Beckham. 'We were like kids in a sweet shop.'

Because of the history of both countries, these matches are always bruising, over-competitive encounters and this was no exception. Beckham forgot his pain and charged into risky challenges, Nicky Butt and Rio Ferdinand reached new heights and Michael Owen regained his zest. Just before half-time Owen went down under a weak challenge from Mauricio Pochettino and Pierluigi Collina blew for the penalty. If it had gone against England and not Argentina there would have been loud protests.

Owen was keen to take it but Beckham insisted. As he readied himself, Diego Simeone walked up to him and offered a hand. Beckham ignored him. By this time in his career he was blasting penalties, not placing them into the corner like he does with his free-kicks. Goalkeeper Pablo Cavallero was into his dive when he struck his shot straight down the middle of the goal. It was the only goal of the game and Beckham couldn't sleep that night. 'It was better than the 5-1 against Germany,' he said.

England only needed to avoid losing to Nigeria in their final group match and honour was satisfied on both sides when the US referee Hall blew the final whistle with the score goal-less. The temperature was close to 100°F at the packed stadium in Niigata and the players rarely went above a fast walking pace. Afterwards in the dressing room they sat drained, drinking litres of water to revive them. Argentina were out and so were France, the pre-tournament favourites. 'This has opened things up for us,' said Eriksson.

England's second-round opponents were Denmark, familiar punchbags for England sides since 1948. Half the side played their club football in England and they were looking to Thomas Sorensen to produce an upset. The former Sunderland goalkeeper fumbled a weak header from Rio Ferdinand into his own net after only five minutes and it was virtually all over. Owen claimed that Sorensen was his bunny, as he scored regularly against him, and he tucked in the second with Emile Heskey adding a third a minute from half-time. The Danes rallied but there were no further goals. Owen came off at half-time with a sore groin, which was to hamper him in the quarter-final against Brazil at Shizuoka on 21 June. Beckham thought that it was down to two countries – Germany and Brazil. He was right and Brazil beat Germany 2-0, both late goals in the second half, in the final at Yokohama. Except for the semi-finals and final, England drew the biggest attendances and the Japanese fans loved them, particularly Beckham. There was hardly any bad behaviour by English supporters. They gave unstinting support and when Eriksson's exhausted side flopped to a 2-1 defeat they stayed on to applaud them and cheer, including David Seaman who had let in a forty-yard free-kick to give the Brazilians victory.

Owen scored in the twenty-third minute, raising hopes among Beckham's players, before Rivaldo equalised just before the interval. After the pro-longed inquests, Eriksson was blamed by anonymous players and voluble critics for not rousing his men with some passionate oratory. One player was supposed to have uttered the immortal words, 'We needed Churchill but we got Iain Duncan Smith.' Beckham thought the players had nothing more to give. 'We were knackered,' he said. 'The dressing room was like a morgue.' With thirty-three minutes remaining, Ronaldinho had been sent off for an over-the-ball tackle on the combustible Danny Mills but it had made little difference. The Brazilian goalkeeper Marcos didn't have to make a single save afterwards.

In the dressing room at half-time and at the end, Eriksson sat in silence for much of the time and in his book *My Side*, Beckham said, 'He should have done more.' Seaman was in tears at the end and Ferdinand ech-oed the general view, 'He took the blame but he was beaten by a freak goal.' Without Gary Neville and Steven Gerrard and with the injuries to Beckham and Owen, Eriksson's team, the youngest in the tournament, was shorn of its power but there was little debate about whether his players were fit enough. Conditions in Spain and Mexico in the 1982 and 1986 World Cup Finals were similar to Korea and Japan and the previous generation of England players coped better in afternoon kick-offs. The difference today is that the world's stars are being ferried around the world in uncomfortable aircraft, almost fortnightly, and the pressure from television and the other media, feeding the expectations of the watching public, has increased to an unbearable level. Tension saps energy and successful teams need upbeat, positive personalities and inspirational coaches. Without them, something has to give. Smaller leagues and fewer matches must be introduced to pre-serve the quality of World Cup football.

When Eriksson arrived home on 23 June he was greeted with another 'tell and sell' story. Jayne Connery, no relation to the former James Bond, a lapdancer with a 36DD bust, claimed in the *News of the World* that she had had an intimate relationship with him for three months. These stories were becoming tiresome and hardly anyone took any notice of Ms Connery.

After a drab 1-1 friendly against Portugal, with the side ruined by lack of co-operation of Premiership managers including Sir Alex Ferguson, it was back into competitive football with the qualifiers for Euro 2004, the Finals of which would be held in Portugal. The draw gave England a ludicrously easy task, or so it seemed: Turkey, Slovakia, Macedonia and Liechtenstein in Group 7. It could be termed the 'Group of Easy Life' after the Group of Death in Korea and Japan.

The opening match was helpfully arranged for 12 October, later than usual, against Slovakia in Bratislava and it turned out to be a nightmare experience. Eriksson was itchy on the flight out, fearing that the publication of Ms Jonsson's book *Honest* would produce more scandal ahead of the game. However, he was soon back to his usual calm state until two English fans were shot in the street within earshot of the team hotel. On a miserable night, filled with racist chants from the home supporters, Beckham equalised after England had been a goal down and Michael Owen won the game eight minutes from the end. Angry FA officials fired off a complaint to UEFA and the Slovakian FA were eventually fined a pittance. Four days later England were in more trouble, twice going behind to an ordinary Macedonian side at the St Mary's Stadium in Southampton. David Seaman was beaten by an inswinging corner and his distinguished career ended on seventy-five appearances. Alan Smith, the snarler from Leeds, now with Manchester United, was sent off.

In the following weeks Eriksson was thinking of quitting according to his assistant Steve McClaren, who resigned for a while to concentrate on his work at Middlesbrough. Brian Kidd took over in the England set-up. Adam Crozier resigned his position at the FA to head the Royal Mail and Eriksson said he was devastated. On 11 November a meeting at the FA ended with peace breaking out. The all-powerful Premiership chairmen backed off from their idea that they should run the England team and Eriksson promised to stay. The Premiership chairmen still refused to have a mid-season break but the England squad was given one, with the FA splashing out to entertain the players and their wives on a two-night stay at Champneys Health Farm.

There were plenty of lows in Eriksson's reign and one of the lowest was at Upton Park on 9 February when twenty-two men of England lost 3-1 to fifteen men of Australia in an absurd friendly match which *The Sun* called 'one of the most lamentable displays in our football history'. Seventeen-year-old Wayne Rooney came on at half-time but failed to score. Another Scouser, the unfulfilled Francis Jeffers, scored the goal.

The following week it was revealed that Eriksson had agreed to join Manchester United thirteen months previously when Ferguson was intent on retiring. Peter Kenyon, the club's chief executive, said, 'We never concluded a deal with Sven,' but he didn't deny that talks had taken place. Later, Ferguson said he was sure that Eriksson had agreed to go. Ferguson soon changed his mind about retiring, ending any further speculation.

Playing Liechtenstein, a principality of sixty-two square miles with a population of 33,863 and seven football clubs, is like playing Guernsey – and yet England's finest and most extravagantly paid players struggled to beat them on 29 March 2003, finally prevailing by two goals to nil in front of 3,548 spectators. Four days later, England took on Turkey, who have yet to win in ten competitive matches between the two nations (competitive because neither team believes in friendlies with the other). The atmosphere inside Sunderland's Stadium of Light was as hostile as any ground staging a similar international in Turkey. The home fans booed the Turkish anthem and the visiting supporters responded with racist taunts, threats and chants. Local hooligans invaded the pitch to celebrate when the England goals, scored by Darius Vassell and Beckham, went in and fighting broke out outside the ground with ninety-five Englishmen detained overnight. UEFA eventually imposed a record fine of £68,000 for misconduct and Englishman Mike Lee, their spokesman said, 'This is a final warning for England and the FA must realise their track record is deplorable. England came close to being thrown out of Euro 2000 and their place next year may be in jeopardy if this happens again.'

Rooney started the Turkey game and impressed everyone, including Eriksson, but the manager was upset to learn that Everton wanted him to remain at home instead of going on the money-making mini-tour to South Africa at the end of the season. David Moyes, the Everton manager, insisted that Rooney had a knee injury and the FA ordered a medical examination of the knee in London before a decision was made. It caused a lot of friction and finally Eriksson relented. Rooney missed little except a meeting with Nelson Mandela. Only twelve of the England squad bothered to meet the former South African President and Beckham, who wanted to be pictured with Mandela, fell and broke a bone in his wrist in England's unexciting 2–1 win.

Eriksson was derided for much of his time in England but he still attracted multi-million-pound offers from big clubs around the world. The list is impressive: Real Madrid, Barcelona, Manchester United, Chelsea and perhaps others. After Roman Abramovich took over at Chelsea at a cost of £140 million, as the club were about to fold, he wanted a world-class coach to succeed the likeable but eccentric Italian Claudio Ranieri. On 3 July 2003 a very well-informed photographer – there are around fifty who work full-time on the celebrity beat in London – managed to take pictures of a grim-faced Sven walking up to Abramovich's plush house in Knightsbridge. On Sven's left was the Israeli-born agent Pini Zahavi, the man whose annual income is in the same bracket as England's highest-paid footballers. Contacted later, Zahavi admitted it was a fair cop and the news caused a quake or two under Soho Square.

Financial expert Mark Palios, a fifty-four-year-old former footballer born in Birkenhead, had been appointed chief executive in succession to Adam Crozier and the idea was to bring some order to the collapsing organisation. In his 323 matches for Tranmere and Crewe he was known as a tough tackler and his bosses wanted someone of that calibre. In his first press conference, Palios confessed that the FA were thinking of a replacement if Eriksson departed for Stamford Bridge. But Eriksson said, 'Just because I have a cup of tea with someone doesn't mean I am signing a contract as the next Chelsea manager.'

Eriksson was still contracted to the FA until 2006 but most people at the FA thought he was on his way. In more talks with Chelsea, a plan was mooted to allow him to continue as England coach while being in charge of the West London club. Beckham was at Real Madrid by this time and was one of several who pleaded with Eriksson to remain with England. One source at the FA said, 'It was crazy. Everyone was in a complete spin about what was going on.' Palios wanted his colleagues to agree on a new deal for Eriksson to end the Chelsea farrago. The lawyers were called in to settle the details and according to another source, only three people on the FA board formalised the final offer, almost doubling Eriksson's salary of £3 million net. With deductions taken care of, the actual amount paid out was £4.2 million, which would rise if bonuses were due, including ones for earning qualification to major tournaments. The trio were Palios, chairman Geoff Thompson and David Dein. Some of the others were furious and asked to have their objections minuted.

Jurgen Klinsmann, the former Tottenham Hotspur striker who went on to manage Germany, was a pioneer in the field of 'net' salaries. An FA official explained, 'Spurs drew up a contract paying him £24,000 a week. When his first payment arrived, the sum was £16,000. "What's this?" he said. "I need to get the £24,000, not £16,000. Please amend the contract."' It was duly changed. Nowadays many managers and players insist on 'net' salaries. Eriksson had never won an international trophy, be it the European Championship or the World Cup, but now he was the highest-paid coach in the world, earning three times as much as the next national coach. Another source said, 'It meant that Eriksson was virtually unsackable. It would cost the FA a fortune to get rid of him.'

Back at football, England kept up the challenge to Turkey, beating Slovakia 2-1 at Middlesbrough's Riverside Stadium and Wayne Rooney scored in the 2-1 win at Skopje in Macedonia to become England's youngest ever goal-scorer at seventeen years and 317 days, beating Owen's record. Beckham's halo slipped when he announced that he would play against Liechenstein at Old Trafford despite the fact that another booking would have kept him out of the final, decisive qualifier in Istanbul on 11 October. He was roundly criticised for putting himself above his fellow players, who would be expected to wait for the manager to name the side. The part-timers of Liechenstein put up a magnificent display, losing the tie by just two goals to nil.

After surviving a hurricane and a mild quake, English football was now struck by a cyclone precipitated by the Rio Ferdinand affair on the eve of the potentially explosive Turkey match. It led to a threat of strike action by England's multi-millionaire footballers, who were eventually put back in their place by public opinion. On 23 September Ferdinand was told to stay on after training at Manchester United's training ground Carrington for an obligatory drugs test. Ferdinand had a reputation for drinking in late-night clubs but there was no suggestion that he had taken recreational drugs. After being reminded about the test, he sped off to the centre of Manchester and pictures of him shopping were later published in a newspaper. When the FA wanted an explanation he said he forgot. Palios, in his role as tough guy, gave the order to leave Ferdinand out of the squad. Eriksson was livid and Gordon Taylor, the PFA supremo, described the action as 'disgraceful'. Gary Neville, an active member of the PFA executive board, spoke up for withdrawal of labour and the players voted unanimously in favour of not travelling unless Ferdinand was reinstated. Lawyers from all sides piled in, taking money that should be used for better causes.

Soon a furious bombardment of abuse from the written and spoken media came crashing down on the heads of the stunned England players, backed by a vast majority of the public. England could have been expelled from the tournament and common sense prevailed when a smart official urged Ferdinand to issue a statement saying the team should be sent without him. It was an embarrassing climbdown, with the rebels putting out a meek statement saying they were sorry. Eriksson's behaviour was reprehensible. He should have told the players to get on with it. It was a serious miscalculation by him. Ferdinand was found guilty at the subsequent case and was banned for more than half a season.

The game at the daunting Sukru Saracoglu Stadium in Istanbul was no advert for Turkey's application to join the European Union. England refused to allocate tickets to English fans and the hostility of the 42,000 locals reached new heights of noise and nastiness. Eriksson showed his tactical nous by creating a successful blockade which produced the right result – 0-0 – to reach the Finals. Once again Beckham was at the forefront of the controversy. His foot slipped when he took a penalty and the ball sailed over the bar. Aston Villa's Alpay responded, shouting insults at him and when the players approached the tunnel, he screamed at him, 'Go f— your mother!' and pushed a finger in Beckham's face. Beckham chased after him and John Terry saved any further provocation. A Turkish player spat at Ashley Cole and it was a shameful episode. Referee Collina ordered Beckham and Alpay to his dressing room at half-time to tell their players to calm down. Happily for Eriksson, UEFA conveniently overlooked their threat of England being expelled if any more incidents occurred following the Sunderland rumpus. While England were through, Turkey deservedly lost their two-leg play-off against lowly Latvia.

Before the European Championship Finals, there was one more farce to emerge from Soho Square. A friendly game was arranged against Denmark at Old Trafford a month after the Turkey game and Eriksson called up Alan Smith as a replacement for the injured Darius Vassell. Smith arrived at the team's five-star hotel only to be sent home again on the grounds that he had been arrested for throwing a plastic bottle into the crowd at a Carling Cup tie. More embarrassment ensued when Palios was told that Nicky Butt had been permitted to play several games for England while on bail following his arrest for an alleged assault five months earlier, a case which was later dropped. Smith's replacement was James Beattie and Palios was incandescent when he learned that the striker was serving 100 hours of community service for being convicted of drink driving. It was an appalling PR gaffe and Palios's position was totally undermined. The players issued another statement, criticising the FA and, to round off a shocking autumn, they lost 3-2 to the Danes. Four more friendlies in the spring hardly lifted morale. A 1-1 draw against Portugal was followed by a 1-0 defeat in Gothenburg, a 1-1 draw against Japan and a 6-1 rout of Iceland using twenty-two players.

Eriksson's expeditionary force flew off to Lisbon on 7 June for the start of Euro 2004 in a buoyant mood. The players always perform better against top opposition and their first game was against France in the rebuilt Stadium of Light six days later. Eriksson told them they had nothing to fear. 'We play against these players all the time in the Premiership,' he said. The players were impressed by the way he worked on their confidence. When the match started, two-thirds of the 62,000 spectators were English, an encouraging sign. France had gone eleven games without scoring and in the thirty-eighth minute Beckham's free-kick was glanced in by the head of Frank Lampard. England were awarded a penalty seventeen minutes from time but Beckham went for power instead of placing his shot and Fabien Barthez beat the ball away to safety. Three minutes later, Eriksson made a bad blunder, taking off the still-frisky Rooney and sending on Emile Heskey. The English cheers were becoming noisier but a minute from the end they were silenced when Zidane equalised from a free-kick. Inside a minute, Gerrard tried a back pass to David James and, instead of trying to pick the ball up, the goalkeeper clattered feet first into Thierry Henry, conceding a penalty. James indicted that the England intelligence planners had been at fault, saying that he hadn't seen video film of any Zidane free-kicks.

Losing like that was like seeing someone's glass of champagne knocked to the ground as he was about to take the first sip. However, the morale of the players was barely affected. They looked on it as a moral victory and five days later they were ready to take on Switzerland. Eriksson wanted to counter the Swiss diamond formation by adopting the same tactic but the midfield players went to see him in his room and asked him to retain the traditional 4-4-2. He agreed, denying afterwards that he had bowed to player power. Rooney blossomed against the functional Swiss, scoring two goals in an efficient 3-0 win. A draw against Croatia in the third game would be enough to reach the next stage but Eriksson wanted an emphatic victory. It wasn't quite that and seventeen minutes from the end it was 3-2 before Lampard thumped in the fourth.

Rooney had scored two more goals in the Croatia game and the hype about him expanded by the minute with Eriksson comparing him to Pelé. The head coach added, 'but he will need to keep his temperament in check.' England's quarter-final opponents were Portugal, who had never beaten England in Lisbon. The first encounter, in 1947, finished Portugal 0, England 10 but the 2004 squad was filled with determined and talented players. The traditional music of Portugal is fado and it expresses the national feeling of sadness when things go wrong. They had to guard against it and it wasn't helped by seeing more than half of the audience cheering for Beckham's team. The mood deepened when Owen scored after only three minutes to end his barren spell.

Rooney had a habit of diving into reckless tackles in his earlier matches but he wasn't at fault when he was injured halfway through the first half. When Jorge Andrade's boot caught his foot it seemed innocuous and he tried to continue. He had to go off in the twenty-seventh minute and the mood of the locals changed abruptly. Portugal were on top and England were struggling. With Beckham flagging, Portugal finally equalised seven minutes from time through a robust header from Helder Postiga, the Portugal striker who failed to make the grade at Tottenham Hotspur. With a minute left on the clock, Michael Owen thundered a header off the bar and Sol Campbell forced the rebound over the line. Swiss referee Meier bravely blew up for a push and the replay confirmed that he was correct.

Graham Taylor had forecast a penalty shoot-out and so it turned out. In extra time, Rui Costa gave Portugal the lead but Lampard made it 2-2. It was England's fifth penalty shootout in fourteen years and, out of the previous four, they had lost three. Beckham should have been substituted before the end but was still volunteering for the first penalty. He had missed two penalties in previous matches and Eriksson should have told him to sit it out. Beckham was first up and blazed the ball over the bar to qualify for a morale-shattering hat-trick. When Vassell's spot-kick, the eleventh of the shootout, was saved, England were rudely knocked out of a competition which they believed was going to be theirs. Once again bad luck hit them where it hurt. The local populace expected to celebrate a first major trophy in the final but were left in their customary sad state after a superbly organised Greece side won 1-0 in a below average match.

Eriksson retreated to his villa in Sunne, in central Sweden, to recharge his batteries and, unbeknown to his employers and the rest of the footballing fraternity, except for a few young ladies, the recharging process wasn't in the arms of Nancy but the clutches of Faria Alam, who boasted about her prowess at blow jobs amongst other social skills. After the story broke, and Eriksson was surprisingly reprieved, he remained on the tightrope. Another nudge might knock him off.

The draw for the 2006 World Cup produced another favourable draw for him – old friends Poland, Austria, Northern Ireland, Wales and Azerbaijan. It was like a list of opponents for a Frank Bruno or an Audley Harrison, not a real champion. England duly qualified but encountered a few natural hazards. A laboured 2-2 draw against Austria in Vienna was followed by a heartening result at Chorzow, 2-1 over Poland, on 8 September. In October, Wales were beaten 2-0 at Old Trafford and Azerbaijan were despatched 1-0 at Baku.

Then on 17 November 2004 England went to Madrid and lost 1-0 in shameful circumstances. The performance was cretinous and for a while everyone doubted whether Rooney would emerge from his Scouse chrysalis into a true footballing champion. He lost his temper after being substituted just before half-time and tore off his black armband – worn as a mark of respect for the late Emlyn Hughes and Keith Weller – and when Beckham tried to calm him down, he told him to 'f—— off'. Even controversy about Ashley Cole and Shaun Wright-Phillips being racially abused failed to divert attention from the central issue, namely, would Rooney soon destroy himself? Eriksson summoned him on the way back home and put him straight in simple, graphic terms. The head coach wasn't given enough credit for his successful counselling. In the following matches Rooney was seen to smile at opponents and pick them up. He started to behave like a normal human being. It was an amazing transformation.

Northern Ireland were whacked 4-0 and a partisan 49,046 crowd at St James's Park cheered Eriksson's men on in a comfortable 2-0 win over Azerbaijan.

But a catalyst for the demise of Eriksson's reign was the 1-0 defeat against 117th-rated Northern Ireland in Belfast on 7 September. What really undermined him was a decision in the friendly in Copenhagen on 17 August when he brought on David James in place of Paul Robinson at the start of the second half. His policy of bringing on countless substitutes finally caught up with him. James was at fault for three of the goals in Denmark's upset 4-1 victory and the confidence of the players was shattered almost at a stroke.

A dodgy keeper is like a landmine. Once the first one goes off it cascades into chaos and Eriksson's players were in turmoil. An outfield player can make mistakes and get away with it. The goalkeeper can't. James's record of calamitous mistakes should have persuaded Sven to ditch him long before. There are few English goalkeepers in the Premiership capable of challenging Robinson's position but that was no excuse. The Championship provides a number of younger goalkeepers who could have performed better than James, who upset the England camp afterwards by complaining that he hadn't been given enough warning to prepare for his second-half appearance.

The setback was England's heaviest defeat for twenty-five years and Sven promised it wouldn't happen again. Just over two weeks later England scrambled a 1-0 win over Wales at the Millennium Stadium and the alarm bells were still ringing. Eriksson, more talkative now the pressure had built up, promised, 'We will be better in Belfast.' Wrong again. It was much worse. Loose talk by Sven about England matching Brazil produced mocking headlines. There were confused messages about the formation, overlooking the key fact that good players win matches, not formations. Beckham was used as a kind of quarterback in front of the defence – reminiscent of Greenwood's use of Hoddle in the 1980s – and the experiment flopped. The England captain has never been a good tackler and sound tackling is required in that role.

Wayne Rooney lost his temper yet again, charging into Keith Gillespie and earning a booking which was to keep him out of the Austria game. He forgot his earlier counselling sessions on how to overcome his anger and swore at the officials and when Beckham told him, 'If you carry on like this, you'll be sent off', he replied, 'F—— off!' The argument continued in the dressing room and Steve McClaren was alleged to have stepped between the two protagonists. Later, Rooney flew to Madrid to watch Beckham in a match and apologised.

One critic made a sound point: the players were no longer enjoying their work. England's cricketers regained the Ashes in the late summer of 2005 playing with smiles on their faces and congratulatory hugs. England's ashen-faced footballers were losing with snarls and oaths. When David Healy, the Leeds striker, scored the only goal in the seventy-fourth minute eight million viewers at home were expecting a reaction from the visiting players. But it was the Ulstermen who ran the hardest in the final minutes. Eriksson looked shocked when he sat down in the interview room afterwards. 'It was my worst performance as England manager because we shouldn't lose, we shouldn't even draw to Northern Ireland,' he said. 'I am very sorry, for the team, for the three points lost and sorry for the fans who have spent a lot of money to watch us. But it was the first defeat in twenty-two qualification games.'

According to Ken Bates, the FA took twenty-two players and forty-two officials to Belfast, occupying all seventy-nine rooms, including nineteen suites, at the stately Culloden Hotel, at a cost of more than £50,000. The next morning the headlines were in the Graham Taylor 'turnip' class with one critic saying 'Sack the Swede'. A more respectable newspaper ran with 'Clueless!' *The Sun* brought round an imitation P45 form to present to Eriksson at the FA building in Soho Square but there was no sign of him. In the past, anyone could walk into the FA offices in Lancaster Gate. Now the door is barred and you have to call up from outside before establishing your credentials. The glass-fronted building looks totally anonymous, barely confirming that this is the headquarters of the ruling body of the national sport.

The Sun also took an Eriksson lookalike to Soho Square, causing confusion as police officers, sent round to keep order if there was any trouble, mistook him for the real England manager. A crowd gathered to see 'Sven' being interviewed by a television reporter. 'A very good impersonation,' said one observer. The mood was jolly. No one wanted to throw an egg at him, unlike John Prescott. A few hours earlier, the real Sven had been smuggled out of Luton Airport, the scene of many England managers' fraught exits. His usual practice was to go to his office after an international game but this time he kept away.

The next day he surfaced and was interviewed by the BBC's *Football Focus* programme. He was asked if was ready to resign (a daft question really on that salary!) and replied, 'Absolutely not, no chance. We have one foot in the World Cup. Why should I resign?' 'Are you worth your salary?' he was asked. 'If you talk about Northern Ireland, no,' he said. 'If you talk about general qualification games, yes. It is a lot of money I know, huge money. But I don't think I am paid more than others in my position.'

When England have a bad result, many people think that the FA switchboard will be jammed from angry callers. After the Belfast defeat, a spokesman said:

> There were some, a score or two. Most of them were quite funny. They say things like, 'I know nothing about football but I am applying for Sven's job.' We get emails but again, it's not a lot. The busiest time was after the Eric Cantona affair, when he tried to kick at that spectator at Crystal Palace in 1995. The switchboard was jammed that day with people saying he should have been sacked or kicked out of the country.

This muted response indicates that popular opinion is often lukewarm about the fate of England managers. But once the critics, from former players in television and radio studios to journalists and website writers, jump in with their stringent views, opinions harden. The phone-ins fill countless hours of listening, mostly ill-informed, and it now becomes a major campaign to get the incumbent out, with the poor fellow attracting more criticism and abuse than almost any prime minister. As Eriksson was earning twenty-five times more than Tony Blair at the time, it is not entirely surprising. Until 1973, the FA's telephone number was ex-directory. Angry critics had to write in.

Earlier in the year Eriksson had invited a small group of journalists to a relaxed lunch in Soho. Oliver Holt of the *Daily Mirror* wrote later:

> Eriksson was fascinating company. He talked a lot about his style of management and how he always preferred to ask the opinions of his players rather than lay down the law. He said he did not believe that a manager could gain authority by shouting and that he did not want to be a dictator. He said the only time his method had run into trouble was when he took charge of Portuguese club Benfica. After a few days, the players were practically begging him to adopt a traditional authoritarian approach and consign consensus management to the dustbin.

Before the match against Austria, played at Old Trafford on 8 October, someone threw a brick through one of the windows in Eriksson's house in Regent's Park, reminiscent of the Duke of Wellington's windows being smashed at Hyde Park 200 years earlier. Eriksson invited the England squad to dinner in Manchester to improve relations and, with David Beckham absent, staying on in Madrid with his son in hospital, the mood was muted. During the week a succession of players were brought to the microphones to defend Eriksson and deny that there had been a bust-up in the dressing room at Belfast. But there was a significant change – the proceedings were filmed by the FA to check how the material was handled in the press the next day. A spokesman said, 'What was written sometimes didn't accurately represent what the players and the manager actually said.' In journalistic jargon, spin was put on it and the FA wanted to expose this practice.

Jose Mourinho and Sir Alex Ferguson were others around that time who complained about the way their words were distorted and they had periods when they refused to be interviewed. A crackdown on spin was long over-due, with offenders being cautioned that if they persisted, they could be barred from future press conferences.

Eriksson said he was 'certain' that England would qualify but, when Beckham was sent off in the fifty-ninth minute of a stumbling game against the Austrians, doubts appeared. England defended for the rest of the match to hold on to their 1-0 lead, taken through a Frank Lampard pen-alty awarded by Spanish referee Luis Medina Cantalejo. The small Spaniard had been in charge of Beckham's debut for Real Madrid two years earlier and had sent him off for two bookable offences in a King's Cup tie for Real in January 2004. Now, at Old Trafford, he repeated his actions, show-ing a yellow card to Beckham for catching Andreas Ibertsberger in the throat with an elbow and then, a minute later, showing another – quickly followed by a red –after Beckham caught the fair-haired full-back with his right foot from behind. Television replays showed there was contact on both counts.

Astonishingly, Beckham went up to the Austrian number 5, shook him by the hand and said, 'Well done.' Afterwards Ibertsberger said, 'The first booking wasn't a yellow but the second time he clipped my foot. I was a bit surprised with his reaction. Maybe he was being sarcastic. I don't know. It gave me no pleasure that Beckham was sent off.'

Beckham became the first England player to be sent off twice, over-taking hard men like Alan Ball, Paul Ince, David Batty and Alan Mullery. At this stage he had been cautioned thirteen times for England, equalling Ince's record, and he recorded fifteen fouls in the 2006 qualification, more than anyone else. But the gentlemanly Beckham is certainly no hard man. He's not even a menacing tackler. And he's not a cynical fouler. Nearly all his offences have caused by pettiness or carelessness.

After the game against the near-anonymous Austrians, no one knew whether Eriksson was right about the qualification and the players and their wives, partners and children, were dining at the opulent Lowry Hotel in Manchester when they heard the news from Prague – Holland's win over the Czech Republic ensured England's place in Germany. Corks exploded from dozens of champagne bottles around the room and a spokesman said, 'It was a pleasant occasion, not boisterous.' Most of the Sunday newspapers failed to carry the news because of the late timing but even on Monday there was hardly any triumphalism among the millions of words written. Jeff Powell pointed out that the BBC should have shown clips from the Czech Republic *v.* Holland match to inform the armchair audience.

A mood of pessimism still lingered. '[England are] not good enough for the Finals,' said a mournful Alan Hansen. Gary Lineker, who rarely criti-cises anyone, asked, 'Does the team reflect the personality of the manager?' – meaning 'boring'. Alan Smith, the former Arsenal striker, now top-quality media man, wrote:

> England expects – it has always been the same. But you can't help wondering if the Mother Country, as far as the national team are concerned, occasion-ally expects a little too much, although the team hadn't functioned well in the previous four matches.
>
> The coach was set upon by a hungry pack who, not unreasonably, wanted a few answers to England's sterile form. As the Swede sat there looking more and more harrassed, you were willing him to hit back in anger. 'Shut up! What do you know? I'll do it my way!'

It brought back memories of 1966 when the critics of that era were say-ing similar things about the boring start by Ramsey's World Cup winners. Remember the 0-0 against Uruguay? Alf would probably have curtailed the interview saying, 'Good evening, gentlemen.' In Ramsey's day the difference was that only two pages, or sometimes only one, were occupied by England football coverage after a big game. On the Monday following the win over Austria, *The Sun* devoted fourteen pages to the subject, the *Mirror* thirteen, and the *Daily Telegraph*, *Times* and *Mail* eight pages apiece. *The Sun* led the front page with a story about Romeo, the ill son of David Beckham, the day after thousands had died from an earthquake in Pakistan and India. The bulk of the television viewers agreed with the suggestion that there is too much football on television these days.

But is there too much coverage in the newspapers? One has to say yes. Quality is needed and less quantity. A proper balance has to be struck. Just now it has gone off the swingometer… into near hysteria.

Eriksson stuck to his script, saying, 'I always said we would qualify and then I said we were one of four, five or six teams who can win it and I still think that is the case.' He thought his boys 'were excellent against Austria, brilliant'. The critics mocked him. He should have stressed the fact that England played the last thirty-one minutes with ten men and without his outstanding player, Rooney.

With both England and Poland having qualified for Germany there was little pressure on either when they met in the last qualifying group game but a higher-tempo performance from England to earn a thoroughly deserved 2-1 win was praised extravagantly. Shearer, who had been damning in his analysis five days earlier, thought it was World Cup class. Hansen agreed. But really, England weren't that much better than the Poles. Eriksson, probably prompted by McClaren, used the English 'pressing' style, pushing the opposition back up the pitch. The danger of that tactic is that speedy opposing forwards, and slow-reacting assistant referees, can cost goals.

Eriksson mentioned good fortune. 'With luck in Germany, we might surprise everyone,' he said. No one mentioned luck when Joe Cole's low shot bounced through several defenders' legs before Michael Owen flicked in his 33rd goal in 74 internationals off the shin of another defender. Frank Lampard's excellent volleyed winning goal followed an untidy piece of build-up play when there were two ricochets off defenders before Owen crossed to him. Thirty-two years earlier at Wembley all the luck went for the Poles as Ramsey's side went out. This time England were conclusive winners and didn't need too much luck. But every team needs it. Most managers decry luck but sometimes they must have it to survive.

Eriksson took more interest in the English game generally in the calm period after qualification. His decision to attend the funeral of Johnny Haynes in Edinburgh late in October was welcomed and he was pictured in most of the newspapers with Bobby Robson, his old mentor. He said, 'I didn't know Johnny. I wish I had. People have told me what a good player he was, how he could pass the ball. Was he like Roberto Mancini? Yes, he was, I have been told, but better.' Roberto Mancini was one of Eriksson's favourite players when they were at Lazio and Sampdoria. David Platt, who played under Eriksson at Sampdoria for two seasons, said, 'I think Sven got his respect from the players from his ruthlessness. He loved Mancini but when he left him out at Lazio that didn't bother him at all. Sven was totally in control of his emotions.'

Owen scored twice in the momentous 3-2 victory over Argentina in Geneva on 12 November. A fortnight before, Eriksson wrote to the Premiership managers asking for their support 'because it will be a competitive game'. They agreed, and the supporters co-operated as well in a match oddly arranged in Switzerland which Roy Collins described as 'worthy of a World Cup final'. Again, luck helped England along. When Beckham won a rare header to provide the first goal for Rooney in the thirty-fourth minute, an England player was standing offside in an active position. No one mentioned that the goal might have been cancelled by a sterner referee than the Swiss Phillippe Leubo.

Five minutes from normal time, with Argentina leading 2-1, Leubo ignored what appeared to be a blatant penalty offence in England's area. Almost immediately England attacked and Owen headed in Gerrard's cross and, in the second minute of added time, Owen glanced in the winner from Joe Cole's cross. From gallant losers, they became world-class winners, ready to beat the world.

In the BBC studio, none of their experts failed to make the point that Roberto Ayala, Argentina's most experienced defender, was substituted in the seventy-fifth minute because he was tired. If he had stayed on, would Owen have scored those goals? These cosy experts spend a lot of time criticising Eriksson but they need to look at themselves sometimes. They are being left behind by the cricketing experts like Benaud, Boycott and new, rising stars like Nick Knight and Michael Slater who tell the viewers what they don't know themselves. Gary Lineker is an exception because he is adept at answering the simple question but a few days later he made some good points about the reign of Eriksson when he was unveiled as the new presenter of BBC golf in place of Steve Ryder. He said:

> Sven has come from a background of Portuguese and Italian football which is different to ours. In the previous two games he finally realised that our players like to play a British-style high tempo game. Being cautious and cagey doesn't really suit us. I am not saying just throw caution to the wind because you have to play sensibly and with discipline, but we have to play to our strengths.

Episode fourteen of England *v*. Argentina was enthralling entertainment but defenders on both sides were guilty of ball-watching, the cardinal sin in the penalty area. Eriksson and his players had to calm everyone down. 'Please don't talk about us winning the World Cup,' he said. 'We are one of a number who could do it.' A thorough check through the prints revealed no mention of the offside goal and the supposed penalty. If the two teams had swapped over, would England's writers have written about the incidents? Of course they would!

After no more eruptions in the first half of a dull winter, Eriksson was hoping for a quiet build-up before the World Cup in Germany, and he had an advantage over some coaches because he learned German at school. But over the weekend of 14-15 January he fell for a well-planned 'sting' by the *News of the World*. The newspaper carried seven pages on how their investigative reporter Mazher Mahmood, posing as a sheikh who claimed to have business interests in Pakistan and Dubai, offered him £5 million a year to act as a consultant for the Dubai Soccer Academy. The discussions led on to Sven's suggestion that his 'backer' could buy Aston Villa and sign David Beckham. Sven made some highly embarrassing comments about Beckham, Michael Owen, Wayne Rooney and Shaun Wright-Phillips, all of whom he had to ring and apologise.

Thirty-three years earlier Don Revie had to go through immigration checks in Dubai trying, unsuccessfully, to avoid recognition before signing up as the national football coach. Sven was excused the normal checks and was whisked away to the world's tallest hotel, 361m in height, named Burf Al Arab at Jumeirah Beach, the suites at which cost up to £5,000 a night. At dinner with his new friends he ate crab cakes and lobster and drank £900 worth of champagne. Every word was taped and he couldn't deny what he had said. On the day the story was published the FA issued a terse statement saying it backed him. Sven issued a similar statement, apologising for the inconvenience and assuring his 100 per cent support of the England team. At 7 p.m. he was due to attend Ladies Night of the Football Writers' Association at the Savoy Hotel to honour Bryan Robson, England's most courageous captain, and many people thought he wouldn't turn up. Gary Lineker was there, joking, and he said, 'How many people have been caught out by the fake sheikh? How naïve of him!' Up to then the list included Sophie, Countess of Wessex, Princess Michael of Kent, Newcastle United chairman Freddy Shepherd, actor John Alford, disc jockey Johnnie Walker and Carole Caplin.

Sven arrived half-an-hour later surrounded by a coterie of FA people and their wives. Nancy, wearing a beautiful pale blue dress, was smiling happily. Sven's face was as red as a new cricket ball, clearly embarrassed. He talked about the day's football matches, Thierry Henry's skill and other subjects, ignoring the main one. Brian Barwick, the new FA chief executive, shook hands without eye contract. The FA party sat next to the *Daily Star* table and, by coincidence, the first course was crab cakes. Bobby Robson made the keynote speech, an impassioned tribute paid to his protégé Bryan of the same name, and he was given a standing ovation.

Around the packed room, the pundits were debating the names of Sven's successor. Steve McClaren, despite signing a new four-year contract at Middlesbrough, was once favourite but the score of Arsenal 7, Boro 0 twenty-four hours earlier was a real blow for him. Robson Senior's tour de force speech mentioned the crippling injuries of Robson Junior, who had worked under him in two World Cups. Later he was being groomed as a possible England manager before he went into club management. Sir Bobby said:

If he had been fit in 1986 Maradona wouldn't have scored that great goal in Mexico. We would have definitely beaten the Argentinians. In 1990 he missed the World Cup in Italy and if he'd been alongside Paul Gascoigne we would have had the best midfield in the world. We could well have won the cup.

Sir Bert Millichip, his lifelong friend, regretted the decision of the FA not to renew Bobby's contract. That was where it all went wrong. If Sir Bobby had won one or even both of those World Cups, he would have stayed for the 1994 tournament. He could have outdone Sir Walter Winterbottom's sixteen years in charge. He could still be involved now as the mentor of the junior Robson. It could have been a winning Robson ticket – Bobby and Bryan.

Instead, the day after the celebrations at the Savoy, the seventy-two-year-old Robson got up at 5 a.m. to catch a 7 a.m. flight to Dublin to start his job as a mentor for the new manager of the Republic of Ireland, Steve Staunton. 'Up to then, I'd never met him,' he said. 'But I'm really excited about it. There are some great people there, fun people like the Cobbolds.' The English FA could have saved themselves a lot of problems over the years if they had stuck with Bobby. It's worth thinking about.

HOW ENGLAND'S MANAGERS HAVE RATED

Highest percentage of wins

1	Ron Greenwood (1977–1982)	60%
	Glenn Hoddle (1996–1998)	60%
	Alf Ramsey (1962–1974)	60%
4	Sven-Goran Eriksson (2001–2006)	57%★
5	Walter Winterbottom (1946–1962)	56%
6	Bobby Robson (1982–1990)	49%
7	Don Revie (1974–1977)	48%
8	Graham Taylor (1990–1993)	47%
	Terry Venables (1993–1996)	47%
10	Kevin Keegan (1999–2000)	38%

★ Up to World Cup 2006 qualification

Man Management

1 Alf Ramsey
2 Walter Winterbottom
3 Terry Venables
4 Don Revie
5 Bobby Robson
6 Sven-Goran Eriksson
7 Ron Greenwood
8 Kevin Keegan
9 Graham Taylor
10 Glenn Hoddle

Coaching Ability

1 Walter Winterbottom
2 Ron Greenwood
   Bobby Robson
   Terry Venables
5 Graham Taylor
6 Alf Ramsey
7 Glenn Hoddle
8 Sven-Goran Eriksson
9 Don Revie
10 Kevin Keegan

PR Skills

1 Terry Venables
2 Walter Winterbottom
3 Bobby Robson
4 Graham Taylor
5 Don Revie
6 Kevin Keegan
7 Sven-Goran Eriksson
8 Ron Greenwood
9 Glenn Hoddle
10 Alf Ramsey

Handling Pressure

1   Sven-Goran Eriksson
2   Alf Ramsey
3   Bobby Robson
4   Walter Winterbottom
5   Terry Venables
6   Glenn Hoddle
7   Graham Taylor
8   Ron Greenwood
9   Don Revie
10 Kevin Keegan

Best Overall

1   Alf Ramsey
2   Bobby Robson
3   Walter Winterbottom
    Ron Greenwood
    Sven-Goran Eriksson
6   Terry Venables
7   Glenn Hoddle
8   Don Revie
9   Graham Taylor
10 Kevin Keegan

Other titles published by Tempus

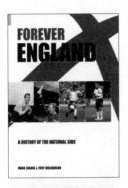

Forever England A History of the National Side
MARK SHAOUL & TONY WILLIAMSON

This insightful and fascinating account is an essential read for anyone interested in the history of the three lions. From the amateur gentlemen of the 1870s to the stars of the early twenty-first century, with many wonderfully evocative illustrations, it is the definitive history of England's national football team.

0 7524 2939 6

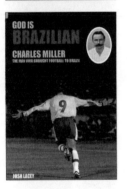

Football Gentry The Cobbold Brothers
BRIAN SCOVELL

John and Patrick Cobbold presided over Ipswich Town FC from 1957 until 1994. Notoriously eccentric, the Old Etonian toffs were pranksters with a thoroughly irreverent attitude. Closely involved with two of England's greatest managers, Ramsey and Robson, the brothers played countless tricks on the pair and led many a young footballer astray with their hard-drinking ways. This account of their lives is suitably hilarious and crammed with anecdotes spanning the four decades of their involvement with football.

0 7524 3464 0

God is Brazilian Charles Miller, The Man Who Brought Football to Brazil
JOSH LACEY

In 1894, Charles Miller arrived in Brazil with a pair of boots, a book of rules and a football. When he reached São Paulo he was shocked to discover that no one knew how to play. So he marked out a pitch, gathered twenty young men and divided them into two teams... Pelé, Garrincha, Ronaldo – all of them can trace their lineage to Miller. This is his story – the profoundly moving tale of a young man, half-English, half-Scottish, who carried a football from Southampton to give Brazil its greatest gift.

0 7524 3414 4

Football Oddities
TONY MATTHEWS

In one of the most individual and irreverent collections of footballing facts ever produced, Tony Matthews has unearthed tales of the unexpected that will delight footy fans everywhere. Did you hear the one about the Argentine full-back who scored a hat-trick of own goals in less than an hour? Remember the England goalkeeper who was sent off after just twenty-seven seconds of a Premiership game in 1995? Read about them – and many, many others – here.

0 7524 3401 2

If you are interested in purchasing other books published by Tempus, or in case you have difficulty finding any Tempus books in your local bookshop, you can also place orders directly through our website

www.tempus-publishing.com